D0261153

FAT, BALD and WORTHLESS

Fat, Bald and Worthless is a hugely entertaining and highly original investigation into the vainglorious, unfortunate and sometimes downright insulting names that pepper the history books, from Brandy Nan to Fulk the Surly, and from Hugh the Dull to Magnus Barelegs. Anyone with a love of the quirky side of history will enjoy the capricious world of noble nicknames, where military tacticians can be celebrated for their drinking habits (Michael the Drunkard), successful diplomats can be mocked for their diminutive stature (Ladislaus the Elbow-High), and a vicious tyrant can be kowtowed to (John the Good).

Revd Robert Easton (childhood nickname Ridiculous Robert) has spent years gathering together the best and worst nicknames given to the rich and powerful over the centuries, and *Fat, Bald and Worthless* is the result: a uniquely irreverent look at both history and the inventiveness of the English language.

Charles the Silly and Wenceslas the Worthless at Rheims in 1398.

FAT, BALD and WORTHLESS

WORTHLESS

[*The Curious Stories Behind Noble Nicknames*]

REVD ROBERT EASTON

PENGUIN BOOKS

PENGUIN BOOKS

Published by the Penguin Group
Penguin Books Ltd, 80 Strand, London WC2R ORL, England
Penguin Group (USA) Inc., 375 Hudson Street, New York, New York 10014, USA
Penguin Group (Canada), 90 Eglinton Avenue East, Suite 700, Toronto, Ontario, Canada M4P 2Y3
(a division of Pearson Penguin Canada Inc.)
Penguin Ireland, 25 St Stephen's Green, Dublin 2, Ireland
(a division of Penguin Books Ltd)
Penguin Group (Australia), 250 Camberwell Road,
Camberwell, Victoria 3124, Australia (a division of Pearson Australia Group Pty Ltd)
Penguin Books India Pvt Ltd, 11 Community Centre,
Panchsheel Park, New Delhi – 110 017, India
Penguin Group (NZ), cnr Airborne and Rosedale Roads, Albany,
Auckland 1310, New Zealand (a division of Pearson New Zealand Ltd)
Penguin Books (South Africa) (Pty) Ltd, 24 Sturdee Avenue,
Rosebank, Johannesburg 2196, South Africa

Penguin Books Ltd, Registered Offices: 80 Strand, London WC2R ORL, England

www.penguin.com

First published 2006
1

Set in 10.5/12.5 pt PostScript Adobe Minion
Typeset by Rowland Phototypesetting Ltd, Bury St Edmunds, Suffolk
Printed in England by Clays Ltd, St Ives plc

ISBN-13: 978-0-140-51540-4
ISBN-10: 0-140-51540-2

To
Harry the Dirty Dog

Contents

Preface

I was in the British Library last year searching for material on Charles III, the sixteenth-century duke of Lorraine, and on the reason for his nickname 'the Great'. The catalogue revealed the existence of a work with the promising title *The House of Lorraine* by one Rachel Lindsay, and so I ordered it from the stacks, only to find it was a Mills and Boon romance set in Paris. 'Held close in his arms, her head against his breast,' began the last paragraph, 'Nicole no longer felt any anger against him . . . everything that had happened in the past was suddenly of no importance.' While Lindsay's *House of Lorraine* might not be the best source of information on Charles III, and the heroine's easy dismissal of the past might be a little over the top, her words were a healthy reminder that, as *Fat, Bald and Worthless* demonstrates, recorded history is a veritable minefield of contradictions and injustices.

How cruel of history, for example, to give the well-meaning if naive Anne Boleyn the perpetual moniker 'the Great Whore'. How unjust of it to label for eternity the magnificent Charles II of France not for his devotion to Church and nation but as 'the Bald', for his supposed lack of hair. How kind, on the other hand, has 'nickname history' been to others. Take for example the repulsive king Edward II of England, who, given his spoilt childhood, his callous and cruel indifference to all his subjects (including his wife), and his woefully inept military strategy, was perhaps one of the most embarrassing monarchs in English history. That he is known as 'Edward Carnarvon', referring to the castle where he was born, rather than 'Edward the Atrocious' or 'Edward the Vile', is surely a travesty of nickname justice.

But that's the point. There is no justice in nicknames. Sometimes they are conferred upon an individual on a whim, sometimes after considerable reflection. Sometimes they are bestowed sarcastically; sometimes they couldn't be more serious. A person may be known for a physical attribute over which they have no control, or for an act of cruelty or generosity entirely of their own making. Nicknames. We all have them, whether we know it or not, and more to the point, whether we like it or not.

The English essayist William Hazlitt observed that a nickname is 'the heaviest stone that the devil can throw at a man'. 'Archibald the Loser' and 'Hugh the Dull' would surely concur. 'John the Perfect', on the other hand, might disagree. Thomas Haliburton, the nineteenth-century humorist, meanwhile, noted that 'nicknames stick to people, and the most ridiculous are the most adhesive.' 'Elizabeth the Red-Nosed Princess' and 'Wilfrid the Shaggy' would probably nod their heads in agreement.

And yet I would suggest that nicknames ('bynames', 'soubriquets', 'cognomens', 'monikers' or 'epithets' – while they all mean slightly different things, they are used for the most part interchangeably) should not be disregarded as mere onomastic trivialities, but celebrated as adding colourful detail to history – history that can so often be presented as bland and dull. The first three kings of Portugal, in many history books, are listed as

Alfonso I

Sancho I

Alfonso II

when they *could* be referred to as:

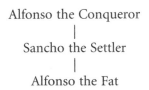

Alfonso the Conqueror

Sancho the Settler

Alfonso the Fat

This book pays homage to the humble yet capricious nickname. It champions and delights in a system of nomenclature that pays no heed to social status nor indeed to historical accuracy. It rejoices in a world where monarchs do not have numerals after their names but appellations such as 'Bald' or 'Worthless', and where nobles are prominent not for their military genius or diplomatic success but for their moral fibre or the size of their nose.

While the word 'nickname' itself (deriving from *eke name*, meaning 'also name' or 'additional name') is only a few hundred years old, nicknames themselves are as old as the hills ... or at least as old as the time since people have occupied hills. For nicknames have been around for as long as people have wanted to find an affectionate, familiar or spiteful way of describing each other. Before the fourteenth century, hereditary surnames were extremely rare and so people used soubriquets and epithets to tell people of the same name apart. In Viking culture, men called 'Einar' were two a penny; only one as far as we know rejoiced in the intriguing extra name of 'Buttered Bread'. The eleventh-century Domesday Book often singled people out by profession or, as in the case of Roger 'God Save the Ladies', by other, less specific qualities.

Fat, Bald and Worthless focuses on history's nobility, a group of people who, on the face of it, have no need for nicknames. Mass acquaintance, however, and therefore public scrutiny, has provided no protection whatsoever from the slings and arrows of outrageous nickname fortune. Chroniclers, it seems, and the common people whom they cited, have felt compelled to comment via a nickname on those in power, even though they have needed no additional identification.

Some of these aristocratic nicknames are galling in their obsequiousness. Outlandish, hagiographical cognomens such as 'Light of the World' and 'Father of Letters' (as in the cases of the emperor Sigismund and Francis I of France respectively) fail to tell us much about the recipient, but instead only serve to highlight the fawning nature of their historians. Mercifully, these are in the minority. Other nicknames, meanwhile, give a fairly obscure figure of the past a more prominent place in history than might be expected. It is almost exclusively because of their nicknames, for example, that 'James the Dead Man Who Won a Fight' and 'Black Agnes' are known by more than a clutch of scholars and a few descendants researching their family history.

This book considers some 400 aristocratic individuals and considers whether their epithets fit the bill. Their nicknames fall into a number of loose categories.[1] These include:

The Toponymic

Usually pretty uninteresting, and therefore rarely given much space in the following pages, these are names stating the geographical origin of the individual. They are not what one might call 'true' nicknames inasmuch as the aristocracy regularly conferred such names upon themselves: they denoted not only their place of origin (such as the linguistically aberrant 'John of Gaunt') or place of residence (such as 'Henry Bolingbroke'), but also stated that they owned land and were therefore people of importance.

Where these nicknames were not self-conferred, as in the case of 'Emma the Gem of Normandy' or 'William the Rake of Piccadilly', the stories behind them are usually worth greater examination. But even this seemingly straightforward giving of names has its foibles. That there is a character called 'John the Scot', who wasn't Scottish at all, reinforces the fickle nature of this genre.

The Physical (General)

A host of nobles in this book have nicknames which fall into this category, some deservedly, some without any merit whatsoever. These are nicknames that refer to an individual's general appearance, for example 'Philip the Handsome', who was, by common consent, pretty good-looking, or 'Richard Crookback', whose disability appears to have been a certain playwright's fabrication.

1. A note on the entries. Most names have been anglicized for ease of reading, and where the dates of an individual are open to question, I have plumped for those given in the *Encyclopaedia Britannica*. Where a person's dates are truly vague, I have used the term *fl.*, short for the Latin *floruit* denoting the high point of a person's life or career.

It's hard, but fun, to imagine one of the more uncomplimentary of this species of nickname being used within earshot of its recipient. Only the bravest or stupidest of subjects, for example, would have addressed Henry I, king of Navarre, by his nickname of 'the Fat', even though by most accounts it was an entirely fair epithet. And though indeed vertically challenged, King Ladislaus I of Poland would surely not have thanked anyone who reminded him of his moniker 'the Elbow-High'.

The Physical (Specific)

Here the nickname refers to one particular physical attribute or abnormality. A royal bouffant or aristocratic coiffure has often proved a rich quarry for the nicknaming fraternity, with many soubriquets, such as 'William Rufus', 'Sven Forkbeard' and 'Boleslav the Curly' commenting on the colour, style or quality of a person's hair. Lack of hair, similarly, has not gone unmentioned, even when, as with 'Charles the Bald', its suitability is a matter of debate. 'Haakon the Broad-Shouldered' and 'Antigonus the One-Eyed' also fall into a category that singles out history's leaders not by their deeds but by their deportment or deficiency.

The Moral

This is perhaps the most slippery of categories. Chroniclers sometimes conferred nicknames upon people not with cold, rational even-handedness but out of politically motivated whimsy. We therefore find the utterly repellent John II of France known to history as 'the Good' and the rather charming William I of Sicily wholly unjustly labelled as 'the Bad'. The French, moreover, enjoyed the habit of nicknaming some of their monarchs sarcastically. Louis XV, for instance, was not 'Well-Beloved' at all, but universally considered a knave.

Some people, however, have clearly deserved their moral cognomen. Few would rush to the defence of Wenceslas of Bohemia for being dubbed 'Worthless', and Peter of Castile's soubriquet of 'Cruel' was by all accounts entirely justified.

The Animalistic

A small but select group, which divides on gender lines. Those few men who come within its remit, such as Louis the Universal Spider, have nicknames that generally portray them in a neutral if not positive light. Noblewomen, on the other hand, from the queen consort to Charles the Silly ('Isabella the Great Sow'), to one of Bluff King Hal's wives ('Anne the Mare of Flanders'), are referred to as other members of the animal kingdom in less than complimentary terms.

The Military

'Victorious', 'Fierce', 'Slayer of the Bulgars' . . . many nicknames understandably refer to the military prowess (real or otherwise) of history's fighting nobility. Some are accurate, such as 'Mehmed the Conqueror', while others are way off the mark, as in the case of 'John the Fearless'.

The Great

Dozens of people down the centuries have been dubbed 'the Great'. Only some seventeen have earned their place in these pages for having an interesting story to support – or undermine – their epithet.[2] With such a collection, one cannot help but be tempted to judge who exactly was the greatest. Catherine and Peter of Russia, Charlemagne and Henry of France must surely be in everyone's top ten, if for nothing but sheer entertainment value.

The Occupational

From 'Caulker' to 'Astrologer', 'Baker' to 'Wizard', occupations, often incidental to the main line of work of many nobles, have proved a rich mine for nicknames. Some, like 'Troubadour' and 'Farmer', hint at those professions that the rulers of nations would

---

2. Thumbnail sketches of a further twenty-four appear in a separate entry entitled 'Great . . . but not that Great'.

have preferred had history not demanded otherwise. Others, such as 'Steward', are marvellously misapplied.

The Behavioural

Into this category fall those nicknamees who are known by the content of their character rather than any specific deed or occupation. 'Fulk the Surly', 'Erik the Meek', 'Louis the Indolent' ... their potted biographies suggest whether they are deserved or not.

The Gem

Just occasionally there is a gem of a nickname that refuses to fall into any category, for example the enigmatic 'Christopher the King of Bark' and 'Athelfleda the White Duck'.

This collection reflects the bias of history in that the percentage of female entries is miserably low. Those women who do appear do so not merely because of their bloodline but, as with their male counterparts, because of their military courage (e.g. 'Black Agnes') or beauty ('the Fair Rosamund') or cruelty ('Elizabeth the Blood Countess'). That so many women have received dismissive nicknames – not least 'Isabella the Great Sow' and 'Mary the Queen of Tears' – reflects how much the nicknames of history's nobility are the product of a male-dominated and occasionally misogynistic culture.

Leafing through this list naturally leads to the consideration of what nicknames current members of the aristocracy should be known by for centuries to come. The satirical magazine *Private Eye* has not been backward in coming forward with monikers for today's British royal family. While Prince Charles enjoys the appellation of 'Brian', Her Majesty herself is referred to as 'Brenda'. But these, I venture, will be short-lived, as was the nickname 'Cheryl' for 'Diana the People's Princess'.

What, therefore, might be the long-term soubriquets for today's nobility? Will Prince Charles be known as 'the Green' for his concerns for the environment? Will Queen Elizabeth be hailed in perpetuity as 'the Steadfast' for her firm grasp of the British royal tiller for more than fifty years? Will Queen Beatrix of Holland be known for the colour of her hair or the quality of her reign? Only time will tell, because, as this book amply demonstrates, nicknames are never forced, but acquired.

Fat, Bald and Worthless is by no means a comprehensive collection. Limited space prevents individual entries on 'Olaf the Slippery', 'William the Delightful' and 'Charlotte the Warrior Lady of Latham'. Rather, it is a select miscellany where the depraved seventh-century empress 'Lady Wu the Poisoner' and 'Poor Fred', the hapless eighteenth-century prince of Wales, make interesting alphabetical bedfellows. Nor does this gallery give greatest attention to those individuals who have proven to be historically most significant. The focus is on nickname rather than place in history. The one-eyed Bohemian reformer John Zisca is thus given more space than King Henry VIII.

Emulating the chroniclers and the common people who, down the centuries, have bestowed epithets upon their nobles, this collection doesn't let the truth get in the way of a good nickname or a good story. Instead it embraces the quirky, the fickle, and the occasionally downright wrong, with the same intensity that the love-stricken Nicole of *The House of Lorraine* embraces the man of her dreams.

Acknowledgements

During my Glasgow childhood, initiation into the semi-secret society of the 'Excellent Eastons' involved jumping off the roof of the potting shed in our garden into the compost heap alongside it. This I achieved, aged about seven, and joined my sibling band of 'Marvellous Mark', 'Wonderful William' and 'Super Susie'. Nowadays, when I need to be humbled, my brothers and sister remind me that my nickname was 'Ridiculous Robert'. Perhaps this early moniker was the embryo of this book.

In the late 1980s and early 1990s I worked for Boydell & Brewer, an academic publisher that specializes in scholarly works on medieval history and literature. It might well have been here that my curiosity and interest in historical nicknames and how people got them was rekindled.

Certainly, were it not for my dear friends 'Hamish the Catalyst' and 'Frances the Splendid', *Fat, Bald and Worthless* would still be a jumble of anecdotes in my head. It was they (as well as 'Anthony the Motivator', who at our first meeting told me to write a book, though I doubt he was thinking of one like this) who encouraged me to stop talking about the thing and actually sit down and compile it. 'Robbie the Affable' and 'Carol the Charming' of the Fox Reformed, and several of my friends from St Mary's Church, Stoke Newington, meanwhile, egged me on and plied me with fine wine.

I am grateful to the staff of the British Library and the University of Sussex Library, where much of my research was conducted, and to all my colleagues and students at Brighton College who have been subjected to my occasional ramblings on the subject. Special mention must go to my Upper Fifth religious studies class of 'Lexy the Loon', 'Jonno the Mad', 'Jo the Great', 'Bobcat', 'Andrew the Eagle', 'Joshua of the Four Kinds of Love',

'Sophie the Sophisticated' and 'Sam the Sensational' – maverick, hilarious and A* in equal measure. I am also indebted to publishing supremos 'Simon the Shaken but not Stirred', 'Martin the Midwife' and 'Sophie the Great Overseer', who, in their different ways, have brought this work to fruition. Thanks, too, to 'Kate the Considerate' and 'Caroline the Thoughtful' for their careful reading of the manuscript.

'Kai the Wonderful Princess', my wife and best friend, has cheerfully read various drafts and gently suggested how I might put bounce and clarity into leaden and convoluted prose – all of this in the midst of the challenges of an intercontinental commute between England and South Africa. My deepest gratitude, however, goes to Harry, who has been by my side throughout the entirety of this project. Without his companionship and constant demands to go for walks on Brighton Beach and the South Downs, this work would have been finished in half the time but with half the fun.

[A]

¶ *Charles the* Affable
Charles VIII, king of France, 1470–98

Sickly, short and very, very ugly, Charles was not admired for his physical attributes. But the people of fifteenth-century France looked beyond the bulbous black eyes, the immense nose and the pockmarked face, and liked what they found. Here was a young monarch who was not only genial and charming (more charming to women than his wife Anne, the duchess of Brittany, would have wanted), but also a cavalier man of adventure.

Charles was known for cooking up madcap schemes, and one of them was claiming to be the rightful heir to the kingdom of Naples. To realize this absurd ambition, he borrowed pots of money and signed disastrous treaties, eventually arriving in Italy amid outlandish pomp and ceremony in February 1495. After only a few weeks, however, a bemused coalition of regional leaders (including the pope) had had enough of his pretensions and drove him back to

Charles the Affable

France. In retreat Charles, who during this time was called by some 'Flagellum Dei' or 'the Scourge of God', barely escaped with his life after the battle of Fornovo where he proved himself to be a brave, if not tactically astute, leader of men.

Back home, 'the Scourge of God' spent much of his time playing tennis or, when it rained, reading legends and romances. And it was while watching a game of tennis at his chateau in Amboise that tragedy struck. Charles went to use the latrine and smashed his head against the lintel of the low doorway. He returned to the tennis match seemingly none the worse for his collision, only to collapse and die later that day. Charles was only twenty-eight, and an entire nation mourned the loss of, if not a great ruler, an approachable, fun-loving dreamer of a man with a zeal for justice and a love for his subjects. The chronicler Philip de Commynes summed up the general opinion of Charles when he wrote that 'he was but a little man, both in body and understanding, yet so good natured that it was impossible to meet a better creature.'

❡ Alaric-Cotin *see* Frederick the GREAT

❡ Alexander II *see* PTOLEMAIC KINGS

❡ *Charles the* Alexander of the North
see Charles the MADMAN OF THE NORTH

❡ *Philip the* Amorous
Philip I, king of France, 1052–1108

Philip was 'amorous' in the same way that Nero was 'naughty'. Contemporary chroniclers unanimously condemn this obese and indolent monarch who was above all a man of conspicuous immorality. His hostility towards the reforming elements of his Church, demonstrated by his plundering of monasteries, caused much ecclesiastical alarm. His political duplicity, meanwhile, was renowned. According to William of Malmesbury, Philip came 'hiccoughing' and 'belching from daily excess' to the side of Robert CURTHOSE in support of his claim to the English throne, but was swiftly bought off by William RUFUS and merrily 'returned to his feasting'. But his moral nadir came when he abandoned his wife Bertha of Holland to live openly with, and then marry, Bertrada of Montfort, wife of Fulk the SURLY. In 1095 the Council of Clermont, comprising 200 bishops and headed by Pope Urban II, demanded that Philip leave Bertrada. The amorous Philip refused, and the Council excommunicated the king. Curiously, almost all the bishops in France supported his liaison with Bertrada, hoping, perhaps, that even though he already had one male heir in the shape of Louis the FAT, a second marriage might doubly safeguard the royal succession.

¶ *Frederick the* Antichrist *see* Frederick the
WONDER OF THE WORLD

¶ *Albert the* Astrologer
Albert III, duke of Austria, 1349–95

As well as a scholar of theology and mathematics, Albert was an expert on the meaning of the movement of the stars, and much preferred the quiet of his study and the solitude of his garden to the noise and splendour of the court. However, appearing at court was an essential part of his duties, and there he was better known as 'Albert with the Tress' or 'Albert the Braided' because he wore a lock of his wife's hair (scurrilous rumours held that it belonged to another woman) entwined with his own. Stemming from this symbolic act of devotion, the Society of the Tress, not unlike the Order of the Garter, was established.

¶ *Alfonso the* Astronomer
Alfonso X, king of Castile and León, 1221–84

Medieval Spain's most culturally significant contribution to the history books was the worldwide dissemination of classical knowledge and Muslim learning. At a host of monastic centres and seminaries, most notably the School of Translators in Toledo, ancient Jewish and Muslim works of astronomy, botany, law and medicine were assembled and translated for the first time. The

Toledo centre was at its peak of creativity during the reign of Alfonso, who was known as 'the Astronomer' because he sought to improve the planetary tables created by the ancient astronomer Ptolemy. The results of this massive undertaking were in part published as the 'Alfonsine Tables'. Unfortunately, they proved to be no more accurate than the original versions.

Chroniclers also dub Alfonso 'the Learned', 'the Philosopher' and 'the Wise' because he was the only true philosopher-king to grace the throne of Castile. During his reign, serious study of history and the arts was encouraged for perhaps the first time in Western Europe, and his personal scholarly interests were considerable and diverse: as well as works on astronomy, he compiled a history of Spain, a sweeping history of the entire world prior to the birth of Christ, and a book on board games including chess, draughts and backgammon.

¶ *Edgar the* Atheling *see* Edgar the OUTLAW

¶ *Philip* Augustus *see* Philip the MAGNANIMOUS

¶ Auld Blearie *see* Robert the STEWARD (under NOBLE PROFESSIONS)

¶ *The* Austrian Wench *see* the BAKER AND THE BAKER'S WIFE

¶ *Ivan the* Awesome *see* Ivan the TERRIBLE

[**B**]

¶ *William the* Bad

William I, king of Sicily, 1120–66

William was actually a ruler of considerable merit. It was the island's barons, including the contemporary historian Falcandus, who, purely out of malice and envy, titled him 'Guglielmo il Malo', spreading rumours of bacchanalian banquets and excessive sexual indulgence.

During the reign of his father, Roger II, the island aristocracy had vociferously complained that they had not been allowed to build castles without his consent. This policy, they claimed, strained their authority over their tenants. As Roger had intended, it also prevented them from seriously considering rebellion against him. And so, when Roger died, the barons conspired to revolt against their new monarch and grab more independence for themselves.

Two major uprisings followed, in the second of which William's chief minister, Maione di Bari, was stabbed to death and his corpse torn to shreds by a Palermo mob. Soon, however, the rebels fought among themselves and William regained power. Continuing, unsurprisingly, to exclude the troublesome barons from the government, William became an active patron of letters and the sciences, and gained a reputation for religious tolerance by welcoming members of both the Christian and Islamic faiths into his court. All in all then, 'William the Bad' was rather good.

The Baker and the Baker's Wife

Louis XVI, king of France, 1754–93

Marie Antoinette, queen consort of France, 1755–93

On 6 October 1789 Louis and his Austrian wife, Marie, distributed bread to a starving mob at Versailles. This may have earned them the nicknames 'the Baker' and 'the Baker's Wife', but not the admiration of a republic which four years later sent them to the guillotine.

A more apposite trade-related nickname for Louis was 'the Locksmith King', since at Versailles he converted a room into a metalwork shop where he would merrily tinker away for hours on end, making locks and mending clocks. Louis was a tubby, short-sighted man who also enjoyed reading English periodicals and colouring maps – hardly the sort, one might think, to engender the vitriol of a people. And yet, since he could prohibit any decree submitted to him, he was nicknamed 'Monsieur Veto' by the republicans, and eventually lost his head.

The unpopularity of Marie, the daughter of Maria the MOTHER OF HER COUNTRY, began when she was unable to produce any children for an expectant France. Even though the cause was found to be a medical condition of

¶ *Charles the* Bald

Charles II, king of France, 823–77

Was Charles the Bald really bald, or was his nickname, as some have suggested, not descriptive but sarcastic, signifying instead that Charles was actually rather hirsute? There are nine portraits of Charles the Bald, and in them he is generally depicted as having a heavy-jowled face, a square chin, a big nose and a long, thin, imposing moustache. Furthermore, there is a small painting of him on what is commonly accepted to be his throne

Louis's, which prevented conception (quickly rectified by minor surgery, after which Marie gave birth to a daughter), the public denounced her, not for lack of fertility but for lack of loyalty. Rumours became rife that she was having a number of affairs (at least one with another woman), and a fake autobiography of hers was circulated which claimed she was a whore.

The French, moreover, blamed 'the Austrian Wench' for the country's financial woes, calling her 'Madame Deficit' and holding her personally responsible for propelling the country to near bankruptcy. Come the Revolution, Marie – branded 'Madame Veto' for reasons outlined above – could do no right, and public animosity against her reached boiling point after her supposed comment 'Let them eat cake' when told that her people had no bread. Her jailers vindictively separated her from her infant son (whose cries she could hear from the cell below) and stuck the head of her best friend, the Princess de Lambelle, on a pole and paraded it in front of her.

Marie was bored with the formal French court, which couldn't match its livelier Austrian counterpart, and she may have been occasionally indiscreet, but she was certainly not callously unpatriotic. Nevertheless, she followed her husband to the guillotine.

in which he boasts a full head of hair as well as a moustache.

The chronicler Lupus of Ferrières noted that Charles was a devout man and a devoted husband, and another contemporary nickname of his was 'the Most Christian King'.

¶ *Constantine the* Bald
Constantine III, king of Scotland, d. 997

Like his hair, Constantine's reign was very short. Chronicles suggest he ruled for a mere two years between kings Kenneth II and Kenneth III, possibly killing the former and being killed by the latter.

¶ *Edward the* Bankrupt
Edward III, king of England, 1312–77

Parliament dubbed Edward 'the King of the Sea' because he supported the navy when they defeated the French and Spanish fleets at Sluys and Winchelsea respectively. Merchants knew him as 'the Father of English Commerce' for promoting trade and enabling foreign businesses, especially from Holland and Belgium, to set up shop in England. Unfortunately for him, the rest of the world nicknamed him for his financial ruin when he defaulted on his debts after heavy losses in the Hundred Years War.

¶ Barbarossa
Frederick I, king of Germany and Holy Roman Emperor, *c.*1123–90

According to his biographer, Rahewin, Frederick was 'shorter than very tall men, but taller . . . than men of medium height'. From this somewhat vague description, Rahewin then goes on to mention the physical detail that brought about the emperor's nickname: we are told that as well as having golden curly hair, piercing eyes and a cheerful face, Frederick sported a *barba rosa* – a reddish beard.

Frederick was a warrior king, and was known as 'the Father of His Country' for his military campaigns for the German cause, including no

Barbarossa

fewer than six invasions of Italy and his spearheading of the Third Crusade against Saladin the CHIVALROUS SARACEN. In June 1190 Frederick unexpectedly died when he was thrown from his horse as he was crossing an ice-cold river in Anatolia. Even though the water was only waist deep, Frederick's armour weighed him down and he drowned.

A well-known legend, however, has it that Frederick is not actually dead, but merely 'asleep' with his knights in a subterranean castle in Thuringia. There he sits at a marble table, waiting to be woken to restore Germany to her former glory. He has been waiting a long time. Some say that his red beard, now snowy white, has grown through the table and touches the floor. Others state that his beard already wraps twice around the table and that he will wake up when it has made a third circumference.

¶ *Magnus* Barelegs
Magnus III, king of Norway, *c.*1073–1103

In 1098 Magnus made a visit to his Scottish territories and was impressed by what he saw, so much so that on his return to Norway he was often seen strolling through the streets of Trondheim in complete Highland dress – kilt, sporran, the works. His subjects were impressed by what *they* saw, and the skimpiness of his outfit gave the son of 'Olaf the Quiet' his nickname. In August 1103 Magnus returned to Britain to see how his son Sigurd the CRUSADER was faring, and he was killed in a skirmish while foraging for food in a bog, his bare legs knee deep in mud.

¶ *Boleslav the* Bashful
Boleslav V, prince of Poland, 1226–79

In the thirteenth century the princes and princesses of Poland enjoyed only limited authority, owing in part to a unified Church that played free and easy with threats of excommunication. All they could do was live a good, devout life and possibly be beatified or indeed canonized for their Christian example. Two such holy people were Kinga, the daughter of Bela IV of Hungary, and Boleslav V, who, though married, upheld their mutual vows of virginity.

Among her many good deeds, Kinga founded a church for Franciscan nuns from the Order of the Poor Clares. Boleslav, meanwhile, built the Franciscan friars a chapel in Cracow, and issued a charter of liberties to the region's Jewish population. For *her* ministry, the Church elevated Princess Kinga to 'the Blessed Kinga'. For *his* work, and possibly because of his sexual abstinence, the Church gave Boleslav the nickname of 'Wstydliwy' meaning 'the Bashful' or 'the Chaste'.

¶ *William the* Bastard *see* William the CONQUEROR

¶ Beaky *see* Arthur the IRON DUKE

¶ *Arthgal the* Bear
Arthgal, first earl of Warwick, *fl.* fifth century

Arthgal, first earl of Warwick, supposedly strangled a bear with his bare hands, and the Warwick coat of arms sports a bear in recognition of this achievement.

¶ *George the* Beau of Princes
George IV, king of England, 1762–1830

During his dissolute youth and equally dissolute middle years, before he succeeded to the throne of the occasionally insane FARMER GEORGE, the Prince of Wales – raconteur, bon viveur and source of scandal – was known as 'the Beau of Princes'. In his later life his nicknames were less flattering.

At the age of eighteen George was already, by his own admission, 'rather too fond of women and wine', enjoying a series of brief affairs, including one with the actress Mary Robinson and another with Lady Melbourne. In 1784 he met his one true love, a Roman Catholic called Maria Fitzherbert, whom he married a year later, although the union was kept a secret and later declared invalid because at that time marrying a Catholic made one ineligible for the throne.

In his twenties 'Prinny', as his friends called him, had become a heavy drinker and prolific gambler, and it was to pay off his huge debts that he agreed to marry his cousin Caroline of Brunswick. The marriage was a complete failure. Describing her as 'the vilest wretch this world was ever cursed with', George absolved her of all marital duties, and the couple separated.

By his forties and fifties George had grown immensely overweight, and epithets alluding to his obesity, such as 'the Fat Adonis at Forty', later emended to 'the Fat Adonis at Fifty', were in abundance. An article appeared in the *Morning Post* in 1812, possibly in defence of the prince against these nicknames, describing him as 'An Adonis in Loveliness'. The essayist Leigh Hunt was not impressed by this piece of sycophancy and wrote in the *Examiner*, 'This Adonis in loveliness is a corpulent man of fifty.' Leigh Hunt spent the next two years in jail.

Charles Lamb learnt from Hunt's mistakes, and published the following ditty anonymously:

Not a fatter fish then he
Flounders round the polar sea
By his bulk and by his size
By his oily qualities
This (or else my eyesight fails)
This should be the Prince of Whales.

When he finally became king in 1820, George started to exhibit signs of the insanity that had so plagued his father, and he lost any remains of the charm that had won him so many hearts in his youth. Nothing, for instance, would persuade him to allow his wife Caroline at his coronation, and when she attempted to take her place in Westminster Abbey, the doors were slammed in her face. Amid great public sympathy, Caroline retired to

Hammersmith where she died the very next month. A nation that had once championed their prince now despised their king.

Towards the end of his life, addicted to alcohol and laudanum, George's bouts of madness grew longer, and he would tell whoever would listen, for instance, that he had fought at the battle of Waterloo. He became more and more of a recluse at Windsor Castle and eventually died, a deeply unpopular king, in 1830.

¶ *Henry* Beauclerc *see* NOBLE PROFESSIONS

¶ Bell the Cat
Archibald Douglas, fifth earl of Angus, *c*.1449–*c*.1513

Archibald's nickname, possibly conferred upon him by the sixteenth-century historian Robert Lindsay, refers to an incident in 1482 when he and a number of other disgruntled Scots noblemen plotted the downfall of certain 'low-born familiars' whom they believed had too much influence over the king.

One day Lord Gray, one of Archibald's fellow conspirators, told a story in which mice discuss hanging a bell around a cat's neck so as to be warned of its approach. The problem was whether there was any mouse courageous enough to fasten the bell. On hearing this tale, Archibald is said to have leaped up and cried, 'I shall bell the cat.' Later, demonstrating decidedly un-mouselike qualities, Archibald led a posse against King James's favourites, murdered them, and then hanged them from the bridge in the Berwickshire town of Lauder.

¶ *Fyodor the* Bellringer
Fyodor I, tsar of Russia, 1557–98

For some societies a young man with learning difficulties, spindly legs and a permanent glazed smile would be an embarrassment. In sixteenth-century Russia, however, such 'feeble-mindedness' was considered an especially inspired form of wisdom – a 'foolishness in Christ' – and those exhibiting it were regarded with respect, if not reverence. The son of Ivan the TERRIBLE, Fyodor was described by a visiting English diplomat as 'hawk-nosed, unsteady in his pace by reason of some weakness of his limbs, yet commonly smiling almost to laughter', and he adored visiting monasteries and churches, taking special delight in ringing the bells that summoned the faithful to Mass.

¶ *Ptolemy the* Benefactor *see* PTOLEMAIC KINGS

¶ Bertie *see* Edward the CARESSER

¶ *Charles the* Bewitched
Charles II, king of Spain, 1661–1700

The reign of Charles II of Spain seemed, for anyone unfortunate enough to be around at the time, interminable. When the king's father, Philip IV, died, he left a four-year-old feeble-minded epileptic as his heir and Spain desperately in need of a regent. Some misguided fools determined that Charles's frequent drooling and convulsive fits indicated that he was possessed by the devil, giving rise to his nickname, 'the Bewitched'. Confessors, exorcists and visionary nuns were dragooned from all corners of the kingdom to employ weird potions and conduct exorcisms

Charles the Bewitched

in an attempt to cast out his supposed devil. Unfortunately for Charles, their efforts achieved only a rapid degeneration of his condition, which left him spending much of his time in a blithering frenzy.

Everyone expected that Charles would die at a young age, but he confounded one and all by ruling, albeit in name only, for thirty-five long years. Given his condition, there was no hope of his wife, Marie Louise, producing an heir, and so his reign was suffused with plots about the succession. At first there were three candidates, an Austrian archduke, a French duke and a Bavarian prince. In February 1699, however, the Bavarian prince suddenly upped and died, leaving a head-to-head contest between Archduke Charles and his rival, Philip of Anjou.

Pathetically, Charles's last days were spent participating in the politics of his successor, and during a rare lucid, frenzy-free period, he named Philip of Anjou, the grandson of Louis the SUN KING, as the sole heir to his dominion. Steadfast amid the howls of outrage made by the pro-Austrian factions of his court, Charles displayed a dignity on his deathbed that had eluded the unfortunate man in his lifetime.

¶ Big Alexander *see* Alexander the WOLF OF BADENOCH

¶ Bertha Bigfoot
Bertrada, queen of the Franks, *c.*720–83

Wife of Pepin the SHORT and mother of Charles the GREAT (Charlemagne), Bertrada was also known as 'Queen Goosefoot' and, as such, was the possible inspiration for the name 'Mother Goose' of nursery-rhyme fame.

¶ *Malcolm* Bighead
Malcolm III, king of Scotland, *c.*1031–93

Above all else, Malcolm loved two things: his wife and the clamour of battle. While Macbeth had been in power in Scotland, Malcolm had bided his time in England learning to speak English and to like the English and their ways. Of all the English he met, however, Malcolm became absolutely besotted with a woman named Margaret, sister of Edgar the OUTLAW, the heir to the English throne, and he married her in 1069. He was so fond of her that he made English, rather than Gaelic, the official court language, kissed the books that she read, and agreed to her saintly demands to spend certain mornings every year washing the feet of six beggars and handing out food to nine orphans. Although it has been suggested that the nickname 'Canmore', stemming from the Gaelic words *ceann* meaning 'head' or 'chief', and *mor* meaning 'great' or 'big', was ascribed to Malcolm because he was a swaggering bully, this was clearly not so when his wife was around.

Malcolm's second love, as with most kings of the time, was fighting, and during his reign he led no fewer than five invasions into the northern part of England. In one of these expeditions it was said that 'old men and women were slaughtered like swine for a banquet.' After comparatively timid military responses from the English monarchs Edward the CONFESSOR and Harold the LAST OF THE SAXONS, Malcolm faced much tougher opponents in William the CONQUEROR and William RUFUS, to whom he eventually ceded Cumberland and by whose forces he was ultimately ambushed and killed. It has been suggested that Malcolm was nicknamed 'Canmore' because he was a 'great chief'. This appears not to have been the case all the time.

Little if any research has been conducted on whether the nickname actually refers to a physical attribute rather than a character trait – it could be that Malcolm simply had a really big head.

¶ *Fulk the* Black *see* COLOURFUL
CHARACTERS

¶ *Halfdan the* Black *see* COLOURFUL
CHARACTERS

¶ Black Agnes
Agnes, countess of Dunbar and March, *c.*1312–69

In 1338 Edward the BANKRUPT sent William Montague, the earl of Salisbury, to capture Dunbar Castle in East Lothian. It looked to be a comparatively simple task since the earl of Dunbar was away, fighting an English army in the north. But Edward and Salisbury had not anticipated the heroic spirit of the countess, whom the English later dubbed 'Black Agnes' for her complexion, hair colour and defiance.

For nineteen weeks Salisbury attacked, and for nineteen demoralizing weeks he was repulsed. In her stout defence of the castle Agnes employed the tactic of mockery. She had her kitchen staff, for example, visibly 'dust' the ramparts with handkerchiefs after every bombardment, and on one occasion she sent Salisbury a fresh loaf of bread and a bottle of wine as a commentary on his attempts to starve her into submission.

A particularly low point for the English must have been when Salisbury menacingly wheeled an arch-roofed war-engine called a 'testudo' towards the walls. The testudo, itself nicknamed 'the Sow', was the pride and joy of Salisbury's men and had seen much success in earlier sieges. But in Agnes the Sow found its match. The countess quickly ordered her colleagues to heave a massive rock from the ramparts on to the battering ram below, and smashed it into kindling. As those manning the war-engine ran for their lives, she is recorded as shouting gleefully, 'Behold the litter of English pigs.'

Salisbury eventually slunk away admitting defeat, cursing the countess's constant vigilance and complaining that:

> She kept a stir in tower and trench,
> That brawling, boisterous Scottish wench,
> Came I early, came I late
> I found Agnes at the gate.

¶ *Charles the* Black Boy *see* Charles the

MERRY MONARCH

¶ *James the* Black Douglas

James Douglas, Scottish nobleman, 1286–1330

James Douglas, who was also known as 'the Good Sir James', supported and served Robert the BRUCE, both before and after Robert gained the Scottish throne. James's exploits, particularly in cross-border warfare, earned him considerable territory in the Border region as well as the nickname 'the Black Douglas', attributed to him both for his dark colouring and for his ruthlessness in battle. Such was his reputation for mercilessness that women in the northern counties would discipline their children by warning that 'the Black Douglas' would come and get them if they did not behave. There are suggestions – sadly groundless – that his epithet actually stems from a military trick he employed to capture Roxburgh Castle in 1314, when he disguised his troops as black cows.

¶ *Edward the* Black Prince

Edward, prince of Wales, 1330–76

Edward's contemporaries knew him as either 'Edward IV', anticipating incorrectly his succession to the throne, or 'Edward of Woodstock' after his place of birth. The title 'the Black Prince', by which he is universally known today, did not gain any currency until the late sixteenth century.

The origins of the soubriquet are unclear. Some suggest that at the battle of Crécy in 1346 King Edward the BANKRUPT put his sixteen-year-old son at the vanguard of his troops in order that he might win his spurs. The teenage prince fought heroically, and for his bravery his fellow soldiers hailed him as 'the Black Prince' after the black cuirass (body armour) he was wearing. Others, however, such as the historian Jean Froissart, write that his designation derives instead from his 'terror at arms' and 'martial deeds'.

In 1361 Edward married his cousin and childhood playmate Joan the FAIR MAID OF KENT and was sent to rule the province of Aquitaine in south-west France. Ten years later he returned to England as bankrupt as his father, having fought against, and lost everything to 'Peter the Cruel' of Castile. After several years of bad health Edward finally died in 1386, passing over the kingdom to his only surviving son, Richard the COXCOMB.

¶ *Charles the* Blackbird *see* Charles the MERRY MONARCH

¶ *Elizabeth the* Blood Countess
Elizabeth, countess of Transylvania, c.1560–1614

While her boorish husband, 'Ferencz the Black Hero of Hungary', was away at war, Elizabeth became fascinated by the occult. Believing that bathing in the blood of virgins was the only way to maintain her creamy complexion, she enticed some 600 local young women to her castle in the Carpathian mountains, where they were ritually slaughtered and employed for cosmetic purposes. When the local peasant population ran out, she lured more upmarket women to her lair, until her dastardly beauty treatment was finally discovered. Elizabeth was tried and found guilty and, as punishment, was walled up in a tiny room of her castle.

¶ *Otto the* Bloody
Otto II, king of Germany and Holy Roman Emperor, 955–83

Otto, sometimes dubbed 'the Red' and 'Rufus', in all likelihood on account of the colour of his hair, was a small, brave man, known for his generosity to the Church, knightly virtuosity and occasional acts of impulsive hot-headedness. One such act, in 981, may explain his third nickname, 'the Bloody'.

Otto travelled to Rome that year in order to thwart a plot

to overthrow him. Upon his arrival, he invited all the chief conspirators, who were blissfully unaware that they had been rumbled, to a banquet. While they were all tucking in, Otto suddenly jumped up and stamped his foot. Armed men rushed into the hall and the emperor unrolled a scroll. Otto read aloud the names of the indicted nobles and, one by one, they were dragged from the table and strangled.

¶ Bloody Abdul *see* Abdul the DAMNED

¶ Bloody Mary
Mary I, queen of England, 1516–58

From an early age Mary demonstrated a devotion to the Catholic faith. Sebastian Giustinian, the Venetian ambassador, reports that when she was only two years old she saw Friar Dionosio Memo, the organist of St Mark's Church in Venice, in the court of her father, BLUFF KING HAL, and she apparently cried out the word 'priest' until Memo played for her.

Later in life, when queen, she considered it her Christian duty to turn the tide of Protestantism which had been flowing through England since the reign of her brother Edward the JOSIAH OF ENGLAND (*see* ENGLISH EPITHETS). To this end she married Philip the PRUDENT of Spain (also a devout Catholic) and, having quashed a Protestant rebellion led by Sir Thomas Wyatt, restored papal supremacy in England and revived the laws against heresy. Over the following three years nearly 300 'heretics' were hanged or burned at the stake, among them Archbishop Cranmer and Bishops Ridley and Latimer. For permitting these executions, Mary was despised in certain quarters and rumours circulated that she had slept with the devil and given birth to a snake.

It appears that her nickname is largely due to the virulently anti-Catholic writings of contemporary historian John Foxe. In his massive work *Acts and Monuments* Foxe gives colourful descriptions of the lives and deaths of the 'English Martyrs' –

those who were executed for their Protestant beliefs. The book, which never specifically uses the name 'Bloody Mary' but refers instead to the queen's 'bloody persecution' and to her successor, GOOD QUEEN BESS, as 'sparing the blood' of religious opponents, was published on the continent during Mary's lifetime and in England a few years after her death. It rapidly became a best-seller in an England that had quickly reverted to Protestantism, and a copy was to be found in nearly every church in the country.

❡ *Harald* Bluetooth
Harald, king of the Danes, c.910–c.985

The name 'Bluetooth' or 'Blåtand' has nothing to do with King Harald's dental discoloration, but refers to his dark complexion and hair – something of a rarity among Vikings. Similarly, this son of Gorm the OLD did not fit the traditional Viking image of a raping and pillaging pagan warrior either. Instead, he was a Christian who after his baptism in 960 strove to convert the Danes to his new faith.

Inscriptions on the famous runic stone at Jelling, carved around 980, claim that he 'won for himself all Denmark and Norway and made the Danes Christian'. This may have an element of truth in it, since for the next fifty years Danish kings were so powerful that they turned their attention away from any domestic strife and towards their English counterparts.

❡ Bluff King Hal
Henry VIII, king of England, 1491–1547

For a short period of time Henry enjoyed the title of 'Fidei Defensor' or 'Defender of the Faith'. It was an accolade conferred upon him by Pope Leo X but later revoked by Pope Paul III when the king divorced the first of his six wives, denounced papal supremacy and became the greatest 'lapsed Catholic' of them all. In 1544 Parliament conferred the title upon Edward VI, and it is a designation still enjoyed by the British monarchy today.

Somewhat more colloquially, and presumably not to his face, Henry was known as 'Old Copper Nose'. This had nothing to do with his ruddy and robust complexion but was rather the result of his command that the mint should produce coins with twice as much copper as silver. With use, the silver would wear away on the most raised part of the coin, namely the nose of the king, which gave rise to the nickname. The more famous moniker 'Bluff King Hal', alluding to the monarch's hearty, barrel-chested charm and no-nonsense personality, was bestowed upon him by later generations.

¶ *Philip the* Bold
Philip II, duke of Burgundy, 1342–1404

As in the case of 'Justinian the Great' and his partner Theodora (*see* GREAT . . . BUT NOT THAT GREAT), Philip's fame as one of the most remarkable men of his century would be considerably more modest were it not for his wife. His creation of a powerful, independent Burgundian state simply would not have been so successful had he not married Margaret of Male, daughter of the count of Flanders.

At first glance, Margaret might not have seemed a real catch for the handsome, tall, broad-shouldered Philip. Some may have gone so far as to suggest that the plain, shabbily dressed noble-woman who was fond of whistling and sitting on the grass was simply too vulgar for the bold soldier and brilliant statesman. But Margaret possessed a quality that made many a suitor blind to any imperfections: as daughter of the count of Flanders, she was by far the richest heiress in all of Europe, and in 1384 the couple owned not only Flanders, the most highly industrialized part of Europe, but also Artois, Nevers, Rethel and several other regions of the Holy Roman Empire.

¶ *Philip the* Bold *see* GALLIC PRACTICE
Philip II, king of France, 1245–85

❡ *Henry* Bolingbroke
Henry IV, king of England, 1366–1413

Three miles west of Spilsby in eastern Lincolnshire nestle the remains of a Norman castle dismantled after capture by parliamentary troops in 1643. This is Bolingbroke Castle, birthplace of Henry and origin of his rather unimaginative epithet. The castle was the chief seat of the duchy of Lancaster, and it was said to be haunted by a ghost that looked a bit like a hare or a rabbit, which would race between the legs of whomever it came across, sometimes knocking them over as it made its escape.

❡ Bomba
Ferdinand II, king of the Two Sicilies, 1810–59

Ferdinand's oppressive reign sparked off numerous political disturbances, culminating in a popular uprising in Sicily in 1848. His response – a massive bombardment of several cities, especially Messina – earned him the nickname 'Bomba', while his son Louis was given the diminutive title 'Bombalino' for a similar attack on Palermo in 1860.

❡ *Ivar the* Boneless
Ivar, king of Dublin and York, c.794–872

Identifying the historical Ivar is problematic since he lived in an era in the no man's land between possible fact and probable legend. According to the late tenth-century *Chronicle of Aethelward* and other sources, Ivar was the leader of the Danish 'Great Army' which invaded England in 865, and the *Anglo-Saxon Chronicle* names him as the brother of Halfdan the BLACK (*see* COLOURFUL CHARACTERS). Theories on the origin of his nickname abound:

- The sexual theory: he was impotent.
- The sarcastic theory: he was actually a giant.

- The scribal-error theory: some monk confused *exos*, meaning 'bonelessness', with the Latin *exosus*, meaning 'detestable'.
- The hubristic theory: a ninth-century story tells of a sacrilegious Viking whose bones shrivelled up inside him after he had plundered the monastery of Saint-Germain near Paris.
- The medical theory: he was a disabled dwarf who suffered from brittle bone disease.

His deeds are similarly confusing. Was he really responsible, as some sources attest, for the murder of St Edmund, who was tied to a tree, filled with arrows and then decapitated? And did he and his men really slaughter babies as they went on their conquests, and practise cannibalism? The problems of separating truth from fiction remain.

❡ Boney *see* Napoleon the LITTLE CORPORAL

❡ Bonnie Prince Charlie

Charles Edward Stuart, pretender to the English throne, 1720–88

Charles Stuart was a handsome young man and was very popular with some of the ladies of Edinburgh when he captured the city in 1745 as part of his vain attempt to secure the throne for his father, James the WARMING-PAN BABY. Some of the women went to great lengths to lay their hands on a lock of his hair, and miniature portraits of 'the Highland Laddie' were all the rage.

After his crushing defeat at the battle of Culloden Moor against 'William Augustus the Bloody Butcher', his popularity waned significantly. Popular legend has it that one Flora Mac-Donald helped him escape by disguising him as her maid Betty Burke, and as a result Charles ended his days in Italy not as a bonnie 'Young Pretender' but as an old, worn-out and unattractive alcoholic.

¶ *James the* Bonny Earl

James Stewart, second earl of Moray, d. 1592

Suspecting that James, the second earl of Moray, had been involved in a plot against his life, James the WISEST FOOL IN CHRISTENDOM issued a warrant for his arrest, and asked George Gordon, the sixth earl of Huntly, to oversee the matter. Huntly was more than happy to oblige since he hated the Bonny Earl with a passion. When he found James, who had holed up at his mother's house on the coast of Fifeshire, Huntly did more than just arrest him. He set the building on fire, causing James to rush out and race to the beach where he was hacked down at the water's edge.

James was a good-looking man (hence his appellation 'bonny') and it is said that when Huntly gashed James's cheek with a sword, James proudly exclaimed, 'You have spoilt a better face than your own.' His distraught mother took the corpse to Holyrood Palace, where it lay exposed to the elements for months.

The Bonny Earl's death has given rise to a new word in the English language. It originated in a mishearing of a line from the ballad 'Geordie', which records his murder:

Ye Hielands and ye Lowlands
O, whaur hae ye been?
They hae slain the Earl o' Moray,
And laid him on the green.

In an article for *Harper's Magazine* in 1954 the American writer Sylvia Wright admitted that she had misheard the last line as 'And Lady Mondegreen' and had gone on to tell friends that she thought it unfair that James's innocent wife had also been killed. And thus the term 'mondegreen', referring to a misheard song lyric, was born.

¶ *Albert the* Braided *see* Albert the
ASTROLOGER

¶ Brandy Nan

Anne, queen of England, 1665–1714

At the age of eighteen, Anne married Prince George EST-IL-POSSIBLE? of Denmark. She bore him seventeen children. Eleven were stillborn, five died in infancy and the only other, little William, duke of Gloucester, died of hydrocephalus in 1700 at the tender age of twelve. Some have suggested that this series of misfortunes was what drove Anne to drink, bringing about her nickname 'Brandy Nan'.

Brandy Nan

A common contemporary portrayal of Anne was that of a dull, massively overweight, heavy-drinking queen with a duller, fatter husband who, not to be outdone, possessed an almost unlimited capacity for hard liquor. It was a depiction that gained further currency when some humorist wrote the following graffiti on her statue in St Paul's churchyard, which used to have a gin shop directly in front of it:

> Brandy Nan, Brandy Nan,
> Left in the lurch
> Her face to a gin-shop
> Her back to the church.

Some would counter, however, that this is an unfair character sketch, resting primarily on Jacobite malice. The duchess of

The Battle of Bravalla

The battle of Bravalla, as recorded by the medieval historian Saxo Grammaticus, took place around the beginning of the eighth century. The Danish king 'Harald Wartooth' fought his nephew Ring, whom he had made sub-king of Sweden. In the fighting, the aged and blind Harald was clubbed to death by his own charioteer, a man called Brun, who some suspected was the god Odin. Saxo Grammaticus lists a number of the most notable nobles who fought on each side. They include:

On Harald's Side
> Olvir the Broad
> Gnepia the Old
> Tummi the Sailmaker
> Brat the Jute
> Ari the One-Eyed
> Dal the Fat
> Hithin the Slender
> Hothbrodd the Furious

On Ring's Side
> Egil the One-Eyed
> Styr the Stout
> Gerd the Glad
> Saxo the Splitter
> Thord the Stumbler
> Throndar Big-Nose
> Hogni the Clever

Marlborough, otherwise known as QUEEN SARAH, makes it clear that while Anne's husband ate and drank heavily, Anne herself did not drink to excess, preferring hot chocolate last thing at night. For her gout, however, she did take laudanum on toast floating in brandy.

Rokar the Swarthy
Rolf the Woman-Lover
Sven of the Shorn Crown
Thorulf the Thick
Thengil the Tall
Birvil the Pale
Thorlevar the Unyielding
Grettir the Wicked
Hadd the Hard
Roldar Toe-Joint
Rafn the White
Blihar Snub-Nosed
Erik the Story-Teller
Holfstein the White
Vati the Doubter
Erling the Snake
Od the Englishman
Alf the Far-Wanderer
Enar Big-Belly
Mar the Red
Grombar the Aged
Berg the Seer
Krok the Peasant
Alf the Proud
Othrik the Young
Frosti Bowl, also known as Frosty Melting-Pot

The Swedes, under Ring, won, losing only 12,000 men to Harald's 30,000.

In an emphatically drunken age, Anne, some contest, was a comparatively sober individual with a sober outlook on life. Deeply religious, she loathed the Whig politician Lord Wharton on account of his lecherous immorality; rumour has it that, as well as chasing married women, he once defecated in a church

British Kings of the Dark Ages

From the Roman invasion of 55 BC until approximately AD 900 the first names, let alone nicknames, of kings of Britain are more often matters of conjecture and legend than fact. Some names and nicknames can be found in Geoffrey of Monmouth's *History of the Kings of Britain*, although this too is thought to be as much the stuff of legend as actual history. Geoffrey's work was completed in 1136 and, among other things, provided the basis for the stories of King Arthur. Below is a list of those kings from this period that were accorded nicknames.

The Earliest Kings
Beli the Great
Lucius the Great
Macsen the Leader
Coel the Old (better known as Old King Cole)
Gurgust the Ragged

Northern Britain
Bran the Old
Morcant Lightning
Merchiaun the Lean
Eleuther the Handsome
Dunaut the Stout
Mynyddog the Rich

South-west Wales
Tryffon the Bearded
Aircol Longhand

North-west Wales
Cadwallon Longhand

Maelgwyn the Tall
Rhun the Tall
Idwal the Roebuck

North-east Wales
Brochfael of the Tusks
Cynan the Cruel
Cyndrwyn the Stubborn

Minor Kingdoms of Wales
Rhun Red Eyes
Gwrin of the Ragged Beard
Glitnoth Longshanks
Gwrgan the Great

South-west Scotland
Dumnagual the Old
Rhydderch the Old

West Scotland
Fergus the Great
Eochaid the Yellow-Haired
Domnall the Pock-Marked
Ferchar the Long
Eochaid Crooked-Nose
Aed the Fair
Eochaid the Poisonous

East Saxons
Sigebert the Little
Sigebert the Good

It appears that Mercians, Northumbrians and West
Saxons, until Alfred the GREAT, were not interested in
nicknames.

pulpit. Rumour has similarly tarnished the reputation of Anne, a decidedly ordinary person with her fair share of weaknesses who became known as little more than a gargantuan old soak.

¶ *The* Bread-Soup King *see* Louis the KING OF SLOPS

¶ *Haakon the* Broad-Shouldered
Haakon II, king of Norway, *c.*1147–62

Much was placed on the small but broad shoulders of Haakon when he was elected king of Norway at the tender age of ten. His main concern was the claim of 'Inge the Hunchback' to the throne, but that fell away in 1161 when Inge died after losing his temper. His death occurred when he and his men were ranged against Haakon's across an ice-covered river. Incensed by accusations of cowardice, Inge's champion, one Gregorius Dagsson, raced forward, fell through the ice and was slaughtered as he tried to clamber back up. In a rush of blood to the head, Inge furiously hurtled towards the enemy and was also killed. Haakon's relief was short-lived, however. Another pretender, Magnus Erlingsson, defeated and killed him in battle the next year. Haakon was fifteen years old.

¶ *Ptolemy the* Brother-Loving *see* PTOLEMAIC KINGS

¶ *Robert the* Bruce
Robert I, king of Scotland, 1274–1329

Allegedly inspired by the determination of a spider that he saw in a cave while gloomily assessing his military fortune, Robert won a famous victory against the English in 1314 at the battle of Bannockburn. The origins of his epithet 'the Bruce' are regrettably less colourful. Originally thought to be of Flemish extraction, his ancestors settled in Brus, near Cherbourg, in Normandy. One of these forebears, also called Robert, came over to England in the early eleventh century and served as right-hand man to Prince David, later King David 'the Saint', during his stay at the court of Henry BEAUCLERC (*see* NOBLE PROFESSIONS). For obvious reasons he was known as 'Robert de Brus', and the name of his descendants was anglicized to 'the Bruce'.

❡ *David the* Builder *see* NOBLE PROFESSIONS

❡ Bungy Louis *see* Louis the KING OF SLOPS

❡ *Leo the* Butcher *see* NOBLE PROFESSIONS

❡ *George the* Button-Maker *see* FARMER GEORGE

[C]

¶ *Edward the* Caresser
Edward VII, king of England, 1841–1910

In an allusion to his ancestral namesake Edward the CONFESSOR, Edward VII was dubbed 'the Caresser' for his womanizing ways. His parents, Victoria the WIDOW OF WINDSOR and Albert the GOOD, were determined to prevent him from becoming wayward or profligate like so many of his relatives, and so must have been very disappointed with both their son and his epithet. Britain, on the other hand, thought he was rather special.

After a regimented childhood during which his good looks had women wrapped around his little finger, Edward, or 'Bertie' as the prince was known, was sent to Cambridge University, where he lodged some four miles outside town to minimize any frivolous or dissolute behaviour. Four miles proved a mere step for Edward, who rapidly developed Rabelaisian appetites for food, cigars, gambling and female company. Midway through his studies he was sent to Ireland, where he was enlisted in the army. Here he also signally failed to reach expectations, most notably when Nellie Clifton, a local 'actress', was found one night in his quarters.

His marriage to Princess Alexandra of Denmark did not appear to diminish his sexual appetite, and a long list of mistresses included society belle Lillie 'the Jersey Lily' Langtry, Daisy 'Babbling' Brook and French tragic actress Sarah Bernhardt, otherwise known as 'the Divine Sarah' or 'Sarah Heartburn'. Once, when Bernhardt was playing Fedora in Paris, Edward confessed that he had always wanted to be an actor. Few in the audience the next night would have noticed that the corpse of

Fedora's dead lover was in fact none other than the heir to the British throne.

For all his misdoings and dalliances, the British liked their prince immensely, especially after the death of his father, when Victoria slumped into a life of mourning. In a drab and dismal court, 'Bertie' was a splash of colour. His practical jokes raised giggles in a palace bereft of laughter, and his fashion sense and love of the good life set the trend for an English society eager for fun. In later life 'Bertie' – now Edward – helped to orchestrate the *entente cordiale* with France, and in recognition of his diplomatic efforts he was dubbed 'the Peacemaker'. He was also known as 'the Uncle of Europe', and this was almost literally true as he was uncle to the German kaiser, the Russian tsar and the king of Spain.

Less laudatory was another of Edward's nicknames, 'Tum Tum', which referred to the monarch's corpulence. On one occasion the chubby Edward gently admonished Sir Frederick Johnstone, one of his guests at Sandringham, with the words, 'Freddy, Freddy, you're very drunk', to which Johnstone allegedly retorted, 'Tum Tum, you're very fat.' The king did not appreciate the remark.

Great Britain, on the other hand, did appreciate Edward. As the foreign secretary Sir Edward Grey wrote, the bubbly king 'had a capacity for enjoying life . . . combined with a positive and strong desire that everyone else should enjoy life too'.

¶ *Edward* Carnarvon
Edward II, king of England, 1284–1327

Given his inept soldiery (his ill-disciplined troops lost the famous battle of Bannockburn to Robert the BRUCE), his alienation of the nation's nobility, or even his alleged homosexuality, Edward could have been nicknamed many things. As it is, his soubriquet, like that of Henry BOLINGBROKE, derives from the castle in which he was born – in Edward's case Carnarvon Castle in North

The Catholic Kings

Ferdinand II, king of Aragon, 1452–1516

Isabella, queen of Castile and Aragon, 1451–1504

The marriage of King Ferdinand II of Aragon and Queen Isabella of Castile in 1469 united the two largest provinces of the Iberian Peninsula and paved the way for the eventual unification of Spain. The Moorish kingdom of Granada finally capitulated to the couple in 1492, and two years later Pope Alexander VI granted them the title 'Reyes Católicos', or 'Catholic Kings', signifying that Spain, united under their dual monarchy, was now subject to the Catholic faith. Both monarchs took their religion very seriously indeed.

Underneath Ferdinand's cold and flinty exterior burned an ardent passion for the Virgin Mary. Unfortunately for his subjects (especially those of the Jewish faith) this zeal was accompanied by a cold and flinty determination to spread his religious beliefs, and in tandem with Isabella he established the notorious Spanish Inquisition to ensure that Catholicism was followed religiously by all.

The austere Isabella 'la Católica', meanwhile, considered herself a moral role model to her subjects. Appalled at their 'lack of faith' and 'inordinate luxury', she promoted frugality and devotion. Despite her immense wealth, for instance, she personally mended one of Ferdinand's tunics seven times, and whenever he was out of town she took great pains to have it known that she slept surrounded by her daughters and ladies-in-waiting.

The couple's faith was sorely tested by the misfortunes of their offspring. Of their five children, their son John died in his late teens (his death popularly ascribed to his physical passion for his young wife), their daughter Catalina (Catherine of Aragon) had her marriage annulled by BLUFF KING HAL, and poor Joan, heiress to the throne after the death of her brother, married Philip the FAIR and then went stark raving mad.

Wales. Edward also died in a castle, namely Berkeley Castle in Gloucestershire, where he was hideously murdered on the orders of his cruel wife, Isabella the SHE-WOLF OF FRANCE.

¶ *Ferdinand the* Catholic *see* the CATHOLIC KINGS

¶ *Isabella the* Catholic *see* the CATHOLIC KINGS

¶ *Michael the* Caulker *see* NOBLE PROFESSIONS

¶ *Peter the* Ceremonious
Peter IV, king of Aragon, 1319–87

Peter considered authority to be effective only if seen to be so, and therefore busied himself with pomp, ceremony and self-celebration to prove that he was in charge. He enjoyed making grand gestures, and founded a couple of universities, had the Qur'an and other major works translated into Catalan, and placed the crown upon his own head at his coronation. But he was also a stickler for detail: when, for example, King James III of Majorca came to court to pay homage, Peter made him sit on a small, unimpressive cushion as a reminder of his lowly status.

Many of his demonstrations of rank and power were shocking in their cruelty, so much so that some nicknamed him 'Peter el del Puñal' or 'Peter of the Dagger'. Once he summoned some Valencian nobles whom he suspected of double-dealing to his court. On their arrival he had one of the palace bells that had summoned them melted down, and the hot lead poured down the unfortunate dignitaries' throats.

¶ *Alfonso the* Chaste
Alfonso II, king of Asturias, 759–842

Early in his reign Alfonso made Oviedo the new capital of the kingdom of Asturias. It was from here that he made the first pilgrimage to Compostela, where the supposed tomb of the apostle St James had recently been discovered. As one might expect from a chaste and devout king, Alfonso died without heirs.

¶ *Boleslav the* Chaste *see* Boleslav the BASHFUL

¶ *Le* Chevalier de St George *see* James the WARMING-PAN BABY

¶ *Ptolemy the* Chickpea *see* PTOLEMAIC KINGS

¶ *Louis the* Child
Louis IV, king of the east Franks, 893–911

Louis was indeed a child – barely six – when he ascended the throne, and he relied upon Liutpold, the margrave of Bavaria, to run the kingdom and keep marauding Magyar horsemen at bay. When Liutpold died in battle in 907, the Magyars ran amok. And when Louis himself, still in his teens, died four years later, the whole of the eastern part of the Frankish Empire sank into desperate lawlessness.

¶ *Saladin the* Chivalrous Saracen
Saladin, Saracen leader, c.1138–93

Saladin was pitted against Richard the LIONHEART in the Third Crusade and earned his nickname when he allegedly saw Richard without a horse and sent him one of his own steeds, saying he would not see such a worthy opponent without a mount.

He was not all sweetness and light, however: his hatred of Christians was absolute. 'Let us purge the air that they breathe,' he told his troops, 'until there shall not remain on this earth one unbeliever in God.'

¶ Citizen Equity
Philip I, duke of Orléans, 1747–93

In an attempt to recoup the vast fortune that he had squandered, Philip built an arcade of shops and cafés in his palace

Saladin the Chivalrous Saracen

grounds. Business proved to be brisk, and the gardens soon became a popular meeting place. However, they also became a crucible of liberal dissent, and as the French Revolution grew in intensity, so did murmurings against Philip, with rumours flying that he secretly harboured ambitions to be king. To stem the tide of unpopularity, Philip publicly renounced his hereditary titles, assumed the name 'Citizen Equity' or 'Égalité' and, as a member of the National Convention, voted in 1792 for the death of Louis XVI, 'the Baker' (*see* the BAKER AND THE BAKER'S WIFE). His efforts were in vain, however, and Philip followed the monarch to the guillotine the very next year.

¶ *Louis Philip the* Citizen King
Louis Philip I, king of France, 1773–1850

Together with the likes of Maximilien Robespierre and Jean Paul Marat, Louis was a member of the Jacobin Club. He fought in the Revolutionary army but, feeling alienated by the more radical policies of the Republic, deserted, and in 1793 went into

Colourful Characters

Erik the RED, Edward the BLACK PRINCE, Harald BLUE-TOOTH and many others with a colour-related epithet are mentioned elsewhere in this book. Below is a collection of other nobles whose main soubriquet is 'black', 'red', 'green' or 'white'. As with the longer, individual entries, the origins of these nicknames vary, from hair colour to dress sense.

Fulk the Black
Fulk III, count of Anjou, c.970–1040

Even the most bloodthirsty of barbarians would blanch when they considered the dark deeds of Fulk, a man who burnt his wife at the stake, waged war with his son, and sent twelve thugs to assassinate the favourite minister of Robert the PIOUS.

Halfdan the Black
Halfdan III, king of Norway, d. c.860

Details about Halfdan's life, as recorded by medieval Icelandic historians such as Snorri Sturluson, are, at best, sketchy. We can be fairly sure, however, that he had black hair and that aged forty he drowned after falling through the ice of a frozen lake.

Amadeus the Green and Amadeus the Red
Amadeus VI, count of Savoy, 1334–83
Amadeus VII, count of Savoy, 1360–91

Amadeus VI adored tournaments almost as much as he did Savoy, and his nickname 'the Green' derives from the vivid emerald colour of his ensign at these events and his customary livery when at court. At his son's wedding he turned up resplendent in his customary green taffeta with cloth-of-gold embroideries on the sleeves. Not to be outdone, Amadeus VII emulated the paternal example, but chose bright red instead of green for his signature colour.

Thorstein the Red
Thorstein, Norse king of Scotland, d. 900

The little we know about Thorstein comes from later Icelandic sources. Quite possibly, he married Thurid, the sister of a woman called 'Helgi the Lean'. In all probability his nickname denotes the colour of his hair.

Elizabeth the Red-Nosed Princess
Elizabeth, princess of the Palatine, 1618–80

Elizabeth, the daughter of 'Frederick the Winter King' (*see* the WINTER MONARCHS), possessed a monstrous aquiline nose that had the disturbing habit of turning cherry red at the most inopportune moments. When it did so, she would run away to her bedroom and hide.

Donald the White
Donald III, king of Scotland, c.1033–99

When he became king on the death of Malcolm BIGHEAD, the first act of the sixty-year-old, white-haired 'Domnall Bán' (meaning 'Donald the White' and sometimes anglicized as 'Donalbain') was to expel all the Englishmen from his court. The red-haired English king William Rufus was furious and sent an entire army north to get rid of him.

White Hands
Godred, king of Man and Dublin, c.1040–95

Godred 'White Hands' was so named because of his habit of wearing white gauntlets into battle. A slightly more outlandish choice of battledress was that of 'Sebastian the Madman', the sixteenth-century king of Portugal who dressed in green armour, in order that he might be clearly visible to one and all.

exile in Switzerland. For a number of years he travelled under a pseudonym, first as 'Chabaud Latour' and later as 'Herr Müller', only returning to France after the restoration of the Bourbons over twenty years later.

On his arrival in Paris in 1830, the son of CITIZEN EQUITY received two nicknames. The first was 'the King of the Barricades', after the form of mass protest that occurred before he was declared lieutenant-general of France. The second, 'the Citizen King', was conferred upon him ten days later when the people elected him their monarch.

After a cautious and conservative reign, Louis Philip was ousted by the Revolution of 1848. Again he used a pseudonym to ensure safety. When he arrived in England, his immigration papers stated that he was a humble citizen called 'William Smith'.

❡ Clicquot
Frederick William IV, king of Prussia, 1795–1861

Often depicted as a romantic aesthete rather than a hard-headed politician, Frederick William had specific tastes and strong views: he appreciated organized religion but believed in the divine right of kings; he liked the order of the German nation but disliked parliaments; and he loved champagne (for which the British satirical magazine *Punch* gave him his brand-specific nickname) but absolutely loathed France.

❡ *Omar the* Commander of the Faithful
Omar I, second caliph, c.581–644

Succeeding Abu Bakr the UPRIGHT, Omar was the first of several caliphs to enjoy the title 'the Commander of the Faithful'. His reign was marked by significant Islamic territorial expansion, including into Persia, but an obviously unfaithful Persian slave assassinated him.

¶ *Edward the* Confessor
Edward, king of England, *c.*1003–66

It is widely accepted that Edward did not love the military life. It is also generally agreed that Edward did not love his wife, Edith (indeed their unconsummated marriage dissolved completely when he sent her off to a convent). Instead, Edward had one passion: the Church. The most enduring expression of his passion for Christianity is Westminster Abbey in London, the construction of which he personally financed.

The term 'confessor' can mean someone who makes their confession to a priest or it can denote a priest who hears confession. In Edward's case, however, it describes a man whose entire life was a confession of his faith.

¶ Conky *see* Arthur the IRON DUKE

¶ *Alfonso the* Conqueror
Alfonso I, king of Portugal, *c.*1109–85

Qualities of boldness, persistence and guile made Alfonso an excellent first king of Portugal. His most famous conquest was that of Berber-controlled Lisbon in 1147 when, accompanied by soldiers originally recruited by St Bernard for the Second Crusade, he took the city after a four-month siege. His success assured him of a nickname and the continuity of the Portuguese monarchy.

Alfonso was a big man with a big beard who enjoyed a reputation of possessing Herculean strength. In 1169, however, the muscle-bound monarch trapped his leg in a gate and broke it so badly that he was never able to ride again. With his military career and conquering days at an end, Alfonso knighted his sixteen-year-old son Sancho the SETTLER (*see* NOBLE PROFESSIONS) and prepared him for the throne.

¶ *Mehmed the* Conqueror
Mehmed II, sultan of the Ottoman Empire, 1432–81

Ottoman tradition demanded that each new sultan had to embark on a great conquest, and Mehmed plumped for the greatest prize of them all: Constantinople. It was a tall order, since the thickness of the city's walls had foiled many a Turkish assault. Nevertheless, on the orders of the new sultan, Ottoman troops once more laid siege to it in April 1453.

At first, history looked like repeating itself. Heavy bombardment of the walls using a 28-foot-long monster of a cannon proved largely ineffective, and the inhabitants had no trouble in repairing the destroyed fortifications every night. However, on the night of 22 May there was an eclipse of the moon. The Byzantines had credited their success in repulsing the Turks to the legend that Constantinople would never fall while the moon was waxing – that is, with its 'horns' to the east. But with the eclipse, their morale was instantly and utterly crushed. During the next few days someone, in his or her despondency, left a gate in the stockade open. It was only a small gate, but all that Mehmed needed. The sack of Constantinople lasted three days, and from that moment onwards Mehmed was hailed as 'the Conqueror'.

After Constantinople Mehmed continued his military conquests. Among the territories to fall under Ottoman control were Serbia, Greece and Wallachia, where Vlad the IMPALER finally met his match. In 1481 Mehmed was embarking on new campaigns against Rhodes and southern Italy when he suddenly died – some say poisoned by an undercover Venetian doctor, others say from a self-administered overdose of opium. Not everyone mourned his passing. On news of the death of 'the Conqueror', the pope ordered that every church bell should be rung in jubilation for three days and nights.

❡ *William the* Conqueror
William I, king of England, *c*.1028–87

In his day William was known as 'the Bastard' since he was the illegitimate son of 'Robert the Devil' (the duke of Normandy) and the daughter of a local tanner. 'Conqueror', however, would have been an apt contemporary soubriquet as well, as long before the Norman had turned his ambitious gaze over the English Channel he had orchestrated a string of military victories that significantly enhanced his power in France.

His conquest of England was no fait accompli. Under the command of Harold the LAST OF THE SAXONS the English forces were one of the most aggressive armies of Europe; however it was Harold's bad luck that within weeks of his success at the battle of Stamford Bridge his men had to face the Norman forces at Hastings. After William's famous victory of 1066 he worked hard to ensure there were children to inherit his new territories. To that end William (who stood five foot ten) and his wife Matilda (who was no more than four foot two inches tall) produced ten children, including two future kings, William RUFUS and Henry BEAUCLERC (*see* NOBLE PROFESSIONS).

❡ Copper Nose *see* NOSE ALMIGHTY

❡ *Napoleon the* Corsican General
See Napoleon the LITTLE CORPORAL

❡ *Richard the* Coxcomb
Richard II, king of England, 1367–1400

In 1394 Anne of Bohemia, Richard's first wife, succumbed to the Black Death, and such was his grief that he ordered the palace at Sheen, where she had spent her last days, to be razed. The tragic event turned out to be a critical moment in Richard's life and reign. The popular king and loving husband descended into melancholy and became a despotic, arrogant fop, whose disastrous second marriage to Isabella, the young daughter of Charles the SILLY, was marked by wanton cruelty.

If for no other reason, however, this son of Edward the BLACK PRINCE and Joan the FAIR MAID OF KENT should be celebrated in history as the inventor of the handkerchief – the must-have accessory for any self-respecting coxcomb. It may have found much service when, having been ousted by the forces of his cousin Henry BOLINGBROKE, Richard spent his last days starving to death in Pontefract Castle.

¶ *Richard* Crookback
Richard III, king of England, 1452–85

William Shakespeare is largely responsible for the popular image of Richard as a limping hunchback with a withered arm. The playwright's sources for *Richard III* may well have included Thomas More's biography of the king, which depicted Richard some decades after his death as 'little of stature, ill-featured of limbs, crook-backed ... envious and, afore his birth, ever froward'. Contemporary chroniclers, however, such as Philip de Commynes and the Italian monk Dominic Mancini make no mention of any deformity, and even his enemies agreed that he demonstrated considerable prowess on the battlefield. Clearly, then, Richard was not sufficiently impaired to be unable to use his weapons or control his horse, and it is quite possible that More was participating in some propaganda, playing on the medieval belief that a twisted mind must dwell in a twisted body.

In his play Shakespeare has Richard maligned as a 'wretched, bloody and usurping boar'. Here he is basing his portrayal on the king's heraldic device of a boar *passant argent*. A contemporary satirist called William Collingborne also alluded to this nickname when he penned a little ditty that included the lines:

The Cat, the Rat, and Lovel our Dogge,
Rules all England under an Hogge.

The first three animals refer to contemporary nobles. 'Hogge' was clearly a none-too-complimentary reference to the king, and for this clumsy piece of doggerel Collingborne paid with his life.

¶ *Boleslav the* Crooked-Mouthed
Boleslav III, prince of Poland, 1085–1138

Boleslav 'Krzywousty' heroically defended Silesia against German invasion, and his heavy defeat of the imperial forces in 1109 must have left a big grin on the royal asymmetric jaw. His rivalry with his brother Zbigniew gave him little reason to smile, however. Terrified that he might stage a coup, Boleslav had Zbigniew blinded. Tragically, his henchmen did such a careless job that Zbigniew died of his wounds.

¶ *Christian the* Cruel *see* Christian the
TYRANT

¶ *Henry the* Cruel
Henry VI, king of Germany, 1165–97

Cold and calculating, mean-spirited and money-grabbing, Henry was considered one of the cruellest men in what were cruel times. His successful invasion of Sicily, financed by the huge ransom he exacted for the release of his prize prisoner Richard the LIONHEART, might have been enough to earn him the nickname 'the Conqueror'. However, history remembers him as 'the Cruel', perhaps for his blinding and castration of Sicily's four-year-old King William, possibly for his desecration of the corpses of Tancred and Roger the GREAT COUNT (*see* the SONS OF TANCRED), two of the island's former leaders, but mostly probably for the merciless vengeance he took on the ringleaders of a failed coup against him in May 1197.

¶ *Peter the* Cruel
Peter I, king of Portugal, 1320–67

Peter was a popular king who liked to dance in the streets with his people and whose love affair with his 'mistress' Ines de Castro became the subject of legend and poetry. When he learned that Ines had been murdered on the orders of his father Alfonso the FIERCE, his twin nicknames of 'the Just' and 'the Cruel' proved especially apt. Two of the assassins, who were found hiding in the lands of his namesake 'Peter the Cruel' of Castile, were brought back to Portugal and summarily executed by having their hearts ripped out, one through his chest, the other through his back.

Peter then publicly revealed that he had been secretly married to Ines for a number of years, and commanded, somewhat grotesquely, that her body should be exhumed and translated to a sumptuous tomb at Alcobaca where all were solemnly to acknowledge her as queen.

¶ Crum-Hell *see* NOSE ALMIGHTY

¶ *Sigurd the* Crusader
Sigurd I, king of Norway, c.1089–1130

In 1099 Sigurd's father, Magnus BARELEGS, left him in charge of the southern Hebrides and the Isle of Man and headed back to Norway. Three years later Magnus returned to Britain and, in order to consolidate his territories, arranged a marriage between Sigurd and Blathmina, the daughter of the Irish high king. Sigurd was thirteen, Blathmina five. The following year Magnus died and the young couple returned to Sigurd's homeland. Only then did his crusading really begin.

According to the medieval Icelandic historian Snorri Sturluson, Sigurd set sail on a crusade to Jerusalem, fighting and defeating the 'heathen' along the way. One of his most famous exploits was the capture of a seemingly inaccessible cave halfway up a cliff face, which was defended by pagan robbers who mocked their enemy on the beach far below. In order to defeat them, Sigurd stealthily hoisted a ship on to the top of the cliff, filled it with soldiers and then lowered it on ropes in front of the mouth of the cave. His men then leaped out and easily overpowered the very surprised thieves.

After a brief spell in Jerusalem where King Baldwin I gave him a splinter of the Holy Cross, Sigurd returned to Norway and ruled without opposition.

¶ *Robert the* Cunning *see* the SONS OF TANCRED

¶ *Boleslav the* Curly
Boleslav IV, prince of Poland, *c.*1120–73

Little is recorded of Boleslav 'Kedzierzawy' except that he had to pay homage to the Holy Roman Emperor Frederick BARBA-ROSSA. This involved sending him a regular financial tribute, furnishing him with 300 knights for his Italian campaign, and appearing at his court when, in what must have been literally a hairy moment, the curly-locked prince came face to face with the red-bearded king.

¶ *Robert* Curthose
Robert II, duke of Normandy, *c.*1054–1134

Contemporary historians William of Malmesbury and Orderic Vitalis agree that Robert was small and rotund, and that his father, William the CONQUEROR, once derisively called him 'Brevis ocrea', literally 'short-boot', a term which developed into the nickname 'Curthose'. Orderic Vitalis gleefully adds that Robert was also nicknamed 'Gambaron', which, based on the Italian word for lobster, possibly refers to the duke's possessing some crustacean-like characteristic.

On his deathbed William expressed his conviction that, under his son Robert, Normandy would be wretchedly governed . . . and wretchedly governed it was. As a ruler Robert proved magnificently inept, following the line of least resistance and allowing barons to do as they pleased. Captured by his brother Henry BEAUCLERC (*see* NOBLE PROFESSIONS) in 1106, Robert spent nearly thirty years of his life a prisoner in various castles in England and Wales. His last few years were in Cardiff Castle, where he appears to have employed his considerable free time in learning Welsh, since a pathetic little poem in that language is attributed to his authorship. The line 'Woe to him that is not old enough to die' is a miserable reflection on the life of a man better known for the size of his footwear than the size of his character.

¶ *Henry* Curtmantle
Henry II, king of England, 1133–89

The extravagances of courtly dress held no charms for Henry, and one of the first innovations he made when king was to introduce the utilitarian knee-length cloak – the 'curt mantle' – of Anjou, as opposed to the ankle-length variety of his predecessors. Troubadours and tournaments he found dreary, preferring instead simpler entertainments such as those provided by a jester called 'Roland the Farter' to whom Henry gave thirty acres in Suffolk, for which, records state, 'he used to leap, whistle and fart before the king.'

Walter Map, one of Henry's courtiers, described him as 'resplendent with many virtues' but also 'darkened by some vices'. When annoyed by one of his court attendants, for instance, the furious king 'threw the cap from his head, untied his belt, hurled his mantle and other garments from him, removed the silk coverlet from the bed with his own hand and began to chew the straw of the bedding'.

Walter Map was in fact one of a paltry few who could find any good qualities in a king who otherwise garnered nothing but contempt: it seems that the weather-beaten, bow-legged, barrel-chested huntsman of a king had an innate ability to offend. According to the chronicler William FitzStephen, Henry once took immense delight in forcing his chancellor to hand over his magnificent, brand-new grey and red cape to a pauper who just happened be passing. Certainly Henry was not on the Christmas-card list of St Bernard of Clairvaux, who is reported as saying, 'From the Devil he came and to the Devil he shall return.'

[**D**]

¶ *Peter* of the Dagger *see* Peter the
CEREMONIOUS

¶ *Abdul the* Damned
Abdul Hamid II, sultan of the Ottoman Empire, 1842–
1918

No Ottoman sultan was more loathed than Abdul Hamid. Some condemned him as 'Abdul the Damned', a man destined for

Abdul the Damned

hell for such acts of callous cruelty as instigating a campaign of terror resulting in the execution of some 25,000 Armenian villagers, and having the head of his imprisoned grand vizier sent to him in a box labelled 'Japanese Ivories'.

Others despised 'Bloody Abdul' for his cowardice. Paranoid about assassination, he rarely ventured out of his palace-cum-fortress, which he kitted out with trapdoors, observation posts and power-

ful telescopes, and he never slept more than one night in the same room. Dour, doleful and universally despised, Abdul Hamid died not from an assassin's bullet but in exile, deposed by a people that found such an abject and venomous ruler quite intolerable.

¶ *James the* Dead Man Who Won a Fight

James Douglas, second earl of Douglas, *c.*1358–88

During the reign of Robert the STEWARD (*see* NOBLE PRO-
FESSIONS) there were several border clashes between the
Douglases of Scotland and the Percy family of Northumberland.
One confrontation in 1388, known as the battle of Otterburn,
which was otherwise entirely forgettable, inspired a ballad in
which James Douglas, who won the battle but lost his life, is
made to say:

> But I have dreamed a dreary dream
> Beyond the Isle of Skye
> I saw a dead man win a fight,
> And I think that man was I.

Doggerel drivel has thus bestowed celebrity status upon an epi-
sode and an earl of little consequence.

¶ *Edmund the* Deed-Doer *see* Edmund the
MAGNIFICENT

¶ *Aud the* Deep-Minded

Aud, Norse queen, *fl.* 850s

When her son Thorstein the RED (*see* COLOURFUL CHARACTERS)
was killed while fighting in Scotland, the thoughtful Aud set sail
for Iceland to start a new life there, with a mission to marry off her
many grandchildren. In this she was wholly successful, with two of
them finding partners en route – one on the Orkneys and the other
on the Faroe Islands. Once in Iceland Aud searched for a place to
settle, and a number of places on the island are named after little
things she did there – 'Kambsnes' or 'Comb Headland', for example,
where she lost her comb, and 'Dögurdarnes' or 'Breakfast Headland' where presumably she ate, rather than lost, her breakfast.

Soon all her granddaughters had found husbands. Her youngest grandson, Olaf, however, had yet to meet a suitable partner and so the ever-considerate Aud held a party – a singles night with a difference. At the gathering Aud announced that she was leaving her inheritance entirely to Olaf, and then she encouraged her startled guests to drink up and have a great time since the festivities were also her funeral feast. With that, she took herself to bed. The next morning she was found leaning against her pillows, as dead as a doornail.

¶ *Henry the* Defender of the Faith

see BLUFF KING HAL

¶ *Louis the* Desired *see* Louis the KING OF SLOPS

¶ *Demetrius the* Devoted

Demetrius II, king of Georgia, 1269–89

Bastinado is a form of torture consisting of the beating of the victim's soles with a stick, an ordeal which Demetrius underwent when he surrendered to the Mongol il-khan Arghun in order to save his people from invasion. But Arghun was not a man to keep his word. Although he had promised that his forces would not attack Georgia if their young king came to his court in Mughan and paid homage, he had Demetrius first tortured and then beheaded.

The Georgians bewailed the loss of their tall, fair-haired and generous king, and for his sacrifice they styled him 'Tav-dadébuli' – 'the Devoted' or 'the Man Who Sacrificed His Head'. Sadly his sacrifice was in vain. With Demetrius headless so was Georgia, and without an effective monarch the kingdom sank into squabbling anarchy.

¶ *Charles A* Discrowned Glutton
see Charles the HARLEQUIN

¶ *Heneage the* Dismal
Heneage Finch, first earl of Nottingham, 1621–82

Heneage was a lawyer who took no part in the troubles of the English Civil War, concentrating instead on building up a lucrative private practice. In 1660 he was elected Member of Parliament for Canterbury and was made Solicitor General and later Lord Chancellor. Lawyers remember him for his just and systematic administration. Almost everyone else remembers him for looking like death warmed up.

¶ Divine Sovereign *see* Lady Wu the
POISONER

¶ *Clovis the* Do-Nothing King
Clovis II, Merovingian king, c.634–57

Clovis was the first of ten *rois fainéants* (do-nothing monarchs) who passed the time in idle luxury in secluded villas while the real power lay with the mayors of the royal palaces. Occasionally these kings made public appearances in oxen-drawn chariots, but it was only with the arrival of Pepin the SHORT in the early eighth century that royal authority meant anything again in France.

¶ Dollheart *see* John LACKLAND

¶ Dona Juana
Maria Louisa, queen of Spain, 1751–1819

Don Juan was a legendary heartless Spanish philanderer; 'Dona Juana' was a very real heartless philanderer who regularly and

Domesday Characters

The Domesday Book mentions a multitude of minor personages in eleventh-century England. We learn about Nigel, a priest who was William the Conqueror's physician. We find men styled 'the Crossbowman' or 'the Engineer', who must have held responsible posts in the royal army. Others, also named for their professions, include 'the Fisherman', 'the Cook' and 'the Interpreter'.

Some people are referred to by a nickname. Richard 'Poignant', meaning 'biter', suggests that the tenant of Trow Farm in Wiltshire was not the most mellow of characters. One can only hazard a guess, meanwhile, as to what earned Roger the epithet 'God Save the Ladies'. Below is a sample list of other epithets and nicknames gleaned from the census:

Eadric the Blind
Alwin the Devil
John the Doorkeeper
Robert the Fair
William Hosed
Berdic the Jester
Geoffrey the Little
Leofgifu the Nun
Richard the Reckless
Godfrey the Scullion
Alwin Stickhare
Magnus the Swarthy
Walter the Vinedresser

often cheated on her husband, Charles IV. One of her favourite sexual playmates was a former guardsman dubbed 'the Sausage Man'. Some say this was because his home province of Extremadura was famous for its sausages. Others propose a more earthy reason.

❡ Dracula *see* Vlad the IMPALER

❡ *Michael the* Drunkard
Michael III, Byzantine emperor, 838–67

'Basil the Macedonian' was an upstart, a former groom who jockeyed his way into the good graces of those in power and finally persuaded 'Michael the Drunkard' to crown him co-emperor, whereupon he had Michael murdered in his bed. Byzantine sources, writing to justify Basil's dastardly deed, portray Michael as a dissolute sot who partook in drinking bouts, horse races and religious burlesques while completely ignoring affairs of state. Yet modern scholars suggest that he was far from completely irresponsible, especially when it came to military matters. In 861, for instance, Michael and his uncle Bardas invaded Bulgaria and secured the conversion of the king to Christianity. A few years after their return, however, both fell prey to Basil's henchmen.

❡ *Wenceslas the* Drunkard *see* Wenceslas the
WORTHLESS

❡ *Hugh the* Dull
Hugh, lord of Douglas, 1294–1342

'Dismal' or 'Worthless', particularly if undeserved, must be hard nicknames to accept, but being known to history as 'the Dull' must surely be the most painful slap in the face. Annals of the great Douglas family of Scotland do not dwell on Hugh's tenure as the head of the clan. 'Of this man,' wrote the early seventeenth-century historian David Hume of Godscroft, 'whether it was by reason of the dullness of his mind . . . we have no mention at all in history of his actions.' It appears that he was gormless. Without doubt he was heirless, handing over the mantle of authority to his nephew William.

[**E**]

¶ *Napoleon the* Eagle *see* Napoleon the
LITTLE CORPORAL

¶ *Napoleon the* Eaglet
Napoleon François Bonaparte, titular king of Rome,
1811–32

Napoleon 'l'Aiglon', the sickly offspring of 'the Eagle' (also known as Napoleon the LITTLE CORPORAL), was never in robust health. This painfully thin 'king of Rome' suffered from a persistent cough for most of his life, then contracted tuberculosis in his teens, and died aged just twenty-one when, in the winter of 1832, he literally caught his death of cold while watching a military parade.

¶ *Ladislaus the* Elbow-High
Ladislaus I, king of Poland, c.1260–1333

Ladislaus may have been small in stature, but he stood tall among his contemporaries as a skilful diplomat, courageous warrior and revered king. At a time of feudal disunity he forged a union between Little Poland and Greater Poland, and won the approval of the pope, paving the way for Polish territorial expansion under his son Casimir the GREAT.

His tactics were not always conventional. In suppressing a revolt by Germans in Cracow, for instance, he used a simple language test, echoing the 'Shibboleth' test found in the Book of Judges in the Bible. Anyone who could repeat and correctly pronounce '*soczewica, kolo, miele, mlyn*' was free to go. Those who could not were presumed guilty and duly punished.

¶ *Edward the* Elder

Edward, king of Wessex, d. 924

Danish aggression was running slack, the Mercians (ruled by Edward's formidable sister Aethelflaed) were in a compromising mood, and the hitherto independent residents of Northumbria and East Anglia were no match for his military supremacy. Peace on all sides ensured an uncommonly calm monarchy for Edward, whose neighbours acknowledged him as their 'father and lord' and, denoting rank rather than family relationship, their 'elder'. Continuing the work begun by his father, Alfred the GREAT, Edward was able to prime England for complete unification, a goal achieved during the reign of his son and successor, Athelstan the GLORIOUS.

¶ *Sophia Charlotte the* Elephant

Sophia Charlotte, mistress of King George I of England, 1675–1725

The people of England were surprised when they learned that their king, George the TURNIP-HOER, was enjoying more than a platonic relationship with his half-sister Sophia Charlotte, not only because she was his sibling but also because she was ugly and enormous. The masses referred to her in elephantine terms while Horace Walpole, that connoisseur of fine things, wrote that she had 'two acres of cheeks and a swollen neck'.

¶ *Alexander the* Emancipator

Alexander II, emperor of Russia, 1818–81

The emancipation of the Russian serfs by Alexander II was, according to *The Times* of London, 'the first and greatest . . . of Russian reforms', but it literally came at a cost, not least to those it was intended to help. Most of the liberated peasants thought that Alexander, whom they referred to as 'Little Father', had given them not only their freedom but also their land. To their dismay

English Epithets

Below are five English noblemen with somewhat florid national epithets. In each case the individual is compared to an ancient hero. Whether their achievements warrant such comparison is a matter of debate.

Henry Our English Marcellus
Henry, prince of Wales, 1594–1612

Given his impressive political acumen and artistic insight, the young Roman Marcus Claudius Marcellus was expected to go far; however, he died aged nineteen, leaving his many virtues to be celebrated by a host of writers, not least by Virgil in *The Aeneid*. Henry was similarly a multi-talented young man: a superb swordsman, a keen patron of the arts and a man of deep piety. But, like Marcellus, he also died young, in his case at just eighteen, of typhoid, leaving a nation to mourn and muse on what might have been.

Robert the English Achilles
Robert Devereux, second earl of Essex, 1567–1601

French soldiers called Essex 'the English Achilles' because of his acts of valour on the battlefield. But, like his Greek mythological namesake, he had a fatal flaw: his Achilles heel was his hot-headedness, which regularly got him into trouble and finally resulted in his execution after he publicly stated that conditions in England were 'as crooked as [Queen Elizabeth's] carcase'.

Henry the English Alexander
Henry V, king of England, 1387–1422

Like Alexander the GREAT, Henry was a man of military action. At the age of ten he was given his first sword, and at sixteen he fought in his first battle. Soon after coming to the throne he invaded France and in October 1415 won a famous victory at Agincourt when the French, outnumbering the English three to one, used disastrous tactics against Henry's longbowmen.

Like Alexander, Henry was also over-fond of alcohol. Chroniclers furthermore state that in his youth he 'fervently followed the service of Venus as well as Mars' and a bevy of contemporary records, telling of his waywardness, leave little doubt that there is some truth to his reputation as something of a drunken wastrel.

Henry followed his namesake by dying in his thirties, in Henry's case almost certainly of dysentery.

Henry the English Solomon
Henry VII, king of England, 1457–1509

The Lancastrian victory at the battle of Bosworth Field brought the Wars of the Roses to an end and Henry to the throne. With admirable Solomon-like diplomacy Henry succeeded in uniting the houses of Lancaster and York by marrying Elizabeth of York, daughter of Edward the ROBBER.

Edward the Josiah of England
Edward VI, king of England, 1537–53

In the Second Book of Kings in the Bible one reads of the young King Josiah ordering the demolition of pagan temples and instigating a comprehensive set of religious reforms. Similarly, in histories of the Tudor period one reads of King Edward ordering the destruction of all shrines and images of saints as he continued the reforms of his father, BLUFF KING HAL.

they found they had to pay taxes, and that annual payments were higher than their former rents.

¶ *Robert the* English Achilles *see* ENGLISH EPITHETS

¶ *Henry the* English Alexander
see ENGLISH EPITHETS

¶ *Edward the* English Justinian
see Edward the HAMMER OF THE SCOTS

¶ *Henry the* English Solomon *see* ENGLISH EPITHETS

¶ *George* Est-Il-Possible?
George, prince of Denmark, 1653–1703

'James the Popish Duke' (*see* the POPISH AND PROTESTANT DUKES) noticed a peculiar trait in his son-in-law. Every time the consort of BRANDY NAN was relayed a piece of bad news, he would invariably shake his head and sigh, '*Est-il possible?*' This occasional mannerism became something of a daily occurrence during the Glorious Revolution of 1688 when the prince heard report upon report of military mismanagement or desertion.

¶ *Erik* Evergood
Erik I, king of Denmark, 1056–1103

While England was decidedly a Christian nation in the eleventh century, the Church had yet to establish a firm footing in Denmark, and the task of embedding the faith in the nation's culture fell to Erik 'Ejegod'. As his nickname suggests, Eric was a pious monarch – so pious in fact that he is noted as the first European king ever to go on a pilgrimage to the Holy Land. Pilgrimages usually involve a return journey, but not for the good Erik, who never again set foot in his kingdom, ending his days instead on the island of Cyprus.

[**F**]

§ *Charles the* Fair *see* GALLIC PRACTICE

§ *Edwy the* Fair

Edwy, king of the English, *c.*941–59

Edwy came to the throne when a precocious teenager and almost immediately fell out of favour with all his senior advisers. Dunstan, the abbot of Glastonbury, was notably and understandably irked when, during Edwy's coronation ceremony, he discovered his royal charge 'consorting' with a young lady. By 959 most of the elders had had enough of Edwy and put their support behind a Northumbrian and Mercian conspiracy to replace him with his far more genial brother Edgar the PEACEABLE.

When Edwy died, in unknown circumstances, his obituaries were universally disparaging – with the exception of that of Athelweard the Chronicler, his unctuous brother-in-law, who dubbed him 'the Fair', alluding not only to his complexion but also to the overblown assertion that he was rather pleasant company.

§ *Philip the* Fair

Philip IV, king of France, 1268–1314

Philip's good looks elicited both praise and his nickname, but his deeds evoked disapproval from a number of quarters. Some of the criticism was comparatively mild. The bishop of Poitiers, for instance, wrote that Philip was 'an owl, the most beautiful of birds but worth nothing'. Others, however, who saw his generosity to the Church as motivated entirely by politics rather than piety, were more forthcoming in their damnation of Philip 'le Bel'. Dante, for example, did not hold back. In his *Purgatorio* he describes him as 'a malignant plant which overshadows all the Christian world', and elsewhere in the poem compares him, in his persecution of the Order of the Knights Templar, with Pontius Pilate.

In this business Philip's behaviour truly was abhorrent. The Master of the Knights Templar, Jacques DeMolay, demanded that Philip make public his private allegations that the Order was teeming with thieves, heretics and homosexuals. Testily, Philip did so and then embarked upon a barbarous crusade upon the crusaders. He reserved his most heinous act of cruelty for DeMolay himself, whom he dragged to an island on the Seine and slow-roasted to death over a smokeless fire.

¶ *Joan the* Fair Maid of Kent
Joan, countess of Kent, 1328–85

One of the most beautiful, though perhaps not the most virtuous, wives and mothers to grace history's pages, Joan married her cousin Edward the BLACK PRINCE and soon gave birth to Richard the COXCOMB. Her subjects dubbed her 'the Fair Maid of Kent' because she was considered 'the fairest lady in all the kingdom'. It was public knowledge, however, that she was also one of 'the most amorous', having produced five children with her first husband, Sir Thomas Holland, and then contracted a bigamous marriage with the earl of Salisbury, William Montague, prior to any union with Edward.

¶ Fair Rosamund

Rosamund Clifford, mistress of King Henry II of
England, *c.*1140– *c.*1176

Legend tells us that Henry CURTMANTLE was besotted with the
ravishing Rosamund and kept her prisoner in a maze in

Woodstock near Oxford. Legend similarly states that Eleanor
of Aquitaine, Henry's wife, was
beside herself with jealousy and
that she mastered the maze and
offered Rosamund two equally
unappealing options: death by
dagger or death by poison. This
is codswallop. As the historian
Giraldus Cambrensis, among
others, makes clear, Henry
lived openly with the beautiful
Rosamund, while the dumped
Eleanor lived under a form of
house arrest.

Fair Rosamund

¶ *Harold* Fairhair

Harold, king of Norway, *c.*860–*c.*940

Stung by the rejection of the princess of a neighbouring country
to his romantic advances, Harold vowed not even to comb, let
alone cut, his hair until he became the sole ruler of Norway. For
ten long years Harold battled against other local, petty kings for
national supremacy, and for ten long years his hairstyle alarmed
all and sundry. But then, in 872, Harold won a famous victory
at Hafrs Fjord and seized control of the entire nation. After what
must have been a dramatic wash and set, the new-look Harold
so delighted his subjects with his clean flowing locks that they
instantly changed their nickname for him from 'Shockhead' to
'Fairhair'.

¶ *Denis the* Farmer *see* NOBLE PROFESSIONS

¶ Farmer George
George III, king of England, 1738–1820

An avid interest in botany and agriculture earned George his nickname but also the disapproval of many of his senior officials, who grumbled that he preferred country pursuits to politics. Certainly George did not like city life, preferring cricket and flying kites to court functions and the theatre. He was in fact one of the first London commuters, regularly galloping twenty miles back to rural Windsor after eating a hasty supper at St James's Palace. There he would pen articles for the scholarly periodical *Annals of Agriculture* and prepare parliamentary speeches on diseases among horned cattle.

In his later years George used a lathe to make a set of ivory buttons, for which some dubbed him 'the Button-Maker', but most people today remember him for the last years of his life when he was intermittently mad. Anecdotes from this period abound. In a particularly popular story, he was said to have got out of his coach in Windsor Great Park and – in a notable lapse of botanical know-how – shook hands with an oak tree because he was under the impression it was Frederick the GREAT.

¶ *Charles the* Fat
Charles III, Frankish king and Holy Roman Emperor, 839–88

Incongruously, the vastly overweight Charles was known during his own lifetime as 'Karoleto' or 'Little Charles' to distinguish him from Charles the BALD. It was not until some four centuries later that he received his more common epithet of 'the Fat'. Obesity, however, was not his most pressing medical condition.

Charles suffered from a debilitating illness that exhibited itself in regular savage headaches and the occasional spectacular seizure. His condition made it virtually impossible for him to rule, and so in early 887 the emperor underwent a surgical skull incision – a trepanation – in the hope that this might bring relief. If it did, it was temporary. Charles died the following year while in exile in Swabia.

¶ *Henry the* Fat
Henry I, king of Navarre, *c.*1210–74

After a four-year reign, marked, it is said, by dignity and diplomacy, 'Enrique el Gordo', or 'Henri le Gros', died. According to most of the received accounts, this youngest son of Theobald the TROUBADOUR (*see* NOBLE PROFESSIONS) suffocated on his own fat.

¶ *Louis the* Fat
Louis VI, king of France, 1081–1137

Philip the AMOROUS, Louis's father, was so overweight that he was forced to hand over the day-to-day administration of the kingdom to his comparatively trim son. But Louis was no slouch in the obesity stakes either. Predisposed to both gluttony and corpulence, he was so fat that after the age of forty-six any horse that he sat on simply buckled.

In his account of the deeds of Louis, the abbot and historian Suger wrote that in 1126 his body was so 'weighed down by burdensome folds of flesh' that 'no-one, not even a beggar, would have wanted or been able to ride a horse when hampered by such a dangerously large body.' Presumably the horse would have had similar objections.

¶ *Sancho the* Fat
Sancho I, king of Castile and León, d. 967

When Sancho came to the throne in 956 he was so fat that he could hardly walk, let alone ride a horse. As such, he could only sit and, with difficulty, raise a finger in protest as rebels under his cousin Ordono stormed the palace and forced him into exile. A few years of dieting later, however, and Sancho was back. The new, improved and slender Sancho marched on León with a large Muslim army and successfully recovered his kingdom.

¶ *George the* Fat Adonis at Fifty
see George the BEAU OF PRINCES

¶ *George the* Fat Adonis at Forty
see George the BEAU OF PRINCES

¶ *Edward the* Father of English Commerce *see* Edward the BANKRUPT

¶ *Frederick the* Father of His Country
see BARBAROSSA

¶ *Christian the* Father of His People
Christian III, king of Denmark, 1503–59

When Christian assumed control of the kingdom in 1536, the predominantly Catholic Danish state council was understandably rather cagey about having an ardent Lutheran as their king. Their fears were well founded. Within two weeks of his accession he had every bishop arrested and thrown into prison, their offices abolished and their lands permanently confiscated. The Roman Catholic Church in Denmark was no more.

The official Church in Denmark was now the Lutheran State Church, in which priests were elected and allowed to marry, and congregations were encouraged to read the Bible in their own language. Such events ushered in the last phase of the Danish

Reformation and gave rise to Christian's nickname – although this epithet was not used within Catholic circles, which considered his actions decidedly lacking in fatherly concern.

¶ *Francis the* Father of Letters
Francis I, king of France, 1494–1547

Francis was given this nickname as well as that of 'the Maecenas of France' because, like the first-century BC Roman statesman who supported such luminaries as Virgil and Horace, he was a munificent patron of the arts and learning. One of the court painters was Leonardo da Vinci, who brought his *Mona Lisa* and *The Virgin and Child with St Anne* along with him. Works by Raphael and Michelangelo graced the halls of his palace at Versailles and various chateaux, and his private library of nearly 3,000 volumes became the basis of the Bibliothèque Nationale.

A generous patron maybe, but Francis had many, many faults. One of these was his shameless unfaithfulness to his charming wife, Claude the HANDSOME QUEEN. Although he was extremely ugly and, according to Victor Hugo, possessed 'the largest nose in France, except for his jester, Triboulet', Francis had a multitude of mistresses. A Venetian visiting the court wrote of his daily routine as follows: 'He rises at eleven o'clock, hears Mass, dines, spends two or three hours with his mother, then goes whoring or hunting . . .'

¶ *William the* Father of the Fatherland
see William the SILENT

¶ *Abu Bakr the* Father of the Maiden
see Abu Bakr the UPRIGHT

¶ *Edward the* Father of the Mother of Parliaments *see* Edward the HAMMER OF THE SCOTS

¶ *Louis the* Father of the People
Louis XII, king of France, 1462–1515

In comparison with his ludicrously prodigal predecessor Charles the AFFABLE, Louis was thrifty bordering on penny-pinching. In response to a friend's warning that he was gaining a reputation in court for being parsimonious, Louis is reported to have replied, 'Far better my courtiers should laugh at my parsimony than that my people should mourn for my extravagance.'

His prudent expenditure of the public purse – there was no direct increase of taxation during his reign – coupled with his reform of the courts and tax laws, won him approval among the masses and a nickname suggesting paternal affection.

¶ Fatso *see* PTOLEMAIC KINGS

¶ *John the* Fearless
John, duke of Burgundy, 1371–1419

John received his epithet from his exploits at the battle of Nicopolis against the Ottoman Turks. A cursory examination of his actions there, however, might lead one to think that he should have been dubbed not 'the Fearless' but 'the Stupid'.

In 1396 European powers were laying siege to the main Turkish stronghold on the Danube. Sigismund the LIGHT OF THE WORLD, the organizer of the crusade, urged prudence, but the knights ignored this sage advice and, with John at the vanguard, charged up the steep hill to the fortified town. Although they scattered the first line of Turkish cavalry and infantry, they were no match for the second wave of defence and, exhausted from the climb, most of the knights were cut down. John somehow survived to fight another day.

John the Fearless

The son of Philip the BOLD, John was a little man with a big head and eyes like a frog. According to chronicler Olivier de la Marche, he was 'very courageous' but trusted no one and 'always wore armour under his robe'. Indeed, this man who regularly used assassination as a political tool lived in absolute fear of his own murder, making his nickname 'Sans Peur' a mockery of reality.

And murdered he was. In 1419 he and some Burgundian delegates met on a bridge at Montereau near Paris to sign a peace treaty with counterparts from Armagnac. John walked into a covered enclosure, where his armour could not withstand a torrent of blows from battleaxes.

¶ *Alfonso the* Fierce
Alfonso IV, king of Portugal, 1291–1357

Alfonso may have been fierce and brave (several chroniclers refer to him as 'Afonso o Bravo'), but his reign was marked by austerity rather than ferocity. The son of Denis the FARMER (*see* NOBLE PROFESSIONS), Alfonso continued where his father had left off in strengthening royal authority and promoting justice, but numerous internal revolts and the devastating impact of the Black Death, which claimed at least a third of Portugal's population, left a country weakened and politically unstable. Alfonso deemed it necessary to use severe methods to quash domestic dissent, and it is from these actions that he probably earned his nickname.

Another origin of the name could be the manner in which he treated Ines de Castro, the mistress of Peter the CRUEL, his son and heir. Ines was a Galician and, concerned that her brothers would direct the affairs of Portugal rather than his son, Alfonso went to her estate in early 1355 to talk to her and assess the situation. After a seemingly amicable interview he rode nonchalantly away, while a couple of his hired hands stayed behind and murdered her.

¶ *James the* Fiery Face
James II, king of Scotland, 1430–60

As his nickname implies, the most obvious thing about James was his disfigurement, and in François Villon's *Ballade* the left half of his face is described as 'the colour of an amethyst from the forehead to the chin'. No poetic licence was in operation here: a contemporary drawing provides visual evidence to support the French lyric poet's claim.

James was fiery in appearance and fiery by nature. An uneasy truce with the powerful Douglas family ended when James stabbed William, the eighth earl, to death and demolished the clan's castles. Then, with Scotland mostly under his sway, he turned his attention to England, but died while laying siege to Roxburgh Castle.

¶ *Ptolemy the* Flute Player *see* PTOLEMAIC KINGS

¶ *Lulach the* Fool
Lulach, king of Scotland, *c.*1031–58

When Macbeth was cut down by the forces of Malcolm BIGHEAD, Lulach, Macbeth's stepson, found himself king. By styling him 'the Fool' or 'the Simpleton' chroniclers suggest that he was not up to the task at all. His entire sorry reign was spent battling with Malcolm BIGHEAD, and he was killed in an ambush in Strathbogie some four months after his coronation.

¶ *Louis the* Foreigner
Louis IV, king of France, 921–54

When his father 'Charles the Simple' was deposed from the French throne, Louis's mother Eadgifu whisked Louis off to England where he grew up in the court of Athelstan the GLORIOUS. After thirteen quiet years away from France, for which he was dubbed 'the Foreigner' or 'd'Outremer', Louis returned home to a torrid battle for supremacy, not least with the forces of such luminaries as 'Otto the Great' and 'Hugh the Great' (*see* GREAT . . . BUT NOT THAT GREAT).

¶ *Sven* Forkbeard
Sven I, king of Denmark and England, *c.*960–1014

With an imposing hairstyle to match his imposing North Sea empire, Sven, the son of Harald BLUETOOTH, instigated a mass of incursions against England. The onslaught then intensified when Ethelred the UNREADY ordered the killing of every Dane living in England, in what has come to be known as the St Brice's Day Massacre of 1002. Some scholars think that Sven's sister Gunhilda was one of the victims.

Battered by successive punitive expeditions and ineptly governed, England was ripe for conquest, and on Christmas Day 1013 Sven was pronounced her king. He didn't live long to wallow in royal glory, however. Just six weeks later the great Viking warrior toppled from his horse and died.

¶ *Manuel the* Fortunate
Manuel I, king of Portugal, 1469–1521

As the ninth child of Fernando, the brother of 'Alfonso the African', Manuel was fortunate to have reigned at all, but due to some marriages and murders of convenience Manuel found himself succeeding John II as king of Portugal in 1495. It was Manuel's predecessor who had planned an expedition in search of a sea route to India and had appointed Vasco da Gama to lead it, but fortunately for Manuel, it was under *his* reign that the expedition actually took place. It was fortunate, too, that Vasco da Gama's friend Peter Alvarez Cabral was put in charge of a fleet destined for India, and that he veered so far west that he landed in Brazil.

These were just two of several voyages of exploration during Manuel's tenure that heralded the beginning of an era in Portuguese history of unprecedented imperial wealth, power and vitality. By 1503 Manuel enjoyed virtual control of the spice trade, so much so that Francis the FATHER OF LETTERS was known to call him 'the Grocer King'.

Unfortunately, as a direct result of this international expansion, domestic corruption went unchecked and Portugal's agricultural and industrial welfare was neglected. Manuel's despotic nature, furthermore, as well as his deceitful kowtowing to the demands of Isabella and Ferdinand (*see* the CATHOLIC KINGS) to rid Portugal of its Jewish population, led to untold horrors and the severe depletion of his country's learning, science and artistry.

Manuel is buried in the Jerónimos Monastery together with Vasco da Gama, the man who principally made his rule, and the lives of many (but certainly not all) of his subjects, so happy.

¶ *Henry the* Fowler
Henry I, king of Germany, *c*.876–936

'Heinrich der Vogler' was so named because he was found hunting wildfowl when informed of his election to the throne. Using this principle, Elizabeth II of Great Britain may (or may not) go down in history as 'the Rhino Watcher', as that was her precise activity high in a fig tree at Treetops Hotel in the Aberdare Forest game reserve in Kenya when she became queen.

¶ *Merfyn the* Freckled
Merfyn, king of Gwynedd, *c.*780–844

Merfyn's spotty face is better known to history than his birth-place. According to bardic tradition, he came from 'the land of Manaw', which refers either to the Isle of Man or to a region on the banks of the Forth. Once he had arrived in the Welsh principality, he allied himself to the royal house of Powys by marrying a woman called Nest, and for nineteen years held his position against all rivals and Danish invasion with such authority that, on his death in 844, Merfyn 'Frych' was able to hand over the kingdom of Gwynedd to his son 'Rhodri the Great' in robust health.

[**G**]

¶ *Victor Emmanuel the* Gallant King
Victor Emmanuel II, king of Italy, 1820–78

Victor Emmanuel's popular nickname was 'Guaff', in reference to his podgy, upturned nose, but the statesman Massimo d'Azeglio thought this to be no epithet for a monarch, and tried to convince nineteenth-century Europe that he was in fact a *re galantuomo* – a gallant gentleman king. But it was something of an uphill struggle. For while Victor Emmanuel could be charming when he wanted to be, there are ample records of his decidedly ungallant behaviour. At formal banquets, for instance, he would regularly sit in morose silence and not say a word. He was often tactless towards his subjects in central and southern Italy, speaking to them in French, the language of his Piedmont home, rather than in Italian. Moreover, he was notorious for his boasting. Once he bragged to Victoria the WIDOW OF WINDSOR that he was a better politician than any of his ministers and that he was writing a book to prove it. In actuality, he was a source of consternation to his entire cabinet and, as one historian has put it, 'was incapable of writing a single page of literate prose'.

After a predominantly military education, in which his school reports were hardly effusive ('Always asleep,' complained one teacher; 'Thoroughly bored and indolent,' wrote another), Victor Emmanuel ascended the throne on the abdication of his distant and unloving father, 'Charles Albert the Vacillating King'. In a reign almost devoid of honourable actions, one act of 'gallantry' is worthy of mention. In 1852 he took the momentous decision of handing the control of the government over to the ambitious and politically astute Count Cavour, whose skilful manoeuvrings over the next few years culminated in Victor Emmanuel's

Gallic Practice

The French people appear to have enjoyed the process of nicknaming their nobility. Unlike the flowery soubriquets favoured by the English, Gallic epithets intersperse the straightforward and appropriate with the highly inappropriate and sarcastic. French noble nicknames cannot therefore be taken on face value. Instead, one has to understand something of the person's life in order to determine whether their nickname has been given without irony or with a liberal dose of Gallic humour. In the former category one can place such aristocrats as:

- Charles the AFFABLE, who was delightful
- Louis the FAT, who was obese
- GOOD KING RENÉ, who was truly chivalrous
- Henry the GREAT, who was physically repulsive, but loved for his deeds
- Louis the QUARRELLER, who argued a lot

While in the latter, one can list such 'dignitaries' as:

- John the FEARLESS, who lacked intelligence rather than fear
- John the GOOD, who was very, very bad
- Louis the WELL-BELOVED, who was a national laughing stock

Below are some French nobility who do not appear elsewhere in this book. As with those mentioned above, their nicknames have been awarded capriciously – some with an element of truth about them, others not.

Philip the Bold
Philip III, king of France, 1245–85

'Bold' as well as 'Daring' he may have been in limited measure, but a further nickname of 'Rash' is also apposite for Philip for his ill-considered quasi-crusade against 'Peter the Great' of Aragon (*see* GREAT . . . BUT NOT THAT GREAT). At vast expense he led an imposing army over the Pyrenees towards Gerona, but soon his supply lines were cut and his army stricken with sickness, and Philip had to slope back home.

Charles the Fair
Charles IV, king of France, 1294–1328

Historians of the time concur that, like his father Philip the FAIR,

Charles 'le Bel' was one of the most handsome people in all Europe. They also agree that, like his father, he was one of the most morally reprehensible. Here, then, the nickname may be considered as both objective and derisive.

Louis the Indolent
Louis V, king of France, 967–87

Louis, also known as 'the Sluggard', truly epitomized torpor, a man '*qui nihil fecit*' ('who did nothing') except get embroiled in an argument with an archbishop.

Louis the Just
Louis XIII, king of France, 1601–43

Two explanations have been proffered for Louis's nickname. The first is that, given his dissolute lifestyle, it was bestowed sarcastically. The second, rather more unorthodox, reason is that Louis was so named because he was born on 27 September under the astrological sign of Libra, the scales. Had the English used such a system, his contemporaries Charles the LAST MAN (born on 19 November) and Rupert the MAD CAVALIER (born on 17 December would have been known respectively as 'the Scorpion' and 'the Archer'.

Philip the Lucky
Philip VI, king of France, 1293–1350

Philip 'le Bien-Fortuné' was perhaps the unluckiest of all French monarchs. His fleet was crushed in 1340 at the battle of Sluys, his troops humiliated in 1346 at the battle of Crécy and finally, in 1349 and 1350, a quarter of his entire nation was killed by the Black Death.

Henry the Warlike
Henry II, king of France, 1519–59

Henry was essentially a man of peace, better known for his womanizing than any warmongering. Contemporary historians dwell at length on his long-running affair with the beautiful Diane of Poitiers.

becoming the first king of a united Italy. This, however, could not diminish the contempt with which he was regarded in certain circles. The British diarist Charles Greville, for instance, thought him to be 'the most debauched and dissolute fellow in the world', while the Tuscan politician Baron Ricasoli, who publicly praised his monarch, acknowledged in a private conversation that of the three qualities essential in a good ruler – bravery, honesty and education – Victor Emmanuel lacked them all.

¶ Gambaron *see* Robert CURTHOSE

¶ *John of* Gaunt
John, duke of Lancaster, 1340–99

William Shakespeare is to be credited (or blamed) for this nick-name. No one called the duke of Lancaster 'John of Gaunt' (a corruption of his birthplace of Ghent in Flanders) after he was three years old, but Shakespeare reintroduced the epithet in his play *Richard II*, in which he has John make the famous nationalist speech which ends with the words, 'This blessed plot, this earth, this realm, this England'. John of Gaunt, meanwhile, is to be credited (or blamed) for introducing morris dancing to England from Spain.

¶ *Emma the* Gem of Normandy
Emma, queen of England, d. 1052

One of the few portraits of Emma to survive (a self-commissioned work entitled *In Praise of Queen Emma*) depicts a woman with pretty eyes and an attractive oval face. The picture must have been fairly accurate since the French noblewoman garnered not only a unique nickname from an adoring nation but also offers of marriage from two kings.

Her first husband, Ethelred the UNREADY, was delighted with his beautiful bride and as a wedding present gave her a large chunk of southern England. Her new subjects were similarly delighted and called their new queen 'the Gem of Normandy'. For a while the gem shone brilliantly among her new country-men. Her popularity dipped but then soared when she was first accused and then cleared both of being an accessory to the murder of her son, Prince Alfred, and of 'misconduct' with the bishop of Winchester. Legend has it that she proved her inno-cence by walking unhurt over nine red-hot ploughshares in Winchester Cathedral. A few years later, however, the gem lost much of her lustre when she fled back to Normandy – some chroniclers say because she was disgusted with her husband's drunkenness and lawlessness.

Ethelred died in 1016 and the following year Emma regained much of her shine by marrying 'Canute the Great' (*see* GREAT . . . BUT NOT THAT GREAT), with whom she reigned for a further eighteen years.

¶ *Nicholas the* Gendarme of Europe *see*
Nicholas the IRON TSAR

¶ Gloriana *see* GOOD QUEEN BESS

¶ *Alexander the* Glorious
Alexander III, king of Scotland, 1241–86

Alexander's reign began in sad circumstances and ended in tra-gedy, but the middle years were comparatively glorious. His father, 'Alexander the Peaceful', died when Alexander was a boy, and at ten young Alexander found himself married to Margaret, the daughter of Henry III of England. The alliance that this marriage caused was initially an uneasy one, but after some ugly squabbling and sabre-rattling a pact was drawn up that was beneficial to both nations.

With his relationship with England pleasantly cordial, Alex-ander was able to focus his attention on the north. In 1261 he offered to buy sovereignty of the Hebrides from 'Haakon the

Old'. Haakon, however, was not selling, and instead of making a deal with Alexander he invaded Scotland, claiming the Isle of Man as well as the Hebrides for himself. Some claim that a Viking, trying to sneak ashore stealthily and catch some Scots by surprise, yelped when he trod on a thistle, thus revealing his whereabouts and securing the thistle's status as the national emblem of Scotland. The Viking conquest fizzled out, the aged Haakon caught a fever and died, and Alexander was able to purchase all of the Western Isles for a gloriously paltry sum.

A string of personal tragedies then knocked the stuffing out of the king. Alexander's eldest son died at the tender age of twenty, a second died aged only eight, and his daughter died in childbirth. Finally, while galloping back from a council meeting in Edinburgh, his horse slipped and hurtled off a cliff with him still in the saddle. Alexander and his horse plunged to their deaths; Scotland plunged into a period of bleak and bloody ignominy.

⁊ *Athelstan the* Glorious
Athelstan, king of the English, 895–939

Son of Edward the ELDER (and, scandal-mongers would have us believe, of a humble shepherd's daughter to whom Edward had taken a fancy) Athelstan was the first Saxon king of all England. He was tall and handsome, a courageous soldier and an avid collector of art and religious relics who was generous both to his subjects and to the Church. His greatest legacy, however, has to be his judicial reforms. Extant law codes tell of his drive to reduce the punishments meted out to young offenders and also suggest the existence of a corps of skilled scribes – perhaps the beginning of a civil service. His nickname possibly stems from a eulogy by an anonymous German cleric who compares him favourably to the Frankish Charles the GREAT: 'King Athelstan lives,' he writes, 'glorious through his deeds!'

¶ *Philip the* Godless Regent
Philip II, duke of Orléans, 1674–1723

When Philip became regent to the five-year-old Louis the WELL-
BELOVED, so began one of the most liberal, irreligious and
debauched decades in French history. The stifling hypocrisy
of the court of Philip's uncle Louis the SUN KING was
replaced with a rich mixture of scandal and candour. Banned
books were reprinted, the Royal Library was opened to all and
tuition fees at the Sorbonne were scrapped.

Philip was a Renaissance man, a talented painter who enjoyed
acting in plays by Molière and composing music for opera. As
for his 'godlessness', there is no doubt. A professed atheist, he
celebrated religious feast days by holding orgies at Versailles, and
when forced to attend Mass, would read the works of Rabelais
hidden inside a Bible. New Orleans, a city not known for its
prudishness, was named in his honour.

¶ *Albert the* Good
Albert, prince consort of Queen Victoria of the United
Kingdom, 1819–61

In late November 1861, after a miserably wet day inspecting the
buildings for the new military academy at Sandhurst, Albert, the
prince consort of Queen Victoria, returned home with a bit of a
cold. A few days later, following a visit to Cambridge to admonish
his wayward son Edward the CARESSER, the cold had developed
into something of a severe chill. Within a fortnight he was dead
of typhoid fever.

Two years before Albert's death, the Poet Laureate Alfred Lord
Tennyson had dedicated his work *Idylls of the King* to the prince
with the lines:

> Beyond all titles, and a household name,
> Hereafter, thro' all times, Albert the Good.

And Victoria the WIDOW OF WINDSOR was now determined that her late husband should be known as 'the Good' because of his modest, gentle devotion, both to his wife and to his

Albert the Good

adopted country. She accordingly arranged for a number of his speeches to be published, commissioned an immense biography to be written, and impressed Tennyson to join in the hagiographical chorus.

Sadly for Victoria, England simply did not see Albert in the same light as she did. Yes, he had earned much popularity at the time of the Great Exhibition of 1851, but in general his subjects simply could not forgive him for being a foreigner, a German with disconcerting un-English manners and tastes. Some scoffed at his continental dress while others castigated him as the tool of the Russian tsar.

Be that as it may, Albert clearly did possess a genuine tenderness that brought out the best in many people. Even Napoleon III, 'the Man of December', was compelled to write favourably about the prince after walking with him in the garden at Osborne House. 'One goes away from him,' he acknowledged, 'more disposed to do good.'

¶ *Haakon the* Good

Haakon I, king of Norway, *c*.920–*c*.961

Haakon was a Christian, and on becoming king he attempted to introduce the religion to his subjects, going so far as to invite missionaries from England to his country. But as soon as he gauged the response of his subjects to the idea (they hated it) he promptly embraced his pagan religion of old.

Chroniclers deemed Haakon to be 'good' not by dint of his faith but because of two other factors. First, he was a good administrator, eager for peace and order and energetic in his reform of the military and judicial system. Second, he was a good soldier. One contemporary poet records how, in the middle of a battle against the Danish, Haakon 'threw off his war-gear [and] . . . joked with his men'. Perhaps due to his skimpy battledress, Haakon was mortally wounded while attempting to drive back a third Danish invasion in 960. He was given a lavish pagan funeral.

¶ *Hywel the* Good
Hywel, king of Wales, *c.*882–950

Hywel, the only Welsh king to be named 'Dda' or 'Good', occupied a period in Welsh history remarkable for its stability and harmony. His secret seems to have been his diplomatic good sense in recognizing and respecting the culture and principles of organization of his English neighbours. The first recorded act of his reign, for instance, is a visit to Edward the ELDER to pay him homage. This, however, may be a decidedly English appraisal of Hywel's reign. In Welsh history he is renowned as a great national lawmaker.

¶ *John the* Good
John II, king of France, 1319–64

John the Good was bad through and through, with the fifteenth-century chronicler Pierre Cochon describing him as 'the worst and cruellest king who ever lived'. Why his contemporaries called this son of Philip the LUCKY (*see* GALLIC PRACTICE) 'the Good' is a matter for conjecture. Perhaps it was because of his devotion to the chivalric code – he founded the Order of the Star, a decidedly second-rate rival to the Order of the Garter. Or perhaps it was due to his alleged generosity to the poor – once, we are told, he gave a purse of money to a milkmaid whose pails were knocked over by his greyhounds.

These acts, however, cannot mask a reign of aggression and duplicity. At the outset of his reign, for instance, John alienated his entire nobility by executing the charming and much-loved Constable of France, the Comte d'Eu. He then turned his attention abroad to his two bitter enemies, Edward the BANKRUPT of England and 'Charles the Bad' of Navarre, and spent the following years making and breaking truces with both.

Roundly thrashed by Edward the BLACK PRINCE at the battle of Poitiers, John was imprisoned in England, where he remained for some time because he was unable to raise his ransom money. Finally hostages were accepted in his place but when one of them (John's own son Louis) escaped, John did what he must have considered the chivalrous thing, and returned to England and voluntary captivity. Behind bars once more, he quickly fell ill of an 'unknown malady' and died.

❡ *Magnus the* Good
Magnus I, king of Norway and Denmark, 1024–47

Back in eleventh-century Scandinavia, goodness meant military courage, and Magnus's goodness was amply demonstrated by his fearless exploits when fighting the Wends in southern Jutland. According to legend, the night before a major battle in which Magnus's forces were considerably outnumbered, the king dreamt he saw his father, 'Olaf the Saint', who assured him of victory. Fortified by his vision, the next morning Magnus doffed his mail shirt and strode into battle wearing nothing above the waist except a red silk shirt. According to Adam of Bremen, 15,000 Wendish corpses littered the battlefield that day. Soon thereafter Magnus died of disease at the tender age of twenty-three, leaving the sort of reputation that poets and saga writers loved to eulogize.

¶ *Philip the* Good
Philip III, duke of Burgundy, 1396–1467

Philip enjoyed the good life. His official court chronicler, Georges Chastellain, wrote how he was skilful on horseback, excellent at tennis, and that he 'loved to hunt . . . and linger over meals'. He was also something of a ladies' man, with records showing that he had some twenty mistresses in all, maintaining a number at the same time in different places.

Later in life, when not hearing Mass or watching dancers cavort, Philip loved to amuse himself in a sort of glorified portable shed, a mobile wooden hut in which he would while away the hours simply pottering about, making clogs, soldering broken knives, repairing broken spectacles, and so on. His son 'Charles the Bold' mocked his father for his hobby, and destroyed the whole outfit after his death. The shed may be gone, but Philip's reputation as a good and popular duke remains intact.

¶ Good Duke Humphrey
Humphrey, duke of Gloucester, 1391–1447

Humphrey was famously pious, an excellent soldier (he received a wound at Agincourt in the service of his hero and brother Henry the ENGLISH ALEXANDER – *see* ENGLISH EPITHETS) and a scholar of some merit, with his collection of classical tomes forming the core of the Bodleian Library in Oxford. Despite his notorious promiscuity and his track record as a truly lousy administrator, he was hugely popular among all classes and known throughout the land as 'Good Duke Humphrey'.

He did have his enemies, however, and none more so than Henry Beaufort, the chief minister of the realm. Beaufort found the hot-headed Humphrey contemptible and was constantly on the lookout for a way to stop him meddling in national affairs. His chance came when it was discovered that Humphrey's wife, Eleanor, dabbled in witchcraft. Eleanor, it was claimed, regularly checked her horoscope and had once made a wax figure of Henry the MARTYR and melted it in a fire. For this she was imprisoned for life and Humphrey was discredited and eventually arrested for treason himself. While in jail he fell ill and died.

The phrase 'to dine with the Good Duke Humphrey', meaning 'to go without dinner', has its roots in a case of mistaken identity. Londoners in trouble with the law would often congregate (for discussion rather than for worship) in St Paul's Cathedral, where they were safe from arrest. There they would gather near a monument popularly thought to be dedicated to Humphrey. In fact the good duke was buried at St Albans and the tomb was that of one Sir John Beauchamp. Nevertheless, people who could not afford a meal and instead whiled away the time in the cathedral were said to be dining with the duke.

⁊ Good King René

René I, duke of Anjou and king of Sicily, 1409–80

Once upon a time there lived a king called René. His subjects loved him and called him 'Good King René', not only because he was kind and generous but also because he was the stuff of legend: a romantic dreamer in love with the chivalric ideal; a courageous soldier who wrote love poems and adventure stories; and a man who (in a reverse of fairy-tale convention) was rescued from prison in a high tower by a gallant and brave woman.

After fighting alongside Joan of Arc, 'the Maid of Orléans', in the army of his brother-in-law 'Charles the Victorious', René fought for the right to inherit the duchy of Lorraine, but lost, ending up in Philip the GOOD's fortress at Dijon. Once imprisoned in the high tower of the chateau, René developed an interest in art, painting miniatures on glass (possibly under the tutelage of the Dutch master Jan van Eyck) and decorating one of the rooms in the castle. But while René experimented with interior design, his young wife Isabel feverishly (and eventually successfully) campaigned for his release.

Once free, René spent four fruitless years battling against 'Alfonso the Magnanimous' for the kingdom of Naples. Eventually he cut his losses, headed back to France and established a brilliant court at Angers, where he indulged his love of Arthurian chivalry and courtly splendour; feasts, mystery plays and minstrelsy were crowned by the heroics of the tournament, an event so adored by René that he wrote a handbook on the subject, the magnificently illustrated *Manual for the Perfect Organization of Tourneys*. When his beloved Isabel died, René was inconsolable, though only for a year, after which he became smitten with the very plain and very pious Jeanne of Laval, the daughter of a Breton nobleman, for whom he wrote a 10,000-verse pastoral love poem. The once-storybook prince spent his sunset years as a living legend, one of the last representatives of medieval chivalry and culture, concentrating on his poetry and his art. Fittingly for such a man of romance, 'René d'Anjou' is the name of a rather lovely pink rose.

¶ Good Queen Bess
Elizabeth I, queen of England, 1533–1603

Even those who disliked Elizabeth had to admit that she possessed a special aura. The slim, pale monarch inherited the magnetism of her father, BLUFF KING HAL, and the sheer presence of her mother, Anne the GREAT WHORE, and court and public alike were dazzled by their fascinating and attractive queen. She did have some detractors – a dissident named Edward Deering once famously used a sermon to denounce her as 'An Untamed Heifer' – but in the main Elizabeth was immensely popular. Soon after her coronation in 1559 her subjects dubbed their new monarch 'Gloriana' and 'Good Queen Bess'.

Elizabeth loved pearls above all precious stones and wore them in necklaces, bracelets and earrings, as well as on her clothing and in her hair. It was an appropriate gem for two reasons. First, Elizabeth was commonly known as 'the Queen of the Sea' since, like her father, she had a passion for all things maritime and, once the Spanish Armada had been destroyed, effectively ruled the waves. Second, pearls were a symbol of virginity, and as well as playing the virginal excellently (she was an accomplished performer of pieces by composers such as Byrd and Tallis) Elizabeth played her role as 'the Virgin Queen' very finely too. Some questioned her right to this title, facetiously conferring upon her the nickname 'the World's Wonder'. On the other hand her court favourite Walter Raleigh went so far as to name a territory in North America 'Virginia' in her honour.

As the years rolled on, the good Elizabeth had to work hard to maintain her appearance. She used a solution containing egg white, borax and poppy seed to keep her skin white, and would rub urine on to her face to prevent wrinkles. There was little she could do about her teeth, however: owing to her love for sugar, they turned rotten and black.

¶ *James the* Good Regent

James Stewart, first earl of Moray, c.1531–70

The historian P. Hume Brown writes that soon after James's death 'men spoke of Moray with affection and reverence as "the Good Regent".' Later generations, it seems, have cooled somewhat in their appreciation of this son of James the ILL-BELOVED, principally because of his conduct towards his half-sister Mary the MERMAID.

In 1565 James found himself out of favour and indeed out of Scotland for his vehement opposition to Mary's marriage to the swaggering Lord Darnley. Mary soon forgave him, however, and welcomed him back into her court, apparently unaware of the part he had played in the murder of David Rizzio, one of her chief counsellors.

It was when Mary abdicated in 1567, however, and James became regent, that his true allegiances came to the fore. To the dismay of Mary, James not only forced her to flee south of the border after the defeat of her Catholic forces at the battle of Langside but also did everything in his power to perpetuate her incarceration there, giving his full support to Mary and Darnley's son, the young Protestant James the WISEST FOOL IN CHRISTENDOM.

With Mary incapacitated, James instigated a series of religious reforms that ensured the success of the Reformation in Scotland. To some, therefore, he was a hero. To others he was a traitor, and on a cold January morning in 1570 James was murdered in what is the first recorded assassination with a firearm.

¶ *The* Good Sir James *see* James the BLACK DOUGLAS

¶ *Duncan the* Gracious
Duncan I, king of Scotland, c.1001–40

History, perhaps sarcastically, has given King Duncan I the epithet 'the Gracious', and in his play *Macbeth* William Shakespeare has two characters (a nobleman called Lennox and Macbeth himself) acknowledge him as such. Shakespeare portrays Duncan as a grey-haired elderly king, but here the bard is playing fast and loose with the historical record, for in truth Duncan was in his early thirties when he came to the throne and, far from being mild-mannered, was regarded as impetuous and arrogant. Part of his unpopularity may have stemmed from his marriage to a cousin of Siward, the earl of Northumberland, and his attempt to introduce English ways into the Scottish court.

As a military man he was useless. He was defeated in battle by his cousin Thorfinn, the earl of Orkney, suffered heavy losses in a fruitless siege of Durham, and finally was hacked down by Macbeth at the battle of Pitgaveny. Of the very few who mourned his passing was his son Malcolm BIGHEAD, who avenged his death by killing Macbeth in 1057.

¶ *Victoria the* Grandmother of Europe
see Victoria the WIDOW OF WINDSOR

¶ *Akbar the* Great
Akbar, emperor of India, 1542–1605

In 1556, when only thirteen, Akbar ascended the Mughal throne when his father, Humayun, descended a flight of stairs faster than he would have wished, and died. Akbar defeated three challengers to his office and conquered or annexed (among others) Rajasthan, Gujarat, Bengal and Kashmir, so that the Mughal Empire under him covered the entire Hindustan plain, from the Indus in the west, to the Ganges in the east, and the Himalayas in the north.

In order to govern this vastly increased territory successfully, Akbar developed a bureaucracy second to none. Military governors were put in charge of autonomous imperial provinces, and tax collection was ruthlessly efficient. Alert, meanwhile, to the fact that no Muslim Empire in India would survive without the support of the majority Hindus, he went out of his way to win their favour. This he achieved, in part, by encouraging inter-faith discourse, employing a large number of Hindus in his civil service and, out of some 5,000 wives, electing a Hindu woman to become the mother of his successor. Some historians have acclaimed him as 'the Guardian of Mankind' owing to his promotion of equal justice for all, and for the care he showed for his subjects. An example of his generosity to his people was his compilation of a library of some 24,000 books, even though he himself was illiterate.

Akbar surely ranks alongside his contemporary Suleiman the MAGNIFICENT for the good he achieved. His creation of a new religion, however, in which he was God, and a new calendar which began on the date of his accession, suggest that his estimation of his own self-worth may have been somewhat exaggerated.

¶ *Albert the* Great

Albertus Magnus, German nobleman, *c.*1200–1280

Albertus, a Dominican bishop and philosopher, is perhaps best known as the teacher of St Thomas Aquinas. His writings on philosophy and theology may have been cutting edge, but it was in his writing on the natural sciences that he exercised his greatest influence and earned himself the nickname 'the Great'. He was a modest man, and his soubriquet, given to him while he was still very much alive, must have been something of an embarrassment.

His *Book of Marvels* makes interesting reading. In its pages one can find the necessary ingredients for various potions. If you want to make someone believe that their bed is full of lice, for instance, you will need a quantity of winter cherry and some hawk feathers; to make women dance for joy, the blood of a gannet, a hare and a turtle dove are crucial; and if your intention is to make a man fart ceaselessly, an essential ingredient is snail's blood.

Albert may have been great in mind, but was not so in stature. In some circles he was also known as 'le Petit Albert' because he was so short, and once, when he was paying his respects to the pope, the pontiff thought he was still kneeling when in fact he was standing up.

¶ *Alexander the* Great

Alexander III, king of Macedonia, 356–323 BC

When he was only twelve Alexander tamed a horse called Bucephalus, an animal so wild that no other person could approach let alone ride it. For the remainder of his short life, stories of his mastery over the rebellious and recalcitrant abound.

Educated by Aristotle, Alexander became king of Macedonia aged twenty. One of his first acts was to suppress a revolution in the city of Thebes whose people thought, erroneously, that he was dead. Alexander sacked the city, selling 30,000 inhabitants into slavery and sparing only the temples and the house of the poet Pindar. Then, in 334, his conquest of Persia began in earnest.

Alexander crossed the Hellespont and within a year had taken most of Asia Minor. From there he moved to the mountain town of Gordium where, according to legend, he 'untied' the intricate Gordian knot by slicing through it with his sword. Over the next couple of years he subdued Syria, routing the forces of the Persian king Darius III along the way, and founded the city of Alexandria in Egypt. His travels then took him back through Syria across much of Mesopotamia and into Babylon, which he made his capital.

Thereafter nations and their peoples capitulated to him without much of a fight. Even cities like Susa and Persepolis, hoarding vast amounts of silver and gold, surrendered relatively quickly. Soon Alexander was marching on to the Caspian Sea, and then crossing eastwards into modern-day Afghanistan and Pakistan. At this point his men declared they would travel no further, and Alexander was forced to return to Susa. In 323, aged only thirty-three, he caught a fever and died.

In his brief lifetime Alexander rampaged through the Persian Empire and opened it up to the West. Some, however, have seen his conquests, for which he earned the title 'Macedonia's Madman', as well as 'the Great', as little more than swashbuckling acts of robbery, since he merely ransacked great cities and failed to replace them with anything of value.

It appears that Alexander considered his own achievements not only as outstanding but also as surpassing those of any other mortal. He proclaimed himself a god, and began wearing two rams' horns attached to a band around his head, so that they appeared to be growing out of his blond hair just above his ears. Some Greek and African states did indeed confer divine status upon him, calling him 'Zeus-Ammon' or 'the Two-Horned'. Alexander certainly had one mortal failing, however, namely an unhealthy love of wine, and while he was no alcoholic, as some have portrayed him, he did occasionally drink himself into a stupor.

Without doubt, Alexander was one of the greatest generals of all time. Countless histories record how he brought Greek ideas, customs and laws to the Middle East and Asia. Fans of rock music, meanwhile, have the additional pleasure of listening to 'Alexander the Great' by the heavy metal band Iron Maiden, which outlines his greatest achievements.

¶ *Alfred the* Great

Alfred, king of Wessex, 849–99

Our perception of the greatness of Alfred may be coloured by the story of his accidental burning of a peasant woman's cakes. The briefest of objective analyses, however, shows that, culinary abilities aside, Alfred was a truly notable monarch. In fact, he is the only English king to have been distinguished with the nickname 'the Great', and his reign was one of the most decisive in his nation's history.

He was the most effective opponent of the Vikings since Charles the GREAT, protecting his kingdom with a network of forts, a newly established navy and a standing army. He augmented these military developments with a revival of interest in religion and learning, the king himself contributing a substantial body of prose literature. Such achievements become all the more impressive when one learns of Alfred's chronic physical infirmity, diagnosed by some scholars as Crohn's disease, an intermittent condition characterized by abdominal pains, fever and wasting. In Wantage, the town of his birth, a life-size statue bears a plaque summing up his more public successes:

Alfred found learning dead, and he restored it;
Education neglected, and he revived it;
The laws powerless, and he gave them force;
The Church debased, and he raised it;
The land ravaged by a fearful enemy, from which he delivered it.
Alfred's name will live as long as mankind shall respect the past.

¶ *Anthony the* Great *see* Anthony the GREAT
BASTARD

¶ *Casimir the* Great
Casimir III, king of Poland, 1310–70

In 1869 an overzealous workman digging in the crypt of Cracow
Cathedral accidentally sliced open the tomb of Poland's medieval
king Casimir III. The attendance of tens of thousands of well-
wishers at his re-interment suggests that Casimir was held in the
highest esteem by the Polish people. Such adulation appears well
placed: while being ruled by 'Kasimierz Wielki', or 'Casimir the
Great', medieval Poland reached the pinnacle of her power and
prosperity.

Casimir's achievements beyond his nation's borders were
impressive: he significantly advanced its frontiers in the east and
cleverly sued for peace with Bohemia. But it was his domestic
dealings that won him the most acclaim. Recalling the ideal of
Louis the SAINT, he ruled his country under the motto of 'One
king, one law, one currency' and, through his administrative and
fiscal reforms and encouragement of the arts, he cemented newly
achieved Polish unity and raised his country to a position equal
to other states of Europe.

Casimir was a true leader, a fine legislator and an able econ-
omist. Hailed as 'the Peasants' King' for his concern for the
common people, he was undoubtedly a popular monarch. Three
unhappy marriages, however, and a string of mistresses (the most
famous being the Jewess Esther, possibly invented by chroniclers
to explain his friendliness towards regional Jewry) hint at a
private life less great than his public one.

¶ *Catherine the* Great
Catherine II, empress of Russia, 1729–96

In a letter to a friend in 1871, Catherine half-jokingly detailed her
accomplishments:

Governments set up under the New Scheme	29
Towns built	144
Conventions and treaties signed	30
Victories won	78
Noteworthy edicts ordering new laws or foundations	88
Edicts for the assistance of the people	123
Total	492

By any standards Catherine was an extraordinary woman. In addition to her administrative reform and military success, she expanded her nation by more than 200,000 square miles and vastly increased international trade and communications. She promoted Russian culture; she was a great collector of books (a correspondent of both Voltaire and Diderot, she wrote several plays herself); she was a patron of the arts; she founded schools. And yet her greatness was stained by stories of a prodigal and licentious private life. Her supposedly gargantuan sexual appetite was legendary. With her degenerate husband 'Peter the Mad' dead, Catherine apparently amused herself with a steady stream of lovers, mostly young army officers. All her potential bedfellows were screened by her personal physician and then road-tested by two of her ladies-in-waiting to ensure that their empress would be satisfied. On her death, scandal-mongers spread the false rumour that she had perished when a horse was lowered on her too suddenly while she was trying to have sex with it. Mud sticks, however, and while Catherine made it known that she would like to be called 'the Little Mother of All the Russians', she was commonly dubbed 'the Modern Messalina' after Valeria Messalina, the lascivious empress of ancient Rome.

Catherine should be celebrated, however, if for no other reason than for one particular act of great courage. In 1768 Russia was reeling from an epidemic of smallpox and the empress summoned an English doctor named Thomas Dinsdale to oversee a programme of inoculation. The vaccine was still at an experimental stage, and Russia was nervous. Catherine, however, set an example to her people by being one of the first to have the injection.

⁋ *Charles the* Great

Charlemagne, Charles I, king of the Franks and
Lombards and Holy Roman Emperor, *c.*742–814

At the zenith of his power in the early ninth century, Charles
ruled all the Christian lands of Western Europe except Britain
and the southern parts of Italy and Sicily. A stunning expansion
of Frankish political sway through military conquest was not his
only achievement by a long chalk, however. Charlemagne (from
the Latin 'Carolus Magnus') also brought about a cultural revival
in his empire: his court at Aachen developed into a crucible of
European arts and intellectual discourse that rivalled anything
the Byzantines could muster.

Physically he took after his mother Bertha BIGFOOT rather
than his father Pepin the SHORT, towering over his contemporaries, therefore, both literally and metaphorically. Ever since his
tomb was opened in 1861 we have known that his contemporary
biographer Einhard was not using poetic licence when he wrote
that the emperor was 'seven times the length of his feet' (he was
actually just under six foot four), and so we can accept with a
degree of confidence his further descriptions of Charles's fair
hair, his laughing and animated face with a rather big nose, his
surprisingly high-pitched voice and his pot belly. We can also be
fairly sure that he was a gregarious man, never happier than
when among friends, in the din of the hunt or noisily bathing
his children in the palace.

Charles thought of himself above all as a Christian, and his
greatest desire was to be counted among 'the Just'. To this end
he went to church several times a day, drank in moderation
(something of a rarity in those times), made several pilgrimages to Rome and spent his last days correcting holy books of
any mistakes he found. He was also apparently a devoted
father, although supporters of his son Pepin the HUNCHBACK,
whom he dispatched to a monastery, might wish to disagree.

Charles was indeed extraordinary – a charismatic, convivial
and cultured man whose military campaigns (always accom-

panied by his pet elephant) and internal reforms almost single-handedly paved the way for the mighty Holy Roman Empire. It seems churlish to point out any faults, but it was said that he had an uncontrollable sexual appetite and an unhealthy passion for roast game.

¶ *Clovis the* Great

Clovis I, Merovingian king, *c.*466–511

Clovis inherited the kingdom of his father, Childeric I, in 481 and soon settled down to a life of conquest. He toppled the Germanic peoples east of the Rhine, and his victory over Syagrius, the self-styled 'king of the Romans', united northern Gaul under Frankish thrall. The burgeoning little town of Paris, meanwhile, became the capital of his empire.

Twelve years into his reign, Clovis the pagan king married a princess named Clotilda, the Christian niece of King Gundobad of Burgundy. Clovis was happy for their children to be baptized but, try as Clotilda might, was completely uninterested in converting to his wife's faith; that is, until a few years later in 496 when, on the brink of defeat by a Germanic tribe, Clovis turned his eyes heavenward and prayed to Clotilda's deity. According to the *Chronicle of St Denis*, he bargained with God that he would 'pledge you perpetual service unto your faith, if only you give me now the victory over my enemies'. The very moment these words were said, Clovis's soldiers were apparently filled with burning valour, putting such fear into their enemies that they turned tail and fled the battlefield. The following Christmas Day Clovis, along with 3,000 of his troops, was baptized, during which ceremony, we are told, a white dove appeared out of nowhere, handily carrying a vial of sweet-smelling holy oil in its beak.

Despite his newly found faith, Clovis had a somewhat maverick approach to the commandment 'Thou shalt not kill.' Gregory of Tours writes that, promising untold power and wealth, Clovis persuaded one Prince Chloderic to murder his father, King

'Sigibert the Lame'. That achieved, Clovis ordered the death of Chloderic himself, and the luckless prince tumbled into the open grave that had been prepared for his father. Later, among many other decidedly gruesome and unchristian deeds, he commanded that a prisoner called Chararic should find God by having his hair cut short and being ordained a priest. Chararic burst into tears at this 'humiliation', and so Clovis promptly had his head chopped off.

After her husband's death in 511, Queen Clotilda spent her life caring for the poor and perpetuating the memory of her 'great', if morally dubious, partner.

¶ *Constantine the* Great
Constantine I, emperor of Rome, *c.*280–337

In 312, on the eve of a battle with his imperial rival Maxentius at Milvian Bridge near Rome, Constantine had a vision. The Christian apologist Lactantius writes that the emperor looked at the setting sun, saw a cross emblazoned on it, and then apparently saw or heard the Greek phrase 'Ἐν Τουτω Νικα', meaning 'With this sign, you shall conquer.' Constantine, who was a pagan, had the Christian symbol inscribed on his soldiers' shields overnight, and won a great victory the next day. He was now sole emperor of the West.

Constantine attributed his success to the God of the Christians, and through the Edict of Milan of 313 declared that Christian worship was now to be tolerated throughout the empire. But not everybody was happy that this minor religion was receiving such favouritism. Seven years later Licinius, the emperor of the Eastern Roman Empire, openly rejected the edict and started persecuting those of the Christian faith. This led to a civil war between the two emperors which Constantine won, his forces fired up with Christian zeal. He was now the sole emperor of the entire Roman Empire.

In 324 the great Constantine relocated his imperial headquarters to Byzantium, humbly renaming it 'Nova Roma' or 'New Rome' (it was not until after his death that it was given the title 'Constantinople'). From here he reformed the imperial currency and passed a wealth of new laws, which included the following:

- Easter was to be publicly celebrated
- All pagan religious practices were to be conducted in public
- Christian clergy were to hear all court cases (there was no appeal)
- A condemned man was not to have his face branded, only his feet
- Parents selling their daughters for sex were to have molten lead poured down their throats
- The professions of butcher and baker were to be hereditary

The following year Constantine presided at the First Ecumenical Council of the Church in the palace at Nicaea. This produced what has become known as the Nicene Creed, still at the heart of Christian doctrine today.

Through his military prowess, political acumen and enthusiastic religious conviction Constantine the Great laid the foundations for a strong empire and created a solid platform for post-classical European civilization. As was the norm, he waited until his dying hours to be baptized.

¶ *Cyrus the* Great
Cyrus II, Persian ruler, *c.*585–*c.*529 BC

According to Herodotus, Astyages, the king of the Medes, gave his daughter in marriage to Cambyses, a prince in what was then a small and rather insignificant territory called Persia. The couple produced a baby whom they named Cyrus, meaning 'like the sun'. But then Astyages had a dream. He dreamed that Cyrus would one day conquer Media, and so he gave orders for the child to be murdered. The courtier who had been assigned the job, however, smuggled Cyrus out of the palace at Persis and arranged for a shepherd to raise him.

Many scholars consider this story of Cyrus's childhood to

Cyrus the Great

be nothing more than formulaic legend. Generally accepted, however, is that Cyrus did indeed go on to overthrow his grandfather sometime between 559 BC and 549 BC, and in so doing united the two tribes of the Medes and the Persians. This consolidation of forces gave rise to what we now know as the Persian Empire, a vast domain that expanded dramatically as Cyrus went on to subdue Lydia in Asia Minor and the kingdom of Babylonia.

Although Cyrus is hailed as a great territorial conqueror, his soubriquet 'the Great' is most fitting for the tolerance and mercy he showed towards those he defeated. The Bible, for instance, records his kind treatment of those he captured at Babylon, and how he ensured the safe passage of all the Jewish captives back to their homeland. Cyrus himself saw his achievements as informed by his Zoroastrian belief in religious tolerance. 'I am Cyrus, King of the World,' he wrote on a large clay cylinder now housed in the British Library. 'When I entered Babylon I did not allow anyone to terrorize the land. I kept in view the needs of its people and all its sanctuaries to promote their well being. I put an end to their misfortune.'

Xenophon writes that Cyrus dictated a long will before dying in his bed. But this, like much surrounding the story of his birth, is hogwash. Cyrus died while fighting a war on his eastern frontier. His distraught soldiers carried the body of their beloved king over a thousand miles back home.

¶ *Frederick the* Great
Frederick II, king of Prussia, 1712–86

Frederick the Great remains one of the most famous German rulers of all time, both for his military successes and for his domestic reforms. An absolute ruler who nevertheless lived under the principle that he was *'der erste Diener meines Staates'* ('the first servant of my state'), he hauled Prussia up by its lapels and turned a sleepy backwater into one of the most dynamic European nations.

Lauded for promoting the benefits of taking a deep pride in one's work (his own work ethic bordered on the fanatical) Frederick made Prussia a kinder, gentler nation. He overhauled the outdated judicial system, abolished torture, codified the legal system and lifted stifling constraints upon the press and religions. Culturally, he was acclaimed for his support of the arts. He was himself something of a poet and, until his teeth fell out, he played the flute with a passion, entertaining foreign diplomats with his own compositions. His musical tastes, meanwhile, like his style of government, were absolute. C. P. E. Bach was exalted and a court favourite; Mozart and Haydn were 'degenerate'.

Prussia's territorial expansion and increased prestige on the European stage are the main factors behind Frederick's nickname. His successful opposition to larger forces in the Seven Years War (helped undoubtedly by the death of Empress Elizabeth of Russia) and his seizure of the Austrian province of Silesia (even though this was in flagrant breach of an established treaty) ensured Prussia's growth and the warm-hearted nickname given to him by the Germans of 'der Alte Fritz', or 'Old Fritz'.

The French were more reserved in their nicknames for him. At the outset of his reign some derisively dubbed him 'le Sablonnier', or 'the Sand Dealer', since so much of the land he inherited was desolate and sandy. Voltaire, meanwhile, with whom Frederick had a love/hate relationship, nicknamed him 'Alaric-Cotin'. This is damning with faint praise, since the original Alaric was a ferocious fifth-century Visigoth king, while Charles Cotin was a sixteenth-century poet whose output was decidedly second-rate.

¶ *Henry the* Great
Henry IV, king of France, 1553–1610

A short, none-too-fragrant, lecherous old man with bad teeth and thick spectacles hardly seems the stuff of legend, let alone worthy of the name 'the Great', but to this day Henry IV is one of France's most loved monarchs.

No contemporary achieved more than Henry. His war against Spain and his international political manoeuvring gained France independence and some new territory. His founding of new industries, construction of a new highway system and expansion of foreign trade transformed a bankrupt nation into a financial force to be reckoned with. His religious tolerance and working motto that 'there should be a chicken in every peasant's pot every Sunday', meanwhile, won the acclaim of a grateful people.

But it is as much for his colourful personal life as for his public persona that he is remembered: Henry would hunt during the day, gorge himself during the evening, and wench at night; he was so small that he always needed a mounting block to climb a horse; he was so fond of food, especially oysters and melons, that he often suffered agonizing bouts of indigestion; and he was so sexually prolific that he suffered almost permanently from one venereal disease or another.

Of his sixty or so mistresses, the most famous was Gabrielle d'Estrées (known as 'la Belle Gabrielle'), who called her lover 'Mon Soldat'. Just how she could be so close to 'My Soldier' defies comprehension. Like James the WISEST FOOL IN CHRISTENDOM, Henry had no time for personal hygiene, and it is no surprise to learn that on her wedding night Marie de Medici drenched herself in scent. Although widespread, the story that Henry chewed garlic like sweets, so much so that he once felled an ox at twenty paces, is sadly apocryphal. It is attested, however, that he did have a fondness for onion soup.

Smelly and shabby he may have been, but he also possessed a charm that proved irresistible. Romantic (he once paused in the middle of a battle to write a love letter), courageous ('le Roi des Braves' – 'the King of Brave Men' – fought in more than 200 battles and skirmishes), cultured (he had a passion for cartography and garden design) and brusque ('I rule with my arse in the saddle and a gun in my fist,' he once declared), Henry embodied many Gallic qualities. And a nation loved him.

❡ *Iyasu the* Great
Iyasu I, emperor of Ethiopia, d. 1706

Like his predecessors, Iyasu was a military man, leading his troops in nearly a dozen campaigns to compel warring clans to lay down their arms and work towards a unified kingdom. But what made Iyasu's reign unusual – what earned him the nickname 'the Great' – was his conduct off the battlefield: Iyasu was passionate about financial and administrative reform. He improved the country's judicial system, reorganized the way in which taxes were imposed and collected, and enhanced trade, in part by relaxing the rigidly anti-European policy of his forebears.

Iyasu suffered from a mystery skin disease, and one of the first Europeans to visit his court was a French physician named Charles Poncet, who arrived *c.*1700 to treat him. Poncet reported that, in addition to Iyasu's famed military prowess, the monarch did indeed have other great qualities: a 'quick and piercing wit, a sweet and affable humour [and] . . . an extraordinary love of justice which he carried out with exactness'. Before long, the emperor was completely cured of his troublesome condition and Iyasu was so pleased with Poncet that he gave him some slaves and a young elephant to take home.

❡ *Kamehameha the* Great
Kamehameha I, king of Hawaii, 1758–1819

During her pregnancy with him, Kamehameha's mother had a craving to eat the eyeball of a chief. That particular delicacy being unavailable, she munched instead on the eyeball of a man-eating shark, a dish that led local priests to prophesy that the child would become a killer of chiefs. Alapainui, the chief of Hawaii at the time and the unborn child's grandfather, was understandably worried and hurriedly arranged to have the new-born baby killed. The child, named Paiea, was whisked away at birth, however, and only returned to his grandfather's household five years later when Alapainui had forgotten his fears. There, little Paiea was noted as a joyless, sullen boy and was given the new name 'Kamehameha', meaning 'the Lonely One'.

As an adult Kamehameha became chief of the northern half of the island of Hawaii, but eventually, thanks in part to the counsel of one wife, who was 6 feet tall and weighed 300 pounds, and the presence of another, a frail 11-year-old whom he married for political reasons, he brought the entire island chain of Hawaii under his control. The islands managed to retain their independence by implementing the policy of denying any *haoles* (white men) the right to own land, but this did not prevent Hawaiians under Kamehameha from welcoming foreign visitors and their innovations, such as coffee, pineapples and, rather more sinisterly, muskets. Aided by these guns, Kamehameha became a 'great' conqueror, and his military achievements (though not his size) earned him comparison with his French contemporary and the nickname 'the Napoleon of the Pacific'.

❡ *Llewellyn the* Great
Llewellyn, king of Gwynedd, *c.*1173–1240

By acknowledging the sovereignty of the king of England, early thirteenth-century Welsh chiefs were able to run their territories almost as they pleased. What made Llewellyn so 'great' was his consummate skill in diverting these rulers' allegiances away from the English monarch and to himself – a programme of consolidation that culminated in Welsh independence during the reign of his grandson 'Llewellyn the Last'. Llewellyn the Great was a warrior king, never one to be overawed by English might, and during his forty-year reign regularly repulsed invasions by the armies of both John LACKLAND and Henry III.

Llewellyn may well have been rough-hewn, but he did possess

a tender side. The story goes that, returning to his castle one day, he found his baby son's cradle empty and his favourite dog, 'Gelert', covered in blood. Assuming that Gelert had eaten the child, Llewellyn immediately ran Gelert through, only to hear a baby's wail mingled with the death throes of his faithful hound. After a brief search the king found his son snuggled under a pile of bedding next to the corpse of a fierce wolf, whom Gelert had obviously killed while protecting the little prince. Distraught, the great Llewellyn had Gelert buried with the pomp and solemnity reserved for noblemen.

¶ *Peter the* Great

Peter I, tsar of Russia, 1672–1725

Peter the Great transformed the Russian nation like an actor playing all the parts in a vast play. His roles included:

The General. Through mass conscriptions, Peter increased the Russian army by some 270,000 men. His forces clashed with the Ottoman Empire, Persia and, in particular, in the Great Northern War of 1700–21, Sweden. Russia eventually won the war, making it the undisputed powerhouse of Northern Europe and providing it with a stretch of the Baltic coast, where Peter founded his new capital St Petersburg in 1703.

Peter the Great

Peter gave his enemies individual attention. In 1698 some 4,000 guardsmen rebelled in what became known as the Streltsy Uprising. They were quickly defeated and Peter personally 'interrogated' 1,200 prisoners in purpose-built torture chambers before they were all killed in mass public executions.

The Taxman. To support all his measures, Peter tripled taxes. One of the most painful of the new taxes was his head tax, a levy that nearly every Russian male had to pay solely because he lived in Russia. One of the most controversial was his beard tax: all men, except priests and peasants, had to hand over 100 roubles a year if they wished to keep their beards. Many Christian folk saw this as a religious violation and, once they had had their beards shaved off, kept them and had them placed in their coffins, fearing they would not enter heaven without facial hair. Other economic policies were sometimes underhand. He actively promoted smoking, for instance, and then taxed tobacco.

The Style Guru. Peter spurned traditional, Muscovite fashion and embraced Western styles instead. Out went the ankle-length oriental garments and in came the shorter versions worn in Paris and London. Peter hung across the gate of Moscow a suit cut according to the new fashion; any man who passed through in a suit cut in the old style was publicly humiliated by having any part of their garments that fell below the knee cut off. Women, too, had to conform. He demanded English-style coiffures, as well as the wearing of bodices, stays and skirts. Peter also alarmed much of Russian society by demanding that men and women should mingle together at court functions, banquets and weddings.

The Giant. Peter was a colossus, standing six foot seven in his bare feet and often towering a foot above everyone else. Never afraid of physical labour, he kept in shape: one of his party tricks was to twist a silver platter into a scroll. Perhaps because of his excessive height, he delighted in a contingent of resident dwarves, with whom he entertained guests by having them dance on tables, trot about court on miniature ponies or spring, sometimes naked, out of pies. Once he arranged for a dwarf wedding, rounding up dozens of dwarves from Moscow and transporting them to St Petersburg, where they formed the retinue for the marriage ceremony and brought about the barely muffled guffaws of the (full-sized) congregation and priest.

The Man of Action. Peter was a restless workaholic, from encouraging the mining industry to modernizing the calendar.

Once, he managed to pass himself off as a carpenter while on an incognito tour of European courts. Other professions at which he tried his hand included barber, snuffbox maker and, much to the alarm of his friends, dentist. Companions with toothache were filled with terror lest Peter hear of their discomfort and offer his services. It is said that after his death a whole sackful of teeth was found among his possessions.

The Man of the Sea. His favourite occupation was shipbuilding, and he spared no expense in extending and improving Russia's shipbuilding industry. He even built a ship himself, which he then captained as 'Peter Alekseevich'. The sea was eventually his undoing, however. In November 1724 he dived into the cold northern ocean to assist a ship rescue, an act of courage that led to his final illness and death.

Peter loved the company of friends but also loved participating in barbaric acts of torture. He was a vulgar practical joker and yet a man who took the world and the work of the Church very seriously. He was, above all else, a man of contradictions, and historians continue to disagree wildly as to his greatness.

¶ *Theodosius the* Great

Theodosius I, Roman emperor of the East and West,
347–95

Fourth-century Rome suffered a chronic shortage of bakers and so a plot was hatched by baking magnates to conscript unwitting volunteers. Taverns-cum-brothels were built, and men who visited them to satisfy their thirst or lust fell through a trapdoor into the bakeries beneath, where they were forced to work as slaves. It is the emperor Theodosius who is credited with uncovering, and putting an end to, this deception.

The reign of Theodosius is most notable, however, not for its clampdown on rogue businesses but for its prominence in the history of the Christian Church. Baptized in his thirties, Theodosius soon afterwards vigorously suppressed paganism and made belief in the Trinity the universal test of orthodoxy.

Great . . . but not that Great

The world of nicknames is one of sycophancy and caprice, and nowhere more so than in the field of 'greatness'. Nobles with the nickname 'the Great' crop up regularly in our history books. From ancient Persian emperors to medieval princes, we find individuals who have been given this accolade, whether they warranted it or not. Below is a collection of some 'great' individuals who have not received a full entry for reasons of space. Some were indeed truly great. Others, completely without merit, have had the name thrust upon them.

- Abbas the Great, the Persian shah who at the turn of the seventeenth century succeeded not only in keeping Uzbek and Ottoman troops at bay but also in assassinating his four sons, thus leaving the Safavid Empire heirless.
- Amadeus the Great, the thirteenth-century count of Savoy, hailed for his expansionist policies in Italy.
- Antiochus the Great, the Syrian king who conducted an eastward campaign in the third century BC as far as India, only to lose all his territories to the Western powers.
- Arnulf the Great, count of Flanders, arch-rival of 'William Longsword' and one of the fiercest soldiers of the tenth century.
- Canute the Great, the eleventh-century king of England who commanded the waves to turn back from the shore, knowing that he would fail, in a demonstration to his sycophantic flatterers that even he had no control over Mother Nature.
- Charles the Great, under whose leadership the duchy of Lorraine attained its cultural and fiscal apogee. For more on the House of Lorraine, readers are referred to the Preface.
- Charles Emmanuel the Great, the duke of Savoy who switched sides in the Thirty Years War so blithely that when he died in 1630 he was detested by the French and the Spanish in equal measure.
- Cosimo the Great, a sixteenth-century member of the powerful Medici family under whose ruthless policies Tuscany enjoyed material prosperity as never before.
- Darius the Great, an administrator without equal whose financial and legal reforms of Persia in the sixth century BC consolidated the military conquests of Cyrus the GREAT.
- Ferdinand the Great of León and Castile, who, in preparation for his own imminent death in June 1065, went to a church and lay on a bier covered with ashes until he breathed his last.
- Hugh the Great, duke of the Franks from 936 until his death twenty

years later, who famously helped Louis the FOREIGNER return from exile in England and then threw him in jail.

- Ivan the Great, the fifteenth-century grand prince of Moscow who continued the work of his predecessors in wresting control of Russia from the Mongols.
- Justinian the Great, whose greatness as the emperor of Constantinople from 527 to 565 relies heavily on his wife, Theodora, who took ruthless control of the empire when he was temporarily confined to bed with the bubonic plague.
- Leopold the Great, the short, melancholic seventeenth-century Holy Roman Emperor whose preference for wearing scarlet hose earned him the alternative nickname 'the Little Man in Red Stockings'.
- Louis the Great, king of Hungary, whose military exploits saw him ruling the largest political complex of fourteenth-century Europe.
- Louis the Great, prince of Condé, whose military career in the mid 1600s exhibited outstanding courage, and whose imprisonment of his wife on trumped-up charges of infidelity exhibited true nastiness.
- Maximilian the Great, the Catholic duke of Bavaria whose troops routed those of 'Frederick the Snow King' (see the WINTER MONARCHS) in 1620 during the Thirty Years War.
- Otto the Great, the tenth-century emperor of Germany whose military successes won him incomparable prestige within Europe.
- Peter the Great, the enormously overweight thirteenth-century king of Aragon who also became king of Palermo.
- Rhodri the Great, who managed to unite most of ninth-century Wales while fending off marauding Danes from the west and menacing Saxons from the east.
- Sigismund the Great, the Polish king nicknamed for his forging of the Union of Lublin in 1569, which made Lithuania and Poland one indivisible body politic, with one king, one government and one currency.
- Theobald the Great, the count who united the houses of Champagne and Blois in the twelfth century, thereby posing a significant threat to both Louis the FAT and 'Louis the Foolish'.
- Vladimir the Great, the barbaric ruler of tenth-century Russia who converted to Christianity and forced his entire nation to do the same.
- William the Great, the duke of Aquitaine from 1004 to 1030 who claimed to have discovered the head of John the Baptist in his monastery and paraded it before his subjects. Most scholars consider his find to be utter humbug.

By some contemporaries Theodosius was known as a warm-hearted man who loved to sit at home and read histories, but history itself records him as being cruel, choleric and intemperate. For example, he generously pardoned the fractious citizens of Antioch in 387, but three years later approved of the massacre of some 7,000 people in Thessalonica, an act for which he had to humble himself in the cathedral of Milan in order to have his excommunication lifted.

¶ *Anthony the* Great Bastard
Anthony, Burgundian nobleman, 1421–1504

In the fifteenth century, being a bastard was not a congenital embarrassment. Anthony was unashamedly the illegitimate son of Philip the GOOD and, though not in line to any throne, was held in high regard among the elite of Burgundy. The first part of his soubriquet, 'the Great', celebrates the fact that he was a courageous jouster, a flamboyant patron of the arts and a collector of illuminated manuscripts.

Less celebrated is Anthony's abortive crusade of 1464. In the spring of that year he led eighty-two volunteers out of Ghent and started the long journey to Jerusalem. At Marseilles, however, the valiant soldiers heard the news that Pope Pius II had died, and in the absence of a pontiff the men reluctantly turned about face and plodded home.

¶ *Roger the* Great Count *see the* SONS OF TANCRED

¶ *Arthur the* Great Duke *see* Arthur the IRON DUKE

¶ *George the* Great Patron of Mankind
George II, king of England, 1683–1760

In his poem *The First Epistle of the Second Book of Horace Imitated* Alexander Pope addresses his monarch, George II, with the following lines:

> While you, great Patron of Mankind! sustain
> The balanc'd World, and open all the Main;
> Your country, chief, in Arms abroad defend,
> At home, with Morals, Arts, and Laws amend . . .

This was no panegyric, however, but a scathing attack on the king. In referring to George opening up 'all the Main', Pope was pointing out that the high seas were in fact full of Spanish ships harassing the English fleet. In mentioning 'Arms abroad', he was alluding to the arms of George's long-term German mistress Countess Melusine von der Schulenberg. And in extolling George's involvement in the arts and national legislation, he was merely highlighting George's disinterest in culture and affairs of state.

Indeed, the king was a pedant, an obsessive who spent hours counting the royal treasury coin by coin and who upbraided his officials for even the mildest of breaches of royal etiquette. His preoccupation with order and punctuality meant that court life was stultifying and monotonous. 'No mill horse,' wrote the statesman Lord Hervey, 'ever went on a more constant track on a more unchanging circle.'

The only excitement in court was when George lost his temper. His habit of falling into rages and kicking his wig around the room was legendary.

¶ *Isabella the* Great Sow
Isabella, queen consort of Charles VI of France, 1371–1435

Isabella enjoyed seven years of comparative wedded bliss with her husband Charles the SILLY until his first severe attack of insanity in 1392. Initially she sought both medical and supernatural remedies for his condition, but as his illness worsened (from time to time he didn't even know who she was) she sought comfort in the arms of other men and in so doing earned her reputation and nickname.

One might have expected her to have time for John the FEARLESS, who rescued her from imprisonment by her son Charles, but according to the Monk of St Denis she found John 'hideously repugnant'. Isabella, whom chroniclers variously describe as 'short and brown-coloured' and 'enveloped in horrid fat', fell instead for the charming and sprightly Louis of Valois, duke of Orléans, who happened to be her brother-in-law. They were apparently seldom apart, putting 'all their vanity in wealth, all their pleasure in bodily delight'. A scandal for France and a butt of English jokes, she died mocked by both nations.

¶ *Anne the* Great Whore
Anne Boleyn, queen of England, c.1507–36

Henry VIII tired of his second wife after about three years, and although BLUFF KING HAL and his cronies insisted that she had enjoyed a hundred lovers, only twenty offences of adultery were officially levied against her. It was, of course, a complete pack of lies and yet, even when, on the damnation of her immortal soul, Anne swore on the sacrament that she had never been unfaithful to the king (least of all with her brother George) she won little sympathy. That she was no ravishing beauty – one critic described her as having buck teeth, six fingers on her right hand and a massive wart under her chin – and that she may have shared too many romantic secrets with some of her courtiers may not have helped her cause, but a whore, let alone a great whore, she was not. For failing to produce a male heir (a girl, such as her daughter, GOOD QUEEN BESS, was decidedly second-class goods) Anne simply and spectacularly fell out of favour. On the scaffold she suggested that as well as 'Anne of a Thousand Days' (owing to the length of her reign) and 'the Great Whore', she would rapidly acquire a third nickname. 'Soon,' she quipped in true gallows humour, 'I shall be known as "Anne sans tête" [Anne the Headless].'

❡ *Aurelian the* Greatest Goth *see* Aurelian the RESTORER OF THE WORLD

❡ *Amadeus the* Green *see* COLOURFUL CHARACTERS

❡ *Archibald* Greysteel
Archibald Douglas, sixth earl of Angus, c.1489–1557

During Archibald's tenure as earl of Angus, the Red faction of the RED AND BLACK DOUGLASES was at its zenith. On the death of his grandfather BELL THE CAT the young Archibald became the sixth earl and swiftly married Margaret Tudor, thus allying himself with her brother BLUFF KING HAL. Back in Scotland Archibald established something of a power base in Edinburgh and gained complete control over the twelve-year-old James the ILL-BELOVED. In 1527 Archibald became chancellor and members of the Red Douglas family held every important post in the royal household.

Archibald's soubriquet of 'Greysteel' suggests he was a man who knew how to wield a sword. This was certainly the case at the battle of Ancrum Moor in 1545, when he hacked down English forces led by one Sir Ralph Evers, who had (inadvertently) desecrated the tomb of William, the first earl of Douglas and forefather of the 'Red Douglas' clan. For such sacrilege, Evers was flayed and his skin turned into purses for the Scottish soldiers.

❡ Griff *see* POOR FRED

¶ *Archibald the* Grim

Archibald Douglas, third earl of Douglas, c.1328–1400

Despite his emblem of a bleeding heart, Archibald, the illegitimate son of 'the Good Sir James' Douglas, was far from a liberal sap. Instead he was one of the ablest soldiers of his era. One historian suggests he was nicknamed 'for his swart complexion'. The following entry from the chronicles of Jean Froissart, describing Archibald's behaviour at a battle near Melrose, supports the idea that he was so named 'for his terrible countenance in warfare':

> Douglas was a good knight and much feared by his enemies: when near to the English, he dismounted, and wielded before him an immense sword, whose blade was two ells [seven and half feet] long, which scarcely another could have lifted from the ground, but he found no difficulty in handling it, and gave such terrible strokes, that all on whom they fell were struck to the ground.

¶ *Manuel the* Grocer King *see* Manuel the

FORTUNATE

¶ *James the* Gross

James Douglas, seventh earl of Douglas, c.1371–1443

James the Gross was very fat and very lazy – on the face of it, a combination not conducive to the long-term success of a fifteenth-century Scottish earl. In a time of violent and premature death, however, James surprisingly lived into his seventies.

Just how 'gross' was James the Gross? Well, he is recorded as carrying about him 'four stane of talch and mair' – in other words, some sixty pounds of fat. And there are convincing hints that his morals matched his physical grossness. Many suggest that it was James who was behind the infamous 'Black Dinner', at which a black bull's head was reportedly served up to the sixth earl of Douglas and his younger brother as a portent of their murder that same night.

¶ Guaff *see* Victor Emmanuel the GALLANT KING

¶ *Akbar the* Guardian of Mankind
see Akbar the GREAT

[**H**]

¶ *Wilfrid the* Hairy *see* Wilfrid the SHAGGY

¶ *Charles the* Hammer
Charles, mayor of the palace of Austrasia, c.688–741

Charles's victory at the battle of Poitiers of 732 turned the tide of Islamic advance in Europe and paved the way for Frankish unification under his son Pepin the SHORT and grandson Charles the GREAT. The victory also won him his nickname. The *Chronicle of St Denis* states that the name 'Martel', or 'the Hammer', was conferred on Charles for having hammered (*martelé*) the Saracens. '[A]s a hammer of iron, of steel, and of every other metal,' the chronicle gushes, 'even so he dashed and smote in the battle all his enemies.'

¶ *Frederick the* Hammer of Christianity
see Frederick the WONDER OF THE WORLD

¶ *Thomas the* Hammer of the Monks
Thomas Cromwell, first earl of Essex, c.1485–1540

After early careers as a soldier, accountant and merchant, Cromwell entered the service of Cardinal Wolsey and rose through the ranks to become BLUFF KING HAL's chief minister. In 1534 he was appointed Henry's vicar-general and the activities that earned him his nickname began.

Thomas's remit in implementing the Act of Supremacy of

1534 was the suppression of the monasteries and confiscation of their property and treasures, and this he carried out with such ruthless zeal that he was ruefully dubbed 'Malleus monachorum', or 'Hammer of the Monks'. Initially, all monasteries with an income of less than £200 were dissolved and their contents sold. This did not inflate the royal coffers as much as had been expected, and so in 1539 Parliament passed a law handing all of the country's monastic houses over to the king. Some abbots resisted Thomas and his policies, and Thomas hammered them hard. Richard Whiting, for example, was dragged by horses from his abbey in Glastonbury to the top of a nearby hill, where he was hanged, drawn and quartered. His head was shoved on a spike above the abbey gate, and his 'quarters' were boiled in pitch and put on display in four West Country towns.

Although Thomas's own religious views may not have been strong, his belief in the sovereignty of the king was absolute, and it was to foster his monarch's links with the Protestant states of Europe that he arranged the marriage between Henry and Anne the MARE OF FLANDERS. Perhaps it was because he was brought up in a blacksmith's forge, but Thomas's inability to detect Anne's equine attributes proved his undoing. Henry thought his new wife resembled a horse, and Cromwell was summarily accused of treason and beheaded.

¶ *Edward the* Hammer of the Scots
Edward I, king of England, 1239–1307

The inscription on Edward's tomb in Westminster Abbey reads, '*Edwardus Primus Malleus Scotorum hic est*' – 'Here lies Edward I, Hammer of the Scots'. Scots are quick to remind anyone who would care to listen that while Edward may have hammered their nation, he never conquered it.

On his return from the Crusades (where his wife, Eleanor of Castile, had saved his life by sucking out poison from a dagger wound) Edward quickly subdued Wales and its king 'Llewellyn the Last', and then turned his attention to England. Here his reformation of the legal and tax systems, and establishment of the country's first formal parliament, won him the titles 'the English Justinian', 'the Lawgiver' and the rather cumbersome 'the Father of the Mother of Parliaments'. With both Wales and England now under his sway, Edward finally began his campaign against Scotland in earnest.

In 1296 Edward easily deposed the Scottish king, TOOM TABARD, but the following year his real troubles began when he faced the wrath of Scottish rebel William Wallace and his brave-hearted men. Wallace, who was known by the matching nickname 'the Hammer and Scourge of England', was eventually captured and hanged, drawn and quartered. Scotland, however, refused to cave in.

Edward, who once ripped clumps of hair from the head of his son Edward CARNARVON, was not a peaceful sort, and he spent nearly a decade furiously trying to subdue his northern neighbours, but it was not to be. Trying to quell a rebellion led by Robert the BRUCE in the summer of 1307, he contracted dysentery and died near Carlisle, a short distance from a nation whose conquest he ached for but never achieved.

The more popular soubriquet for Edward did not refer to his notable military exploits but rather to a notable physical characteristic. If this had been followed, the inscription on his tomb would have read, '*Edwardus Primus praeditus pedibus longis hic est*' – 'Here lies Edward Longshanks'.

¶ *Ferdinand the* Handsome *see* Ferdinand
THE INCONSTANT

¶ *Philip the* Handsome
Philip I, king of Castile, 1478–1506

Philip had a long nose, long hair and long limbs. The inhabitants of the Low Countries, over whom he was ruler from 1482, admired the dashing appearance of this son of 'Maximilian the Penniless' and styled him 'Filips de Schone'. Later, the inhabitants of Castile over whom he became king in 1502 similarly titled him 'Felipe el Hermoso'.

His people may have admired him, but his young wife, Joan the MAD, was absolutely nuts about him. Historians with an eye for the titillating recount how the couple behaved when they first met. As soon as they clapped eyes on each other, we are told, they immediately summoned a priest to marry them on the spot. The declaration of their union had barely left the minister's lips before the couple raced into the royal bedchamber to consummate their marriage.

Joan may have been madly in love with the good-looking Philip, but Philip was an inveterate womanizer with a bevy of mistresses. When he died still in his twenties – some say he caught a fever after playing a ballgame and then drinking too much cold water too quickly – many a woman mourned the loss of a sexy sovereign. Joan simply went completely and utterly insane.

¶ *John the* Handsome Englishman
see John the SILLY DUKE

¶ *Claude the* Handsome Queen
Claude, queen consort of Francis I of France, 1499–1524

When Claude, the unattractive daughter of Louis the FATHER OF THE PEOPLE, married Francis the FATHER OF LETTERS, the French people cruelly called her 'the Handsome'. According to one contemporary, the Seigneur de Brantôme, she was 'very small and strangely fat' with an unattractive round face and a squint in one eye. She was also lame, clomping through court with a pronounced limp. The day after their marriage Francis went hunting, and for some years took little interest in his bride except as a mother for his children.

Over time, however, both the king and the French people warmed to their queen. It was not just because she started to produce children at an admirable speed, nor because they had

Harald and the Hair Shirt

Harald I, earl of Orkney, d. 1131
Paul II, earl of Orkney, d. c.1138

The *Orkneyinga Saga* tells the story of a pair of half-brothers, 'Harald the Smooth Talker' and 'Paul the Silent'. Together, the voluble Harald, and Paul, 'a man of few words [who] had little to say at public assemblies', ruled the islands. Sadly, in this case, opposites did not attract and the two men hated each other with a passion.

One day Harald came across Helga, his mother, and Frakok, his aunt, making a beautiful white shirt with gold thread. He asked the women who it was for and they replied that it was a special Christmas present for Paul. Deaf to their protests Harald quickly slipped it over his head. It was only then that the women were able to explain that this Yuletide gift was 'special' in that it had been dipped in poison. For his foolhardiness Harald died in agony. For their treachery Paul sent Helga and Frakok into exile.

grown accustomed to her plain, slightly melancholic face, which in a good light made her look like a rustic Madonna. It was because this long-suffering queen was charming. Claude was an excellent mother who adored her husband (bearing his lecherous infidelities with virtuous resignation) and who was unfailingly kind to all who met her. When she died, worn out by childbearing, in 1524, she died universally beloved, with all France mourning the passing of a woman whom one chronicler described as 'the very pearl of ladies . . . without stain'. From initial facetious disdain, therefore, the French recognized that in their *bonne reine* true beauty lay within. The fruit known as the greengage in English is called *la reine-claude* in French in her honour.

¶ *Harold* Harefoot
Harold I, king of England, d. 1040

Historical records such as the *Anglo-Saxon Chronicle* have little
to say about Harold's short reign except that he entered into a
dispute with the Church over some lands at the southern port
of Sandwich, and that he died in Oxford in 1040. We can deduce
from his nickname, which derives from the Old Norse word
harfotr, meaning 'swift runner', that he was fast on his feet and
possibly fast on his horse when hunting. We can also deduce by
what happened to his body after it was buried that Harthacanute,
his half-brother, hated him.

Harthacanute was the legitimate heir to the thrones of both
Denmark and England. Harold agreed to act as his regent in
England but quickly reneged on his promise and proclaimed
himself king. Three months after Harold's death Harthacanute
arrived in England to claim the throne. Unable to take revenge
on Harold when he was still alive, Harthacanute arranged for
Harold's body to be exhumed, torn apart and flung into a bog.

¶ *Charles the* Harlequin
Charles V, Holy Roman
Emperor, 1500–1558

Charles the Harlequin

While Charles V was certainly
a fearless and indefatigable
warrior, one of his epithets, 'a
Second Charlemagne', would
appear to be based solely on
the two monarchs' sharing the
same Christian name. Whereas
Charles the GREAT was a
devout man of faith, Charles V
spent his retirement at Yuste
Monastery in Estremadura en-

gaged in feasting rather than fasting. And whereas the real Charlemagne drank in moderation, this 'Charlemagne', according to one English traveller, drank 'the best that ever I saw ... his head in the glass five times as long as any of us, and never [drinking] less than a quart at once of Rhenish wine'.

A second soubriquet, 'a Discrowned Glutton', is more apt. After a reign enmeshed in civil strife and foreign upheaval, Charles, who was already decidedly chubby, waddled away from it all and abdicated for a life of culinary overindulgence.

A third nickname, 'the Harlequin', initially seems to be the most inappropriate of all. How could fellow nicknamee Francis the FATHER OF LETTERS liken Charles to a frivolous buffoon when in reality the emperor was a serious, phlegmatic character who rarely spoke since his misshapen jaw made him difficult to understand and, when he did, it was in German and mainly to his horse? The answer is that Francis was using the term 'harlequin' in its Old French sense, meaning 'demon'.

❡ *Amadeus the* Hermit of La Ripaille
see Amadeus the PACIFIC

❡ *Frederick the* Hesitater *see* Frederick the WISE

❡ *Charles the* Highland Laddie *see* BONNIE PRINCE CHARLIE

❡ Holy Mother *see* Lady Wu the POISONER

¶ *Hywel of the* Horseshoes
Sir Hywel ap Gruffyth, Welsh nobleman, b. *c.*1284

Hywel was the son of the wet nurse of Edward CARNARVON. Edward was so impressed with his foster brother and boyhood chum – not least with his ability to break or straighten horseshoes with his bare hands – that he made him a knight of the realm.

¶ *Harry* Hotspur
Henry Percy, English nobleman, 1364–1403

Henry Percy, the eldest son of the first earl of Northumberland, earned his evocative nickname for the reckless courage he showed in battles along the Scottish Borders, including the 1402 victory over the Scots at Homildon Hill, a fight which was lost by Archibald the LOSER. In what turned out to be a rash and impetuous move, Henry conspired with Owen Glendower and others to dethrone Henry BOLINGBROKE, and was killed by the king's troops at the battle of Shrewsbury in 1403.

¶ *Pepin the* Hunchback
Pepin, Frankish prince, d. 811

Despite his deformity, Pepin was initially designated as the future ruler by his father Charles the GREAT, but this was reversed when, thanks to Charles's second wife, the young and fertile Hildegard, another son appeared. Pepin was not pleased with this arrangement and, together with some disgruntled magnates, entered into a conspiracy to seize the throne while Charlemagne was away at war. The plot, however, was discovered and Pepin, according to the biographer Einhard, was 'cruelly scourged, tonsured and sent into a monastery, the poorest . . . in all the king's broad domain'.

A near-contemporary writer known as 'Notker the Stammerer' tells how Charlemagne later discovered another plot against his life and sought advice from his reluctantly monastic son. Pepin, weeding in the garden, apparently told his father's envoys to report back precisely what he was doing, namely digging up useless weeds to enable other plants to prosper. Charles understood his son's cryptic message and promptly got rid of his enemies by having them executed. He then rewarded Pepin by letting him move to 'the most noble monastery then in existence'.

In all likelihood, however, Notker's story is a complete fabrication and Pepin actually died unreconciled and in abject poverty.

[**I**]

❡ *James the* Ill-beloved
James V, king of Scotland, 1512–42

The whole of James's upbringing was conducive to moral delinquency, and it was said that his stepfather, Archibald GREYSTEEL,
actively encouraged him in a precocious career of vice. When he
was still a teenager, he already had three illegitimate sons and,
by the time he died, aged twenty-nine, he had sired seven children, all with different mothers.

Considering his merciless treatment of the inhabitants of the
Scottish Borders and Highlands, his treacherous double-dealings
with BLUFF KING HAL of England and his vindictive domestic
policy of taxation, it is little wonder that he was called 'the
Ill-Beloved' and is generally understood to be one of the most
unpopular monarchs who ever sat on the Scottish throne. 'So
sore a dread king,' the duke of Norfolk wrote to Thomas the
HAMMER OF THE MONKS, 'and so ill-beloved of his subjects,
was never in that land.'

There was another side to James, however, a side that endeared him to many. Stories of 'the King of the Commons'
wandering unknown among his subjects are widespread. Perhaps
the best known tells how a miller called Jock Howieson rescued
the (incognito) king from a gang of thugs and washed and
dressed his wounds. James introduced himself as 'the Gudeman
of Ballangiech', a tenant farmer on one of the royal estates,
and, in gratitude, invited Howieson to Holyrood Palace. James
promised the miller that he would catch a glimpse of the king,
whom he would recognize as the only person wearing a hat.
Once they had arrived at the palace, with James still in disguise,
a group of courtiers all removed their hats and bowed, at which

Howieson, who was wearing a cap himself, exclaimed, 'Then it must be either you or me, for all but us are bareheaded!' For his Good Samaritan kindness, Howieson received the freehold of a royal farm.

But such romantic events were mere interludes in what was otherwise a dark reign steeped in iniquity. The circumstances of James's death were fittingly sad. On hearing that his forces had suffered a disastrous rout at the hands of the English at Solway Moss, James climbed into bed, turned his face to the wall and died, indifferent to the birth of his daughter Mary the MERMAID the week before.

❡ Ill-Fated Henry *see* Henry the MARTYR

❡ *Jamshid the* Illustrious
Jamshid, king of Persia, *fl.* eighth century BC

To Jamshid, the fifth monarch of Persia's Pishdadian dynasty, we owe much. Legend credits him with nothing less than the introduction of the solar year and the invention of most of the arts and sciences on which civilization is based. It is to one of his wives, however, that we owe the discovery of the properties of wine. Suffering from a painful illness, she drank the juice of some fermented grapes in the mistaken belief that it would prove lethal. On the contrary, she fell into a deep sleep and woke up the next morning with a hangover – but cured.

Perhaps it was the drink, but in later life Jamshid elevated his own status to that of a god, and for his pride he was put to a barbaric death. A Syrian prince named Zohak hunted him down and had him strapped between two boards and sawn in half with the backbone of a fish.

❡ *Ptolemy the* Illustrious *see* PTOLEMAIC KINGS

¶ *Yung-cheng the* Immortal
Yung-cheng, emperor of China, 1678–1735

On 8 October 1735 Yung-cheng the Immortal died.

¶ *Vlad the* Impaler
Vlad Tepes, prince of Wallachia, *c.*1431–76

As one might suspect, the origins behind Vlad's nickname are not for the queasy.

In the middle of the fifteenth century the province of Wallachia in southern Romania was self-governed under Turkish suzerainty. It was a brutal time and Vlad, who called himself 'Dracula', meaning 'Son of the Dragon', was the most brutal prince of all. He ruled the province three times. The six years of his principal reign, between 1456 and 1462, were predominantly occupied with combating the Turkish forces of Mehmed the CONQUEROR and quashing repeated rebellions by the Saxon citizens of Brasov. During this period he supposedly put 20,000 people to death, and his methods of maintaining sovereignty were nothing short of stomach-churning.

He loved to watch people being boiled alive in copper cauldrons. He delighted in peeling the skin off the feet of Turkish prisoners, covering their wounds with salt and then bringing goats to lick their soles. Once, some Ottoman ambassadors refused to remove their turbans as a sign of respect for him, so he had their turbans nailed to their heads.

But his favourite modus operandi was impalement. The people of Brasov earned the dubious distinction of being the most popular victims of this form of execution, and the hills surrounding their town carried more stakes than anywhere else in the principality. Here, it is said, Vlad impaled women and their suckling babies on the same stake and then wined and dined with Carpathian vultures among the cadavers. Here, a Russian narrative tells us, a boyar who was unable to endure the smell of coagulating blood any longer held his nose in a gesture of revulsion, upon which Vlad ordered a stake, three times as long as normal, to be prepared. He then presented it to the peasant saying, 'You can live up there yonder, where the stench cannot reach you.' The poor man was immediately impaled and his body left to rot in the sun.

The mechanics of impalement are cumbersome. A sharp stake is thrust through the victim's rectum, and then forced through the body to emerge either through the eye or throat. The stake is then planted in the ground, leaving the victim hanging in agony. Stories of Vlad's impaling some 100,000 people in his lifetime are therefore highly improbable. If a tenth of the tales of his brutality deserve any credence, however, Vlad was one of the most barbaric men of the Middle Ages, and any gory scenes in Bram Stoker's novel *Dracula* are the lightest of entertainments in comparison.

❡ *Ferdinand the* Inconstant
Ferdinand I, king of Portugal, 1345–83

The story of this woefully perfidious king is a tale of three women who had something in common. Ferdinand, also known as 'the Handsome', initially intended to marry Leonor, daughter of the king of Aragon, but under the provisions of a political treaty was compelled to snub her in favour of Leonor, the daughter of the Castilian 'Henry the Bastard'. Ferdinand then rocked royal society by jilting Henry's daughter in favour of the beautiful Portuguese noblewoman Leonor Teles de Meneses. While one may not admire his inconstancy with women, one cannot but be impressed with the constancy of their names.

❡ *Louis the* Indolent *see* GALLIC PRACTICE

❡ *Elizabeth the* Infamous
Elizabeth, empress of Russia, 1709–62

Elizabeth Petrovna was known throughout the courts of Europe as 'l'Infame Catin du Nord', or 'the Northern Harlot', but her reputation as nothing but a trollop is unwarranted. What one can say with certainty is that Elizabeth was a woman of passion.

- She was a passionate patriot. Like her father Peter the GREAT, she was held in the highest esteem by her army and her first years of power showed her to be an astute, if painfully procrastinating, governor of Russia.

Elizabeth the Infamous

- She was a passionate hostess. The beautiful, popular and vivacious Elizabeth provided guests at court with lavish feasts and entertainments. Childless herself, she adored holding children's parties, serving up miniature food on miniature plates on miniature tables.
- She was passionate about her appearance. One of her weaknesses was fine clothes, and unlike most she had the means of indulging it. On her death 15,000 dresses were discovered in her wardrobes.
- She was passionate about matters spiritual. Elizabeth was extremely religious, yet also extremely superstitious. If a fly, for instance, settled on her pen or paper when she was on the point of signing a bill, the document would be put to one side for another day.
- She was a passionate sensualist. The French ambassador found her disgusting, alluding in various dispatches to her deplorable indolence, her delight in being surrounded by riff-raff, and her 'voluptuous vanity'. Her favourite luxury, we are told, was to lie in bed and have her feet scratched by her ladies-in-waiting.

Irish High Kings

Beginning with the extravagantly named, and probably legendary, 'Slainge the Firbolg' of about 2000 BC, royal cognomens in Irish genealogies make intriguing reading. Most Irish histories start with the fourth-century AD king 'Niall of the Nine Hostages', but there is sufficient evidence to trace high kings back several centuries before him. Some of these kings were given nicknames, and below is a list, beginning at AD 1, of those so honoured.

First Century AD
Nuada the White
Lugaide of the Red Stripes
Conchobar of the Red Brows
Crimthann the Modest Warrior
Carbery Cathead

Second Century
Tuathal the Legitimate
Fedlimid the Lawgiver
Conn of the Hundred Battles

Third Century
Art the Solitary
Fergus of the Black Teeth

❡ *William the* Iron Arm *see* the SONS OF TANCRED

❡ *Arthur the* Iron Duke
Arthur Wellesley, duke of Wellington, 1769–1852

Was Wellington named 'the Iron Duke', as one Victorian biographer has proposed, after a steamboat that plied between

Liverpool and Dublin? Or did the press dub him so after he installed iron shutters at Apsley House in 1828 to fend off an angry mob? Without question, Wellington himself would have preferred to believe the name derived from either the harsh discipline he imposed on his regiments or his rigid opposition to parliamentary reforms.

After his famous victory at Waterloo in 1815 over Napoleon the LITTLE CORPORAL, and before any ferrous appellations had become common currency, Wellington had been variously heralded as 'the Great Duke' and 'the Saviour of the Nations'. His most popular nicknames throughout his life, however, celebrated neither his military success nor his political character, but his vast and unmistakable nose. Supporters and critics alike knew him as 'Conky', 'Old Nosey' and 'Beaky', while even poets were fascinated by his immense aquiline proboscis. 'Proud Wellington,' wrote Byron, 'with eagle beak so called / That nose, the hook where he suspends the world.'

¶ Iron-Hand
Götz von Berlichingen, German knight, 1480–1562

No metaphor in use here. The Germans named their hero 'Iron-Hand' precisely because he had an artificial iron hand, replacing one that had been blown off at the siege of Landshut in 1505.

¶ *Ernest the* Iron-handed
Ernest, duke of Austria, 1383–1424

Ernest's uncompromising and relentless warring against his brothers Frederick and Leopold accounts for his epithet, but in a wonderful uxorial nickname transference it is Ernest's wife who really deserves this soubriquet. Cymburga, a Polish noblewoman, was the perfect partner for the adamantine Ernest. Historians record that she could crack nuts with her fingers and drive nails into wood with her bare fist.

¶ *Edmund* Ironside
Edmund II, king of England, *c.*993–1016

The sixteenth-century antiquary William Camden states that Edmund's nickname derived from his valour on the battlefield. Others claim, however, that the king was so called because he wore his armour all day, every day. He undoubtedly had use for it, fighting no fewer than five battles with 'Canute the Great' (*see* GREAT . . . BUT NOT THAT GREAT) within a year of occupying the English throne. At the battle of Ashingdon, a chink in his battered iron armour was found, and Edmund received a fatal wound.

¶ *Frederick* Irontooth
Frederick II, margrave of Brandenburg, 1413–71

At the turn of the fifteenth century Berlin was an unhygienic outpost of the Holy Roman Empire, bogged down in lawlessness and ravaged by plague. In 1411 Sigismund the LIGHT OF THE WORLD asked the noblemen of the House of Hohenzollern to quash the province's robber barons and restore law and order. This they did with admirable speed. When, however, the young Frederick assumed control of the region, some of the more arrogant burghers presumed his inexperience spelled liberality. Not so. Frederick immediately disbanded the courts, seized private property and 'bit off' the hand of anyone who dared to take liberties; hence his nickname 'Dent de Fer'.

¶ *Nicholas the* Iron Tsar
Nicholas I, tsar of Russia, 1796–1855

Nicholas was a big baby. When his grandmother Catherine the GREAT clapped eyes upon him, she marvelled at this 'colossus' and whisked him away to her private quarters to raise him herself. But Catherine died five months later and Nicholas returned to the care of his somewhat indifferent parents. He grew to be strikingly handsome and was a big hit with the ladies when he visited England in 1816. With his Grecian nose, curly moustache and imperial bearing, he could have chosen almost anyone to be his bride. As it was he fell for and married the sickly Princess Charlotte of Prussia, whom he called 'Mouffy', and together they had seven children, including Alexander the EMANCIPATOR.

In December 1825 Nicholas's older brother Alexander died and, after putting down a small revolt by the so-called 'Decembrists', Nicholas was acknowledged as tsar of all Russia. It was a job he took seriously. Nicholas saw himself as something of a guardian against revolution, and his foreign policy of offering his nation's services to suppress any regional uprising earned him the tag 'the Gendarme of Europe'. The name 'the Iron Tsar', meanwhile, stems from his ferociously repressive national policies. Championing the mantra of 'autocracy, orthodoxy, and nationality', Nicholas governed Russia as a police state, and woe betide anyone who stepped out of line. Spies were everywhere and punishments severe. Singing a mildly risqué song at a private party, publishing a literary paper that challenged his supreme authority, or sporting a beard (if one was a nobleman) – all could be sufficient to earn a one-way ticket to Siberia.

[J]

¶ John of Yesteryear
Robert III, king of Scotland, c.1337–1406

Robert's nickname was 'John Faranyei', or 'John of Yesteryear', because his name as a child was John, but he switched it to Robert at his coronation. This 'Robert' did because he was all too aware of the miserable reign of John ' TOOM TABARD' Balliol and concluded that the name of John must be unlucky. However, if he thought a change of name would ensure a peaceful reign, he was sorely mistaken.

In 1394 a horse kicked Robert so violently that he was left physically unable to oversee the day-to-day government of the kingdom. Reluctantly, he handed over the reins of power to his ambitious and corrupt younger brother, the duke of Albany, who immediately imprisoned Robert's son David and left him to starve to death. Another of Robert's brothers, Alexander the WOLF OF BADENOCH, meanwhile, had become the bandit ruler of northern Scotland, tyrannizing the Isles without fear of reprisal.

The whole kingdom, wrote one chronicler, was 'a den of thieves [where] murders . . . fire-raising and all other deeds remained unpunished', and Robert knew he had been a failure. When James, yet another son, was captured by English pirates and sent to the Tower of London, it was all too much for him. He retired to his ancestral home and told Annabella, his wife, that he wanted to be buried in a dunghill with the epitaph, 'Here lies the worst of kings and the most miserable of men.'

¶ *Otto the* Jolly
Otto, duke of Austria, d. 1339

Except in battle, Otto der Fröhliche always had a smile on his face. He reigned – very happily – with his disabled brother Albert the LAME, joyfully marrying Anna, the sister of Charles the PARSON'S EMPEROR, and jovially accepting the added appointment of vicar of Germany when it was offered to him.

¶ *Edward the* Josiah of England *see*
ENGLISH EPITHETS

¶ *Aristides the* Just
Aristides, Athenian statesman, *c.*530–468 BC

The process of ostracism in ancient Athens took the form of citizens scratching on a fragment of pottery the name of the man they wished to see banished. If more than 6,000 ballots were cast, the person whose name appeared most often was exiled for a period of ten years. And in 482 BC Aristides, a statesman known for his honesty, fairness and integrity – and consequently envied and detested by many – found himself a candidate for banishment.

On election day an illiterate country bumpkin approached Aristides, whom he did not know, and asked him to write 'Aristides' on his ballot. The statesman asked the farmer whether this Aristides had ever done him any wrong. 'Oh no,' came the reply, 'in fact, I don't even know who Aristides is, but I'm simply tired of hearing everyone call him "the Just".' Aristides dutifully wrote down his own name and was ostracized. Two years later, however, the statesman was invited back. Athens simply could not live without a man who so eminently displayed the virtues it held most dear.

¶ *Haroun the* Just

Haroun al-Rashid, caliph of the Abbasid dynasty,
c.766–809

Haroun was literally the stuff of legend, with his splendid court at Baghdad playing a central role in the book *The Thousand and One Nights*. His mother al-Khayzuran ruled there imperiously, and his wife ostentatiously lived in the lap of luxury, refusing to have anything but jewel-studded gold and silver vessels on her table. In comparison with these two women, Haroun himself was a rather unassuming man, content to listen to music, write poetry and watch the occasional cockfight.

Legend also has it that Haroun al-Rashid – sometimes anglicized to 'Aaron the Just' – was so anxious that his subjects should be treated justly by his government that he would sometimes disguise himself at night and walk through the city bazaars, listening to people's concerns and complaints.

However, justice in eighth-century Arabia was meted out summarily. On learning of a scandalous relationship between his grand vizier and an Abbasid princess, Haroun had all the leading members of the vizier's family executed. Accompanying the incognito caliph on his fact-finding strolls through Baghdad, meanwhile, were not only a few friends, but also, rather sinisterly, his executioner.

¶ *Louis the* Just *see* GALLIC PRACTICE

¶ *Peter the* Just *see* Peter the CRUEL

[K]

❡ *Christopher the* King of Bark
Christopher III, king of Denmark, Norway and Sweden, 1418–48

The good-natured, easy-going but none-too-enterprising Christopher enjoyed his beer far more than the vexing affairs of state, and discontent with his indolence increased exponentially when a string of bad harvests compelled his peasants to mix ground tree-bark with their flour to make bread. Out of sympathy, the king apparently joined his subjects in eating these 'bark buns' – a practice that may have contributed to his early death.

❡ *Henry the* King of Brave Men *see* Henry the GREAT

❡ *Louis the* King of Slops
Louis XVIII, king of France, 1755–1824

For much of his life Louis was a king without a kingdom, and Europe's elite had little time for him. Occupied with the machinations of Napoleon the LITTLE CORPORAL, they dubbed this brother of Louis XVI 'le Roi Panade' – literally 'the Bread-Soup King'. This was not a gastronomic nickname, however, but an economic one, suggesting that Louis, exiled and without a traditional royal income, was fiscally 'in the soup'. E. Cobham Brewer, the compiler of the famous *Dictionary of Phrase and Fable*, translates 'Roi Panade', somewhat harshly, as 'the King of Slops'.

Modest, yet ever optimistic about the royalist cause despite

Napoleon's success, Louis spent nineteen years away from French soil waiting for the right moment to reclaim the throne. In the spring of 1814 it seemed that moment had come. The English stopped calling the chubby old gentleman who had been quietly living among them 'Bungy Louis' and instead hailed him as 'the Desired', encouraging him to consolidate the peace that Arthur the IRON DUKE had done so much to win for him.

After the battle of Waterloo, Louis returned to France where, apart from the Hundred Days when Napoleon attempted to reclaim power, he spent the next nine years doing his level best to rule as a constitutional monarch. But it was hard work. Louis was in his sixties, obese and suffering from gout, and as his health grew more feeble, so did his influence. On his deathbed in September 1824 Louis is reported to have sighed morosely that 'a king should die on his feet'.

§ *Louis Philip the* King of the Barricades
see Louis Philip the CITIZEN KING

§ *James the* King of the Commons *see*
James the ILL-BELOVED

§ *Edward the* King of the Sea *see* Edward
the BANKRUPT

§ King Oliver *see* NOSE ALMIGHTY

§ *Richard the* Kingmaker
Richard Neville, sixteenth earl of Warwick, 1428–71

Through his marriage to Lady Anne de Beauchamp in 1449, Richard Neville acquired not only the title of earl of Warwick, but also sizeable estates throughout England, making him one of the most powerful men in the country. His increased wealth and political influence enabled him to carve out for himself the role of kingmaker – instrumental in the fortunes of two men who were both vying for the English throne.

Richard the Kingmaker

First, Richard wielded his power to negotiate the deposition of Henry the MARTYR in favour of his own cousin Edward the ROBBER, but when Edward proved treacherously ungrateful, Richard drove him into exile and restored Henry to the throne once more. Richard's military dexterity did not match his brilliant, manipulative political skill, however, and he was killed a few months later, fighting against Edward's forces at the battle of Barnet.

¶ *Anne the* King's King
Anne, duke of Joyeuse, 1561–87

Having wantonly ousted a host of court favourites, the capricious and louche Henry the MAN-MILLINER appointed Anne (a male name in sixteenth-century France) as his new right-hand man, hoping that this ambitious champion of Roman Catholicism would maintain administrative order while he engaged in the serious businesses of fashion design and puppy-training.

As the new duke of Joyeuse, Anne revelled in his near-absolute authority and in his nickname of 'the King's King', which suggested where true royal power lay. But he was as arrogant, selfish and foolish as his monarch and met his nemesis when facing the Protestant forces of Henry of Navarre, the future Henry the GREAT, at the battle of Coutras in October 1587.

Anne amassed a brightly coloured army, double the size of

Henry's plainly dressed and rather shabby Huguenot troops, and, confident in his cavalry and of victory, he and his men scoffed as the Huguenots sang a psalm before the engagement. Disobeying royal orders (not for the first time), Anne had his troops attack, but the better-prepared Protestants slaughtered them in their thousands, and 'King Anne' was killed in the act of surrender.

[**L**]

¶ *John* Lackland
John, king of England, 1167–1216

As the youngest son, John had no immediate inheritance and thus received the nickname 'Lackland' – an entirely appropriate epithet as it turned out, since during his reign he succeeded in losing nearly all of England's territories in France. His exploits in Ireland when still a prince, however, should have alerted his nobles to the humiliations that were to come. Dispatched there in 1185 to conclude the conquest begun by his father, Henry CURTMANTLE, all John managed to do was alienate the friendly native kings by ridiculing their dress and appearance, and infuriate his own soldiers by spending their pay on himself.

If 'Lackland' was an apt epithet, that of 'Softsword' was undeserved. Although certainly no warrior like his brother Richard the LIONHEART, he was no coward either, and it was merely sniping malcontents who dubbed him 'Mollegladium' after he signed the peace treaty of Goulet with Philip the MAG-NANIMOUS in 1200. Similarly, the French unjustly nicknamed him 'Dollheart', in contrast to his lionhearted brother, after he famously retreated from the siege of La Roche-aux-Moines in 1214 even though he had the superior force. A more fitting nickname might have been 'the Restless', since, as attested by his need for many mistresses and his habit of writing notes in church telling the preacher to hurry up as he wanted his dinner, he could never sit still.

¶ *Albert the* Lame
Albert II, duke of Austria, 1289–1358

Until his early thirties Albert was a tall, good-looking man with a commanding presence, but when an illness left him paralysed from the waist down and unable to move except in a litter or on horseback, his ability to govern Austria was in the balance. But thanks, undoubtedly, to the encouragement of his permanently merry brother and co-regent Otto the JOLLY, an undaunted Albert demonstrated for a further fifteen years a deftness and generosity that endeared him to his subjects and won him the additional nickname 'the Wise'.

¶ *David the* Last King of Paradise
see David the MERRY MONARCH

¶ *Charles the* Last Man
Charles I, king of England, 1600–1649

Deliberately avoiding the word 'king', Parliamentarians called Charles 'the Last Man', implying that he would be the last person to sit on the throne of Great Britain as monarch. When he was not, they refused to be daunted and with admirable determination dubbed Charles II 'the Son of the Last Man'.

Unlike his son, Charles was in no way a merry monarch. Standing five feet four inches, his sad, dispirited face with its mournful, heavy-lidded eyes showed no trace of affection even towards his closest colleagues. His stammer, meanwhile, which he tried (unsuccessfully) to cure when a boy by cramming his mouth with pebbles, made strangers uncomfortable. And though devoutly religious, the king did not impress William Laud, the archbishop of Canterbury, who remarked, 'He neither is, nor knows how to be great.'

The morose Charles had few close friends apart from his wife, Henrietta Maria, but had many enemies. Puritans dubbed him 'the Man of Blood' for his leadership in the Civil War, and had him beheaded in January 1649. His many distant supporters, however, considered his execution an act of religious persecution and conferred upon him the title 'the Martyr'.

¶ *Alfred the* Last of the Dandies
Count Alfred d'Orsay, French nobleman, 1801–52

The political and artistic elite of early Victorian London, including Charles Dickens, Benjamin Disraeli and Napoleon III,

'the Man of December', loved to visit Alfred's opulent residence. They were intrigued by his tight trousers, loud waistcoats and strong perfumes, they were thrilled and scandalized by his simultaneous affairs with both the count and countess of Blessington, and they were eager to hear him hold forth on matters of taste in English society. That is, until the money ran out. In 1849 d'Orsay went bankrupt, and he fled back to France where he died fighting off his many creditors.

Alfred the Last of the Dandies

¶ *Harold the* Last of the Saxons
Harold II, king of England, *c*.1020–66

Whether Harold was killed at the battle of Hastings by an arrow in the eye, as the Bayeux Tapestry famously appears to suggest, is a matter for debate. Certainly no mortal arrow wound is mentioned in any contemporary account of the battle. Writing in 1070, William of Jumièges merely states that 'Harold himself was slain, pierced with mortal wounds' by four Norman soldiers. 'The first, cleaving his breast through the shield with his point, drenched the earth with a gushing torrent of blood; the second smote off his head below the protection of the helmet and the third pierced the inwards of his belly with his lance; the fourth hewed off his thigh and bore away the severed limb.' The *Chronicle of Battle Abbey*, meanwhile, records that he was 'laid low by a chance blow'.

Henry of Huntingdon, however, writing some sixty years later, is adamant that a shower of arrows 'fell around King Harold, and he himself sank to the ground, struck in the eye'. And although he does not describe *how* he died, the contemporary historian William of Poitiers writes that the king's body was 'recognized not by his face', suggesting such mutilation as an arrow might cause.

To this day, the precise nature of Harold's death is unclear. What *is* clear is that the death of Harold Godwinson spelled the end of the Anglo-Saxon phase of English history and ushered in Norman rule under William the CONQUEROR.

¶ *Magnus the* Law-Mender
Magnus VI, king of Norway, 1238–80

Magnus is the last Norwegian king to be featured in the Icelandic sagas, but in covering his life, stories of heroic valour and errant knights are noticeably absent. Instead, we learn how he devoted his life to the legal reform of his nation, revising and codifying previous laws and establishing among his nobility a hierarchy along European lines, with the introduction of dukes, earls, knights and barons. We find out that, under him, the punishing of criminals was considered a public affair, meted out by official courts rather than private individuals with a score to settle. We are told, furthermore, that belligerent bishops ensured that the only area of law not to be changed was the governance of the Church. It was a time of serious, unromantic politics, and Magnus – a serious, unromantic king – was the right man for the job.

¶ *Edward the* Lawgiver *see* Edward the
HAMMER OF THE SCOTS

¶ *Suleiman the* Lawgiver *see* Suleiman the
MAGNIFICENT

¶ *John with the* Leaden Sword
John, duke of Bedford, 1389–1435

John with the Leaden Sword

During the Hundred Years War Archibald the LOSER taunted John, the regent for Henry the MARTYR of England, with this nickname. Archibald was feeling confident after winning a couple of morale-boosting, if militarily insignificant, skirmishes, and mocked John for possessing a 'leaden sword', a term suggesting incompetence in the field. In response John invited Archibald 'to dine with him at Verneuil' and in the ensuing battle the nickname lost its validity and Archibald his life.

¶ *Alfonso the* Learned *see* Alfonso the
ASTRONOMER

¶ *Frederick the* Learned *see* Frederick the
WISE

¶ *Baldwin the* Leper
Baldwin IV, king of Jerusalem, 1161–85

For a king to continue ruling when crippled by a debilitating disease, two things are essential: an indomitable spirit and the devotion of his subjects. Baldwin had both in spades. William of Tyre, Baldwin's tutor, writes of his first suspicions that his charge had leprosy when he noticed the prince's failure even to flinch when pinched by his playmates. And leprosy was a very public disease. 'It grew more serious each day,' remarks William, 'specially injuring his hands and feet and face so that his subjects were distressed whenever they looked at him.' Despite his condition, however, Baldwin became not only king but also perhaps the greatest warrior of the age, inspiring his troops to frustrate the dynastic ambitions of Saladin the CHIVALROUS SARACEN.

Baldwin rode at the vanguard of his army, even though he could not remount should he be unsaddled, and he continued to lead his men even when failing sight and the inability to use his arms and legs meant that he had to be carried in a litter slung between two horses. In 1182 he wrote a heartfelt letter to Louis VII ('Louis the Young') of France, humbly recognizing his limitations and offering to abdicate in favour of a healthier man. 'It is not fitting,' he conceded, 'that a hand so weak as mine should hold power when fear of Arab aggression daily presses upon the Holy City and when my sickness increases the enemy's daring.' A replacement failed to arrive, however, and so, aware of his imminent death, he crowned his eight-year-old nephew king. Even though defeat was guaranteed, Baldwin died adored by those he served.

¶ *Henry the* Liberal
Henry I, count of Champagne, 1152–81

Henry's brothers must have been shocked and delighted when, after their father's death, he plumped for the province of Champagne as his inheritance rather than wealthier territories such as Chartres or Blois. But Henry, son-in-law of 'Louis the Foolish', was himself no fool. Recognizing the province's growth potential, he instituted a set calendar for six massive trade fairs and guaranteed the security of all who visited; in so doing, he transformed Champagne into the undisputed commercial centre of Western Europe. The province, and in particular its count, became very rich.

Being a devout Christian, Henry wanted to share his good fortune. So he set about endowing local abbeys and monasteries with land and privileges and, in gratitude, the amazed and delighted monks and abbots were the first to give him his nickname.

¶ *Sigismund the* Light of the World
Sigismund, Holy Roman Emperor, 1368–1437

Sigismund won his grand nickname among chroniclers for his high intelligence, winning demeanour and ability to speak at least six languages, but he died having contributed little to the betterment of his empire or Europe as a whole. One of the main factors behind the dimness of 'the Light of the World' appears to have been his chronic indecision, as demonstrated by his dealings with his half-brother Wenceslas the WORTHLESS of Bohemia.

While king of Hungary and margrave of Brandenburg, Sigismund looked to expand his territories, and debated whether to invade Wenceslas's kingdom. At first he decided not to, and allied himself to Wenceslas, who was at war with most of Bohemia's nobility. But he then threw his support behind the nobles, only to change allegiance again and again until he finally plumped for Wenceslas, whom he then imprisoned and then released again.

On Wenceslas's death, Sigismund inherited the Bohemian crown and undertook a series of wars against John Hus and his followers, but was unable to win a single battle of significance. The Hussites, meanwhile, referred to him as 'the Red Demon' alluding, in part, to the colour of his beard.

❡ Lightning *see* Bejazet the THUNDERBOLT

❡ *Louis the* Lion
Louis VIII, king of France, 1187–1226

In depicting the city of Avignon as 'a sewer where all the muck of the universe collects', the Italian poet Petrarch was referring to its reputation for heresy and debauchery. A century before, in 1226, when Louis laid siege to it and eventually starved its inhabitants into submission, it was literally filthy as well. Though small, pale and often ill, Louis was an effective soldier and, for his ruthless tactics in establishing royal power in Poitou in the west of France, and Avignon and the rest of Languedoc in the south, was dubbed 'a Reborn Alexander' and 'the Lion' by his sycophantic court poet Nicholas of Brai. The capture of Avignon may have been the pinnacle of Louis's military career but it also proved his downfall, for after a mere forty months as king he succumbed to dysentery, which he had contracted while fighting there.

❡ *William the* Lion
William I, king of Scotland, 1143–1214

William was not nicknamed 'the Lion' for his military record, which makes pretty dismal reading. During an invasion of England in 1173, for example, he mistook a group of his own troops returning from a raid as an attacking English force and ran them down with one of his siege machines. The next year, while laying siege to the castle at Alnwick, he foolishly managed to get himself captured. One foggy day he and sixty other men went riding in the castle grounds, oblivious to the dangers of such a jaunt. The fog suddenly lifted, and William found himself surrounded by Englishmen, who whisked off their prey to Richmond Castle. There William languished at the pleasure of their Majesties Henry CURTMANTLE and Richard the LIONHEART until the latter freed him in exchange for money to pay for a crusade.

The nickname of the grandson of 'David the Saint' instead derives from his choice of a red lion *rampant* for his heraldic device, and even though, according to one chronicler, William 'never had much affection for those of his own country', it remains to this day an integral element of the arms of Scotland.

¶ *Haile Sellassie the* Lion of Judah

Haile Sellassie I, emperor of Ethiopia, 1892–1975

The Jesuit missionaries who educated Ras (meaning 'prince') Tafari at the Ethiopian imperial court must have followed their pupil's career with bewildered interest, as claims to divinity, Christian and otherwise, accompanied the entire life of this most extraordinary African statesman.

When he became emperor in 1930, Tafari changed his name to Haile Sellassie – Amharic for 'Power of the Trinity'. At the same time he embraced the additional title of 'the Lion of Judah', a soubriquet that derives from a verse in the Book of Revelation where Christ is described as such. By taking these titles, Ras Tafari was comparing himself with Jesus. The religion of Rastafarianism, which emerged in Jamaica in the early part of the twentieth century, however, goes one step further and claims that Sellassie is indeed the one, true Messiah, and Ethiopia paradise on earth.

Opinion is divided as to Sellassie's success as emperor. Some praise him for his abolition of slavery and his establishment of a national assembly. Others accuse him of being a brutal dictator. Certainly his authority was absolute: even the lions and cheetahs on his estates would allow him to feed them by hand. When he was angry, we are told, he spoke in a low voice. And when he spoke in a low voice, those around him cowered in fear.

Not everyone was scared of him, however. Italy's invasion of Ethiopia in 1935 led to five years of exile, and in 1974 Marxist revolutionaries overthrew his government and slung him in prison. When he died in captivity the following year, his jailers showed their utter indifference to the king by burying him beneath a toilet. To cite the words of the biblical King David, 'How the mighty have fallen.'

¶ *Richard the* Lionheart
Richard I, king of England, 1157–99

Without a doubt Richard 'Coeur de Lion' was a splendid soldier, and his conquests of Cyprus, Acre and Jaffa were the highlights of a crusade that fast acquired mythical status. One story that quickly circulated, and goes some way to explaining his specific nickname, was that on his travels he had physically ripped the heart out of a lion and eaten it.

His epithet 'Lionheart', or the less mellifluous 'Lionhearted', indicative as it is of courage and generosity, is somewhat misleading. In truth, Richard was a brutal and haughty tyrant and his fellow crusading princes deeply resented his limitless insolence. When, for example, Leopold, archduke of Austria, had planted his banners on one of the towers of Acre – as he had every right to do – Richard had them publicly torn down and flung into the latrines. His cruelty, meanwhile, was astonishing. In order to punish Saladin the CHIVALROUS SARACEN for delaying in sending him 200,000 dinars after Acre's capitulation, he had 3,000 prisoners beheaded.

On his death from a crossbow wound while laying siege to some forces belonging to Philip the MAGNANIMOUS, many chroniclers and eulogists praised Richard for his bravery, patronage of the arts and ability to rally his troops when all seemed lost. With greater hindsight, later historians have acknowledged his hot temper, barbarism and irresponsibility, which made him, according to one contemporary source, 'bad to all, worse to his friends, and worst of all to himself'.

¶ Little Charles *see* Charles the FAT

¶ *Napoleon the* Little Corporal
Napoleon Bonaparte, emperor of the French, 1769–1821

'I am the successor, not of Louis XVI,' Napoleon wrote to Pope Pius VII in 1804, 'but of Charlemagne.' Patently he was referring to his military genius rather than physical stature, since Charles the GREAT stood over six foot three, while Napoleon was comfortably a foot shorter. His limited size and propensity to stoutness naturally made him a sitting target for caricaturists (the English derisively referred to him as 'Tiddy-Doll' as well as the less imaginative 'Boney'). And yet, while not physically commanding – his colleague General Lasalle thought he looked more like a mathematician than a general – Napoleon impressed everyone he met with his natural authority and, above all, his large greyish-blue deep-set eyes, which had an almost hypnotic effect. His troops adored him, not least when he used to ride among them, employing his phenomenal memory to address each one by name. Beautiful women, drawn by his magnetism, forgave him his bouts of hysterical cruelty (while never cruel to women, he at least once kicked a priest in the testicles) to be at his side.

To the epithets 'the Corsican General', 'the Eagle' and 'the Nightmare of Europe', 'the Violet Corporal' was added when Napoleon was banished to the island of Elba in 1814. Napoleon vowed that he would return to France when violets were flowering, and his supporters wore the flower in their lapels to demonstrate their loyalty. And he was true to his promise, arriving at the Tuileries in Paris in March 1815, when the violets were in full bloom. After his defeat at the battle of Waterloo, Napoleon allegedly asked to visit the grave of his wife, Josephine, before he was exiled to St Helena. He picked a few violets growing around her headstone and put them in a locket which he wore until his death six years later.

¶ Little Father *see* Alexander the
EMANCIPATOR

¶ *Catherine the* Little Mother of all the
Russians *see* Catherine the GREAT

¶ *Louis the* Locksmith King *see* the BAKER
AND THE BAKER'S WIFE

¶ *Edward* Longshanks *see* Edward the
HAMMER OF THE SCOTS

¶ *Archibald the* Loser
Archibald Douglas, fourth earl of Douglas, *c.*1369–1424

Archibald lost so many battles and was so unlucky a general that
he gained the nickname of 'Tine-man', or 'the Loser', as well as
the sympathy of the historian David Hume of Godscroft, who
wrote that 'no man was lesse fortunate, and . . . no man was
more valorous.' Archibald lost more than battles, however. In
1402 he lost an eye when fighting Harry HOTSPUR at the battle
of Homildon Hill; later that same year he lost favour with Henry
BOLINGBROKE of England when he joined Percy's rebel forces;
and finally, on 14 August 1424, he lost his life while leading the
French and Scottish troops against the English under John with
the LEADEN SWORD in the battle of Verneuil in Normandy.

¶ *Ptolemy the* Lover of his Father
see PTOLEMAIC KINGS

¶ *Ptolemy the* Lover of his Mother *see*
PTOLEMAIC KINGS

¶ *Philip the* Lucky *see* GALLIC PRACTICE

[M]

¶ Macedonia's Madman *see* Alexander the GREAT

¶ *Charles the* Mad *see* Charles the SILLY

¶ *Joan the* Mad
Joan, queen of Castile and Aragon, 1479–1555

As early as 1499 a Spanish priest reported his concern that the young wife of Philip the HANDSOME was 'so frightened that she could not hold up her head', but the first clear signs of her extreme neurosis did not appear until three years later, when she would apparently run up curtains like a cat. Many chroniclers believe that her mental imbalance lay in her profound jealousy of her good-looking but inept husband, whom she suspected of having numerous affairs. Such suspicion was highly justified. Philip was a playboy whose calculating advisers, one ambassador reported, would 'take him from banquet to banquet and from one lady to the next'. When the lusty Philip died aged twenty-eight, Joan went completely insane and refused to have her husband buried. Instead she traipsed his corpse from monastery to monastery (avoiding convents, where she assumed that Philip might seduce the nuns) in the expectation that he would rise from the dead.

⁊ *Otto the* Mad
Otto, king of Bavaria, 1848–1916

Incurably insane when he came to the throne in 1886, Otto invoked his 'royal prerogative' to shoot a peasant every day. His courtiers-cum-guards duly obliged. Using a gun loaded with blanks, the monarch would take a pot at a palace servant dressed as a serf. On hearing the report of the gun, the courtier would topple 'dead' into the nearest bush.

⁊ *Rupert the* Mad Cavalier
Rupert, prince of the Palatinate, 1619–82

Charles the LAST MAN could not have been happier when his nephew Rupert offered his services shortly before the outbreak of the English Civil War. His reputation as an intrepid soldier and horseman during the Thirty Years War had preceded him, and Charles swiftly put the 23-year-old in charge of the royalist cavalry. Once in office Rupert set about making crucial changes to the tactics of the cavalry charge.

Beginning at the battle of Edgehill, Rupert specified that, unlike before, the royalist horse would not use their firearms until they had broken through the opposing ranks. This meant that the cavalry literally charged at the enemy, making contact with them when at a gallop. The shock of such a thundering attack was a major reason behind his many victories.

For his own part Rupert was considered something of a fearless lunatic, gleefully riding into every fresh encounter with nothing but military glory on his mind. Amazingly, he was never wounded badly, and eventually retired to Germany where he dabbled in the printmaking business.

¶ Madame Deficit *see* the BAKER AND THE
BAKER'S WIFE

¶ Madame Veto *see* the BAKER AND THE
BAKER'S WIFE

¶ *Charles the* Madman of the North
Charles XII, king of Sweden, 1682–1718

At the outset of the eighteenth century Charles XII of Sweden
waged the Great Northern War against Denmark, Poland and
Russia, and a succession of victories won him the title 'the
Alexander of the North'. His reckless disregard for his own safety,
however, coupled with the wholesale defeat of his army at Poltava
in 1709, earned him the nickname 'the Madman of the North'.

Some have hailed Charles as a hero and the inspiration behind
all attempts to restore the country's imperial status. According
to the poet Esaias Tegnér, he was 'Svea's [Sweden's] greatest son'.
Others have gone so far as to claim he was something of a
superman, battling like Odin against evil forces. Voltaire glorified
him as 'the only person in history who was free from all human
weakness'. A third element, on the other hand, has condemned
him as a slightly unhinged, unyielding fool, whose refusal to
make peace prior to Poltava, when Sweden had the upper hand,
brought disaster upon the nation.

¶ *Francis the* Maecenas of France *see*
Francis the FATHER OF LETTERS

¶ *Philip the* Magnanimous
Philip II, king of France, 1165–1223

Under Philip, known by some as 'Philip Augustus' because he
was born in August, France doubled in size. The count of

Flanders, Henry CURTMANTLE and John LACKLAND all surrendered lands to him during a reign marked by military success. His nickname, however, reflects his domestic accomplishments rather than his territorial gains. Philip paved the main roads of Paris, continued construction of the magnificent Notre-Dame Cathedral and built the Louvre (as a fortress, not as an art gallery). Trade privileges won him the support of the merchant class, and fair taxation earned him the appreciation of the nation's workforce.

Not everyone was a recipient of Philip's magnanimity, least of all his second wife, Ingeborg of Denmark. Philip married Ingeborg, daughter of 'Waldemar the Great', in 1193. For reasons that are not entirely clear (the English chronicler William of Newburgh suggests that he was furious that he did not receive 'the ancient right of the King of the Danes in the English kingdom' as his dowry) he hastily repudiated his marriage. When Ingeborg protested, Philip confined her to a convent.

Philip then asked the pope for an annulment on the grounds that the marriage had not been consummated. Again Ingeborg protested, claiming that it *had* been consummated, and that she was the rightful queen. Deaf to her claims and in defiance of the pope, Philip married a Bavarian noblewoman called Agnes of Meran. Once more Ingeborg protested. This time the pope agreed with her complaint and in 1200 demanded that Philip take Ingeborg back as his wife. Philip did so, but far from magnanimously, waiting thirteen long years before releasing her from her duties as a nun.

¶ *Edmund the* Magnificent
Edmund I, king of the English, 921–46

A monk by the name of Florence of Worcester styled Edmund both as 'the Magnificent' and as 'the Deed-Doer', and although the king did indeed do deeds – and great deeds at that – Edmund himself would have been the first to agree that neither the start nor the end of his reign was particularly magnificent.

His rule began with a serious military setback when Olaf, the

Norse king of Dublin, captured the kingdom of York shortly after Edmund's succession. Over the next few years, however, things improved territorially. Edmund drove Olaf back to Ireland, crushed a revolt of 'Idwal the Bald' and pushed Scottish insurgents back beyond Northumbria. The succession of his family line was guaranteed, meanwhile, with the birth of future kings Edwy the FAIR and Edgar the PEACEABLE.

His sons were barely toddlers when Edmund died abruptly and in a decidedly undistinguished manner. While celebrating the feast of St Augustine in Pucklechurch, Gloucestershire, the king recognized a thief called Leofa, whom he had exiled six years earlier. An argument started, a brawl ensued, and Edmund was fatally stabbed in the stomach.

¶ *Suleiman the* Magnificent
Suleiman I, sultan of the Ottoman Empire, 1495–1566

Under Suleiman, the Ottoman Empire reached its apogee, a golden age when its administration, culture and military might were simultaneously at their zenith. The imperial fleet controlled the Mediterranean, his army besieged Vienna, and artists, poets and theologians bustled among the new ornamental public buildings which graced Istanbul, the proud capital city of an empire of some 30 million people.

Suleiman the Magnificent

In the West Suleiman was 'the Magnificent', so named not only for his military conquests but also for the splendour of his court. Suleiman ruled there with absolute authority, drinking perfumed water from jewelled cups and watching the antics of dwarves. His life was a composite of suspicion (like Abdul the DAMNED he changed his bedroom every night), opulence (he seldom wore his clothes more than once) and pomp. At a funeral for one of his children (whose death, incidentally, he had ordered) Suleiman commanded that a special ointment should be put into the eyes of the horses which drew his chariots, in order that they should be seen to 'weep'.

In his own country he was known as 'Kanuni', 'the Lawgiver', a leader who, assisted by his grand viziers, set up a remarkable administration and developed a flourishing economy. Using a detailed book of regulations, he divided his vast dominions into several districts, appointed a specific portion of his army to each region, and spelled out the function of each soldier down to the last man.

On Suleiman's death, control of the empire passed into the hands of his son Selim II. There was no rivalry for the succession since Suleiman had arranged for his other children to be murdered. As his nickname 'the Sot' would indicate, Selim oversaw the gradual implosion of the empire that his father had striven so hard to build.

¶ *Margaret the* Maid of Norway
Margaret, queen-elect of Scotland, 1283–90

When Alexander the GLORIOUS plunged off a cliff to his death, the Scottish royal line was catapulted into crisis. Who would be the next monarch? Edward the HAMMER OF THE SCOTS was duly consulted and he declared that little Margaret, then living in Norway, was to be the next queen, and furthermore that she would marry his son. So, Margaret said farewell to her father 'Erik the Priest-Hater' and set sail to succeed her grandfather as ruler. But it was not to be. The rough crossing from Bergen to Scotland proved too much for the little six-year-old maid, and she died on board during a storm off the Orkney Islands.

¶ *Malcolm the* Maiden
Malcolm IV, king of Scotland, 1141–65

In 1152 red-blooded Highlanders were unimpressed with their effeminate-looking new king, and were in rebellious mood when the slim and fair-haired Malcolm ceded English lands, so hard won by 'David the Saint', to Henry CURTMANTLE. Malcolm possessed a kind and gentle disposition, and his vow of celibacy, an oath made much to the chagrin of his mother, gave rise to his nickname. But he was no pushover, and he put down all civil uprisings with swift and brutal efficiency.

Malcolm died after a short illness aged twenty-four. Scotland came under the jurisdiction of his younger brother, William the LION, a man whose fiery temperament was much more to the liking of the kingdom's northern residents.

¶ *Joan* Makepeace
Joan, queen of Scotland, 1321–62

In accordance with the terms of the peace treaty of Northampton, Joan, sister of Edward the BANKRUPT of England, was married in July 1328 to David, son of the Scottish king Robert the BRUCE. The couple enjoyed, and continue to enjoy, the distinction of being the youngest royals ever to wed. Joan had just turned seven and David was only four and a half. Although we do not know for sure whether they liked each other's company, one thing that is certain is that the only product of their thirty-four years of union was Joan's nickname.

¶ *Ptolemy the* Malefactor *see* PTOLEMAIC KINGS

¶ *Henry the* Man-Milliner
Henry III, king of France, 1551–89

Henry 'le Mignon' of France was a spineless, effeminate dandy who spurned public affairs of state to pursue his private passions of fashion design and the training of dogs, parrots and monkeys. 'Maximilien the Iron Duke' was aghast at the sight of this coxcomb of a king caked with cosmetics and drenched with perfume. 'I shall never forget,' he wrote, 'his fantastic equipage. He had a sword at his side, a Spanish hood hung down upon his shoulders . . . and a basket full of little dogs hung to a broad ribband about his neck.' While Henry dabbled in designing hats, Anne the KING'S KING ran the country and acquired his nickname for his efforts.

¶ *Charles the* Man of Blood *see* Charles the
LAST MAN

¶ *Demetrius the* Man Who Sacrificed His Head *see* Demetrius the DEVOTED

¶ *Anne the* Mare of Flanders
Anne of Cleves, queen of England, 1515–57

On New Year's Day 1540 BLUFF KING HAL galloped to Rochester on England's south coast to catch a glimpse of the woman who was to be his fourth wife. Thomas the HAMMER OF THE MONKS had shown him a portrait of Anne painted by Hans Holbein, and now, weighed down with New Year's gifts for her, Henry was eager to meet his new bride in the flesh.

Henry kept the gifts. The woman he saw bore no resemblance to Holbein's picture; in fact, she looked like a horse. Placing politics above pleasure, Henry married the equine Anne, although he made it clear to one and all that he 'left her as good a maid as he found her'. Shortly after Easter the couple were divorced, and Anne trotted away to live a comfortable life, taking advantage of Henry's generous gift of two houses, a substantial retinue and the princely sum of £500 a year. The matchmaking minister Cromwell, meanwhile, was beheaded.

¶ *Charles the* Martyr *see* Charles the LAST MAN

¶ *Edward the* Martyr
Edward, king of England, c.962–78

When the sixteen-year-old Edward visited his half-brother Ethelred the UNREADY at Corfe Castle, an unorthodox welcome party was waiting to greet him. Seeing him approach, the household staff gathered at the main gate and offered him a cup of refreshing mead. As he drank, they proceeded to stab him to death. Few missed the teenager, who is remembered largely for his cockiness and tantrums. Within a few years, however, some people were claiming that miracles were occurring alongside his bones, which had been buried without ceremony in a church in the small town of Wareham. Eager to oblige his people, Ethelred had Edward's bones moved to Shaftesbury Abbey, and declared him a saint and martyr.

¶ *Henry the* Martyr
Henry VI, king of England, 1421–71

Henry was a devout Christian, but when he was stabbed to death while saying his prayers in the Tower of London he was killed not for his faith but for his crown. His was a tragic reign mired in rebellion, in which he mostly played the part of pawn to the ambitions of others. He was born at Windsor Castle, and succeeded to the thrones of both England and France before the age of one, when his father, Henry the ENGLISH ALEXANDER (*see* ENGLISH EPITHETS), and his grandfather Charles the SILLY of France died within months of each other. Two of his uncles –

GOOD DUKE HUMPHREY in England and John with the LEADEN SWORD in France – acted as regents until he assumed royal authority in 1442.

The dual monarchy proved too much for Henry, who preferred cultural pursuits to war. He was passionate about education and founded both Eton College and King's College, Cambridge, but when it came to military matters he simply did not have the fortitude or will necessary to rule in such turbulent times. In France, the revival of French patriotism under Joan of Arc, 'the Fair Maid of Orléans', led to England yielding nearly all its French territories. In England the success of the House of York in the Wars of the Roses resulted in Henry's deposition, imprisonment and eventual murder.

Though Henry was assassinated, the epithet 'the Martyr' seems somewhat inappropriate. More apt is the soubriquet 'Ill-Fated Henry' found in Alexander Pope's poem 'Windsor-Forest', which pleads:

> Let softer strains ill-fated Henry mourn,
> And palms eternal flourish round his urn.

⁋ *Erik the* Meek
Erik III, king of Denmark, d. 1146

Never able to forget the violent death of his uncle Erik the MEMORABLE, Erik 'Lam' was a docile, peace-loving monarch in an age when lambs like him were routinely slaughtered. Thankfully he collaborated with the hard-headed and strong-willed Archbishop Eskil, who helped him both in Church administration and in repulsing a number of invasions before encouraging him to retire to a monastery.

❡ *Erik the* Memorable
Erik II, king of Denmark, d. 1137

Erik is never to be forgotten for his massacre of Prince Magnus and no fewer than five Danish bishops and sixty priests in the bloody battle of Fotevik of 1134. Erik, moreover, will always be recalled for his ensuing brutal three-year reign in which he murdered a brother and a nephew and quelled uprisings with barbaric efficiency. The exact year of his birth has escaped everyone's memory, however.

❡ *Philaretos the* Merciful
Philaretos, Byzantine nobleman, 702–92

The life of Philaretos was written by his grandson, the monk Niketas of Amneia, as a Byzantine version of the biblical story of Job. Philaretos comes across as a mild-mannered and temperate person who shared food and money with the poor, even when he was down on his luck. His generous distribution of his possessions caused many people, including his wife and three children, to consider him a complete and utter fool.

❡ *Mary the* Mermaid
Mary, queen of Scotland, 1542–87

After the death of her first husband, Francis II of France, Mary was dubbed 'the White Queen' because, as prescribed by French custom, she wore only white for six weeks. A longer-lasting epithet, however, was that of 'the Mermaid' – a nickname that, in the sixteenth century, enjoyed an intriguing double meaning.

With her oval face, pale complexion and hazel eyes, Mary was an attractive teenager – so attractive that the courtier Pierre de Brantôme wrote that 'Her beauty shone like the light at mid-day.' As she grew older, she grew more handsome, and the tall, elegant, auburn-haired queen who could dance with such grace was so admired by all for her looks that she was deemed as beautiful and seductive as a mermaid. However, it was not long before some were using the name 'Mermaid' as a term of contempt rather than approval.

Mary married her second cousin, Henry Stewart, Lord Darnley, pronouncing him the 'lustiest and best proportionit lang man that sche had seen'. Darnley's attributes were many – he was tall, slender and an accomplished musician; but so too were his vices – he was arrogant and addicted to sex and the bottle. Mary, looking for solace, met and fell in love with James Hepburn, the fourth earl of Bothwell.

Whether the two were directly involved with the death of Darnley, who was found smothered on the lawn outside his lodgings, has never been proved. There were many, however, who were sure of their guilt and placards soon appeared on Edinburgh's streets, depicting the hare – Bothwell's crest – surrounded by daggers, and Mary as a mermaid. Here the image of the mermaid was being used not in reference to beauty but in its other capacity as a common symbolic representation of a prostitute.

¶ *Charles the* Merry Monarch
Charles II, king of England, 1630–85

Although decidedly melancholic during his period of exile and susceptible to bouts of pessimism in his later life, Charles was renowned for his vivacious lifestyle and good humour, and his enjoyment of active pursuits borders on the legendary. He went for early morning swims, played tennis well into his fifties, enjoyed croquet and bowls in the park, loved hunting and adored going to the races. But his real passion, the thing that made him almost constantly merry, was women.

Barbara Palmer (later the duchess of Cleveland), Moll Davies, Winifred Wells (who we are told had the 'carriage of a goddess and the physiognomy of a dreamy sheep'), Elizabeth Farley, Mary Knight, Mrs Jane Roberts (daughter of a clergyman), Hortense Mancini, Louise de Quérouaille (whom he found it impossible to restrain himself from fondling in public) and the irrepressible Eleanor the WITTY were just some of those who helped to satisfy the king's immense sexual appetite. His fourteen acknowledged illegitimate children and at least thirteen mistresses were fodder for the wits of the day, including the dukes of Rochester and Buckingham – the former dubbing him a 'mutton-eating king', the latter referring to him as a man who could 'sail a yacht, trim a barge and loved ducks, tarts and buttered buns'. Charles similarly became known as 'Old Rowley' after a stallion of that name in the royal stud noted for its many offspring.

Other nicknames conferred upon Charles alluded to his appearance and political status. Charles's natural complexion was so dark that his mother jokingly wrote in a letter that she had given birth to a black baby. Later the soubriquets 'the Blackbird' and 'the Black Boy' were used to describe him, and in England today there are still a few pubs named after him. Parliamentarians, meanwhile, who had dubbed his father Charles the LAST MAN, persevered in their attack on the monarchy by styling Charles 'the Son of the Last Man'.

The poet John Wilmot, second earl of Rochester, had earlier characterized his good friend the king as a 'merry monarch, scandalous and poor'. In 'The King's Epitaph' Rochester continued with his gentle mockery, writing:

> Here lies a great and mighty king
> Whose promise none relies on;
> He never said a foolish thing
> Nor ever did a wise one.

¶ *David the* Merry Monarch
David Kalakaua, king of Hawaii, 1836–91

Fortified beforehand with milk and bowlfuls of the island speciality of poi, King David could consume vast quantities of his favourite tipple of rum without it showing. In this happy state he would then play cards and invariably win, even when the odds seemed stacked against him. Once, for example, he was playing poker against a sugar baron. The baron placed his four aces on the table and claimed the large pot of money. David, however, who held four kings, insisted that four kings plus his own royal person made five kings, thus beating the baron's hand.

Considerable quantities of food and drink were never far from the king on his 1881 royal circumnavigation of the world, during which he visited, among other places, the United States, Japan, China, Egypt and the great capitals of Europe. A man of a naturally convivial disposition, David was fêted every step of the way and was never merrier.

Things were less jolly for him in 1887, however, when a bloodless coup relegated him to the role of figurehead and eventually led to his retirement in a boathouse among some duck ponds in Waikiki. When he died during a second trip to California, the press aptly dubbed him 'the Last King of Paradise'.

¶ *Sigurd the* Mighty
Sigurd I, earl of Orkney, d. 892

Norse sagas agree that Sigurd and the Hebridean Viking ruler Thorstein the RED (*see* COLOURFUL CHARACTERS) were the mightiest warriors of their day. Together they attacked any ships that happened to pass by and made furious raids on the Scottish mainland. Mighty he may have been in war, but the manner of Sigurd's death would have been the last any warrior would have wished. We are told that he cut off the head of an earl called Maelbrigte whom he suspected of treachery, and strapped it to his saddle as a trophy. But as he cantered around, triumphantly showing off his prize, a tooth of the noble Maelbrigte scratched him on the leg and Sigurd died soon thereafter from blood poisoning.

¶ *Christina the* Miracle of Nature
Christina, queen of Sweden, 1626–89

Neither of her parents thought there was anything miraculous in Christina. Having been promised by soothsayers that she was going to give birth to a boy, Queen Maria Eleanora of Brandenburg refused to have anything to do with her daughter, and left her in the care of her father, King Gustav 'the Lion of the North'. The nonplussed Gustav treated her like a boy, taking her on military expeditions and introducing her, at close range, to the sound of cannon fire. When Christina was six, Gustav was killed in battle, and his widow confined herself to her bedroom, reportedly with the king's heart in a golden container. Christina's education then began in earnest.

Christina the Miracle of Nature

She studied twelve hours a day, becoming fluent in five languages, an expert in horsemanship and an accomplished historian, reading Thucydides and Polybius in the original Greek. She studied astronomy, music and literature and oversaw the creation of the nation's first newspaper. Her passion for philosophy resulted in her inviting René Descartes to Stockholm, summoning him at five o'clock in the morning for learned conversations. Many of her adoring subjects deemed such intellectual brilliance as nothing short of miraculous.

Indifferent to the love of her people or notions of patriotic duty, however, Christina stepped down after ten years of rule, sending shockwaves coursing through a bewildered nation. Publicly Christina claimed that she was simply not strong enough to be queen, but privately the real reasons were her aversion to marriage (on the grounds that it was a form of slavery) and her secret conversion from Lutheranism to Roman Catholicism. On the very day of her abdication she disguised herself as a man and left Sweden for Rome, never to return. The pope initially welcomed her but over time distanced himself from a scandalously independent woman who spent more time at the opera than at church, and who openly laughed at his cardinals.

❡ *Catherine the* Modern Messalina
see Catherine the GREAT

❡ *Alfonso the* Monk *see* NOBLE
PROFESSIONS

❡ *Ramiro the* Monk
Ramiro II, king of Aragon, d. 1154

When 'Alfonso the Battler' died in 1134, the kingdom of Aragon fell into a panic. The Battler's will stated that his entire kingdom should go to the military Orders of the Holy Land, but the Aragonese nobles were having none of this and elected his brother Ramiro as king. Ramiro, who happened to be a Benedictine monk, accepted the crown, stating that he did so 'not out of any desire for honour or ambition or arrogance but only because of the needs of the people and the tranquility of the church'.

Ramiro the Monk then proceeded to marry Agnes of Poitiers, daughter of Duke William IX of Aquitaine. The next year Agnes gave birth to a girl, Petronila, whose hand Ramiro immediately offered to Ramon Berenguer IV, count of Barcelona. With the dynasty secured after his three-year secular adventure, Ramiro returned to his monastery, where he died in 1154.

¶ Monsieur Veto *see* the BAKER AND THE
BAKER'S WIFE

¶ *Charles the* Most Christian King
see Charles the BALD

¶ *Maria the* Mother of Her Country
Maria Theresa, archduchess of Austria and queen of
Hungary and Bohemia, 1717–80

When she came to the Austrian throne in 1740, Maria Theresa
found the national coffers nearly empty, the army savagely
depleted, and her own knowledge of state affairs limited at best.
Most of the first fifteen years of her reign, therefore, were spent
learning statecraft, implementing tax reforms and doubling the
size of a military that saw considerable action against her main
adversary, Frederick the GREAT. In 1763 Maria Theresa signed a
treaty that ended all hostilities and recognized Prussian pos-
session of Silesia.

Two years later, however, the sudden death of her husband,
Francis Stephen – a man whom she truly loved – turned her life
upside down. From then on, Maria Theresa was alone. And so,
relying on her maternal instincts, she treated her nation as an
only child.

First, she arranged marriages for her real children in the best
interests of Austria; a major coup was the union between her
teenage daughter Marie and Louis XVI (*see* the BAKER AND
THE BAKER'S WIFE). Next, she bolstered the nation's cultural
programmes by becoming a visible as well as a vocal patron of
Austria's arts and sciences. Third, she reformed what she deemed
to be a nation in moral delinquency, abolishing the gaming
laws as well as the right of sanctuary. Meanwhile, her notorious
'*Sittenkommission*', sometimes referred to as the 'chastity police',
made strict demands on her people: a woman baring an ankle
could end up in jail, and a woman walking unescorted through

the streets of Vienna at night risked being sent to a rehabilitation camp for prostitutes.

Absolute and authoritarian she may have been, but Maria Theresa was a generous and loving mother figure to her country and provided a solid platform for the continuation of the Habsburg Dynasty into the modern age.

❡ **Mrs Brown** *see* Victoria the WIDOW OF WINDSOR

❡ **Mrs Freeman** *see* QUEEN SARAH

❡ **Mrs Morley** *see* QUEEN SARAH

[**N**]

¶ *Kamehameha the* Napoleon of the Pacific *see* Kamehameha the GREAT

¶ *Henry the* Navigator

Henry, prince of Portugal, 1394–1460

Henry's nickname of 'the Navigator' was first given general currency in the nineteenth century. In a work of 1842 the German geographical statistician J. E. Wappäus describes the prince as 'Heinrich der Seefahrer'. It is a misnomer. Henry was actually something of a landlubber, orchestrating the maritime expeditions of others rather than taking to the seas himself.

Henry, the fourth son of 'John the Bastard', was a pious man. He took a vow of celibacy, often wore a hair shirt and became governor of the military Order of Christ, a sort of Portuguese successor to the Knights Templar. He was also a rich man, controlling the nation's tuna-fishing and soap-production industries. In the 1440s he used his wealth to sponsor a number of expeditions along the west coast of Africa in the hope that something might be discovered – perhaps even a new source of gold – that would make him even richer. To further his ambitions, he expanded his home in Sagres on the south-west tip of Portugal to include a shipbuilding yard and a centre devoted to cartography, navigation and exploration.

In 1441 his ship literally came in when a Portuguese vessel returned from sub-Saharan Africa with a small amount of gold. By 1452 African trade was flourishing and enough gold had been shipped back to fund several major journeys of exploration and

Noble Professions

In addition to such luminaries as Albert the ASTROLOGER and FARMER GEORGE, several royals appear in the history books with a professional soubriquet. This appears to be an exclusively male preserve: for an act of domestic policy and for his hobby, for example, Louis XVI of France is known by the two nicknames 'the Baker' and 'the Locksmith King'; Marie Antoinette, on the other hand, is popularly labelled, not for her actions or interests, but for her affiliation to her husband (*see* the BAKER AND THE BAKER'S WIFE). As can be seen by the sample below, not all nicknames are to be taken at face value.

Henry Beauclerc
Henry I, king of England, 1069–1135

As the youngest son of William the CONQUEROR, Henry was singled out for a life in the Church and accordingly was given an excellent education, leading to his nickname of 'Beauclerc', meaning 'fine scholar'. With the convenient death of William RUFUS, and the absence abroad of his brother Robert CURTHOSE, the scholar exchanged the confines of his study for the court.

David the Builder
David, king of Georgia, 1073–1125

In 1121 David liberated the city of Tblisi after more than four centuries of Arab rule and, by means of a massive reconstruction policy, rapidly transformed it into a cosmopolitan metropolis at the centre of a trade route linking Europe with Asia.

Leo the Butcher
Leo II, Roman emperor of the East, c.401–74

Leo was a butcher of people rather than of meat for the table. This lifelong soldier showed his violent streak soon after his coronation by killing anyone who opposed his replacement of the patriarch called 'Timothy the Cat' with one disarmingly called 'Timothy Wobble-Hat'. Later, he was not above butchering his own son Patricius to maintain power.

Michael the Caulker
Michael V, Byzantine emperor, d. c.1042

As far as we know, Michael never caulked in his life – not even once

– since in an odd transplant of nomenclature he was nicknamed after his father's profession, that of sealing ships' hulls to ensure that they stayed watertight.

Denis the Farmer
Denis, king of Portugal, 1261–1325

The sheer energy of Denis's agricultural reforms impressed his subjects into giving him the epithet 'o Lavrador'. His greatest legacy was the planting of the 'Pinhal de Leiria', a pine forest protecting fields of crops from advancing coastal sands.

Alfonso the Monk
Alfonso IV, king of Asturias and Léon, d. 933

Called to the monastic life, Alfonso abdicated the throne in favour of his brother Ramiro. Within a few years, however, secular temptations proved too great, and when Ramiro was away on a raiding expedition, Alfonso slung his habit to one side and tried to seize the throne. The attempted coup failed, and Alfonso was blinded.

Sancho the Settler
Sancho I, king of Portugal, 1154–1211

Wars with the Moors had left much of twelfth-century Portugal a wasteland. Sancho 'o Povoador' spent much time and effort in restoring and repopulating the country, especially in the Algarve.

Robert the Steward
Robert II, king of Scotland, 1316–90

In the same vein as Michael the CAULKER (*see above*), Robert's epithet alludes to his father's profession rather than to his own. Robert was the son of Walter, the sixth high steward of Scotland, and of Margery, the daughter of Robert the BRUCE. His red eyes and feeble appearance gave rise to his other nickname, 'Auld Blearie'.

Theobald the Troubadour
Theobald, king of Navarre, 1201–53

Gertrude, Agnes and Margaret, Theobald's three successive wives, all had their charms, but his one and only true love was Blanche of Castile, the wife of Louis the LION. Theobald 'le Chansonnier' composed dozens of songs in her honour, including one in which he writes of the values of platonic versus physical love by referring to an old hag's crotch and his own pot belly.

bring about Portugal's transformation from a small European country into a significant colonial empire.

¶ *Christian the* Nero of the North
see Christian the TYRANT

¶ *Ptolemy the* New Lover of His Father
see PTOLEMAIC KINGS

¶ *Napoleon the* Nightmare of Europe
see Napoleon the LITTLE CORPORAL

¶ *Jane the* Nine Days' Queen
Lady Jane Grey, queen of England, 1537–54

Just a few weeks before his own death Edward the JOSIAH OF ENGLAND (*see* ENGLISH EPITHETS) amended the will of his father BLUFF KING HAL, dismissing the claim of BLOODY MARY as the rightful heir to the English throne and nominating the fifteen-year-old Jane instead. The codicil proved to be the death warrant for the well-educated, well-mannered Protestant girl from Leicestershire.

On 10 July 1553 she was proclaimed queen. Genoese merchant Baptista Spinola happened to be in London on that day and saw England's new monarch pass by. 'She is very short and thin,' he wrote, 'but prettily shaped and graceful . . . She is now called Queen but is not popular, for the hearts of the people are with Mary, the Spanish Queen's daughter . . . This lady is very heretical, and has never heard Mass.' Nine days later and 'Jane the Quene' was deposed and became 'Jana non Regina'. The following February she was executed for high treason.

¶ *Elizabeth the* Northern Harlot
see Elizabeth the INFAMOUS

¶ Nose Almighty

Oliver Cromwell, Lord Protector of the Commonwealth,
1599–1658

There was something about Oliver Cromwell's eyes. Grey-green,
heavy-lidded, melancholy yet piercing, they were nearly always
mentioned when people described him. But more universally discussed than his eyes – more indeed than the warts near his left eye, which he famously demanded to be included in a portrait – was another unmistakable facial feature. Oliver Cromwell, the driving force behind the revolutionary opposition to Charles the LAST MAN and Charles the MERRY MONARCH in the English Civil Wars, had a very big, and a very red, nose. Its colour fascinated the nation. A poem

Nose Almighty

circulating during Cromwell's time termed it 'the Lancaster rose',
while a contemporary pamphlet spoke of it somewhat less coyly
as 'the glow-worm glistening in his beak'. Its colour, and indeed
his entire complexion, which one later commentator compared
to that of a piece of wood or an unbleached almond, led many
to the misguided assumption that he overindulged in drink.

Popular nicknames focused almost exclusively on his proboscis: 'Nose Almighty', 'Copper Nose', 'Ruby Nose' and simply
'Nosey' became common parlance. Some royalists also nicknamed their arch-opponent 'Crum-Hell' since, in his lifetime,
Cromwell's name was pronounced 'Crumwell', while Rupert the

Norse Sagas

The Norse sagas are veritable treasuries of nicknames. While many characters possess patronymic second names such as 'Ingiborg Finn's-Daughter' and 'Heinrik Haraldsson', many others have an epithet in place of, or in addition to, their filial name. Individual entries for many of the main characters, such as Sven FORKBEARD and Erik the RED, can be found elsewhere in this work. The lists below contain some of the supporting cast.

The anonymous *Orkneyinga Saga* was written around 1200 and tells of the conquest of the Scottish Northern Isles by the kings of Norway in the ninth century and the subsequent history of Orkney. Within its pages we find:

Thorarin Bag-Nose
Einar Belly-Shaker
Svein Breast-Rope
Einar Buttered-Bread
Sigurd the Fake Deacon
Havard the Fecund
Thorkel Flayer
Thorkel the Fosterer
Angus the Generous
Oddi the Little
Arni Pin-Leg
Hugh the Stout
Olaf Tit-Bit

Egil's Saga, thought to have been written by Snorri Sturluson around 1230, describes the Viking world from the middle of the ninth century to the end of the tenth. As well as Egil, the ruthless Viking hero, we learn about:

Sigtrygg the Fast Sailor
Harald Grey-Cloak
Thora Lace-Cuff
Thorvald the Overbearing
Ljot the Pale
Einar the Scale Clatterer
Eyvind Shabby
Atli the Short

The romantic medieval Icelandic *Laxdaela Saga*, composed by an unknown author around 1245, mentions:

An the Black (who, for reasons unspecified, is nicknamed 'Brushwood Belly')
Alf of the Dales
Thorbjorn the Feeble
Audun Fetter-Hound
Ketil Flat-Nose
Thorhalla the Gossip
Asgeir the Hot-Head
Geirmund the Noisy
Olaf the Peacock
Gunnlaug Serpent-Tongue
Thord the Short
Bork the Stout
Hallfred the Troublesome Poet
Gizur the White

Describing the Norse discovery of America, the two *Vinland Sagas* also recount how Erik the Red started a colony on Greenland. They introduce the reader to Erik's son (Leif the Lucky), as well as Hrafn the Dueller – a warrior killed by Erik – and a man by the name of Thord Horse-Head.

Finally, *Njal's Saga* is an Icelandic family saga written in the late thirteenth century. Along with the following:

Orm Box-Back
Thorstein Cod-Biter
Eystein the Noisy
Ref the Poet
Ragnar Shaggy-Breeches
Askel the Silent
Hedin the Sorcerer
Sigurd Swine-Head
Ulf the Unwashed
Bessi the Wise
Haf the Wise

It also features a man called Iron-Grim wearing nothing but a goatskin.

MAD CAVALIER dubbed his adversary 'Old Ironsides' because his ranks at the battle of Marston Moor in 1644 were so impenetrable.

His political supporters, meanwhile, had other names for their hero. Many knew him as 'King Oliver' since he was king in all but name, turning down Parliament's offer of the crown in 1657. Later in life he was affectionately referred to as 'Old Noll', Noll being a familiar form of Oliver.

¶ **Nosey** *see* NOSE ALMIGHTY

[O]

¶ *Gorm the* Old

Gorm, king of Denmark, d. *c.*958

One chronicle describes Gorm as *stultissimus* (very stupid), a second describes him as lazy or indolent, while a third, penned by the eleventh-century historian Adam of Bremen, deems some-one – most likely Gorm – a 'savage worm, a heathen persecutor of Christians' who so angered Henry the FOWLER that Henry invaded Denmark and forced the worm to sue for peace.

However, nickname history has been kind to Gorm. He is most commonly known as 'the Old', an epithet probably given to him at a later time when people looked back to his reign as the distant past, remembering him because of the inscriptions on two large stones at Jelling which bear his name. Our knowledge of Gorm is virtually limited to what these inscriptions tell us – that he was husband of Thyra, father of Harald BLUETOOTH, and that he reigned in the tenth century, with Jelling his seat of power.

The medieval historian Saxo Grammaticus suggests two further things about Gorm: first, that Thyra refused him the pleasures of the nuptial couch in a vain attempt to win her mate over to Christianity, and second, that he was blind for many years, having 'prolonged his old age to the utmost bounds of the human lot'. Modern science casts doubt on the latter claim. Forensic analyses on his skeletal remains show that Gorm the Old probably died in his forties.

¶ Old Copper Nose *see* BLUFF KING HAL

¶ Old Fritz *see* Frederick the GREAT

¶ Old Ironsides *see* NOSE ALMIGHTY

¶ Old Noll *see* NOSE ALMIGHTY

¶ Old Nosey *see* Arthur the IRON DUKE

¶ *James the* Old Pretender *see* James the WARMING-PAN BABY

¶ Old Q *see* William the RAKE OF PICCADILLY

¶ Old Rowley *see* Charles the MERRY MONARCH

¶ *Antigonus the* One-Eyed
Antigonus I, king of Macedonia, 382–301 BC

The works of the Greek painter Apelles, none of which survive, were said to combine Dorian thoroughness with Ionian grace. Of his portraits, about which ancient writers raved, was one of King Antigonus, the former general under Alexander the GREAT who forged a friendship between Macedonia and many of the Greek city-states. The depiction was in profile, because of the king's missing eye. The reason for its absence, like the true beauty of Apelles' oeuvre, remains a mystery.

¶ *John the* One-Eyed
John Zisca, Bohemian reformer, 1360–1424

To lose one eye may be regarded as a misfortune. Some say that John lost one eye in a childhood accident, while others say it was at the battle of Tannenburg in 1410. To lose both eyes seems like carelessness. John lost the other one while leading an army of peasants in a campaign against papal authority in Bohemia. Despite his blindness, he continued to act as general with the same skill, success and ruthlessness as before. His favourite way of executing monks, we are told, was to smother them with pitch and set them alight.

On his death, an element of his rag-tag force called themselves 'orphans', as if they had lost their father. Michel de Montaigne writes that Zisca was with them in later engagements not only in spirit but also literally in the flesh. The reformer, it transpires, had arranged for his body to be flayed and his skin made into a drum for his men to carry into battle.

❡ *Henry* Our English Marcellus
see ENGLISH EPITHETS

❡ *Edgar the* Outlaw
Edgar, king of England, *c.*1052–*c.*1125

Although he was proclaimed king following the death of Harold THE LAST OF THE SAXONS at the battle of Hastings, the teenage Edgar was never actually crowned. Instead he submitted to William the CONQUEROR some eight weeks later. Some chroniclers refer to him as 'the Atheling', meaning 'son of the king', but this is semantically inaccurate, since his father, 'Edward the Exile', was similarly never crowned.

Other chroniclers dubbed him 'the Outlaw' because, like his father, Edgar spent much of his life away from home, often in the Scottish court, where he married Margaret, sister of Malcolm BIGHEAD. In 1106 he returned from the First Crusade and was finally welcomed to England, this time by Henry BEAUCLERC, but only on the condition that he lived in peaceful retirement on his country estate in Hertfordshire.

[**P**]

¶ *Amadeus the* Pacific

Amadeus VIII, duke of Savoy, 1383–1451

Amadeus offered something of an early fifteenth-century concili-
ation service, giving advice and encouragement to leaders of any
European powers who felt that negotiations had come to an
impasse. For this international Solomonic role he was dubbed
'the Pacific', but it could easily have been applied to his domestic
affairs. During his 42-year reign he expanded Savoy's territory
primarily through diplomatic channels rather than military force.

Surviving an assassination attempt, and unwilling to die
as young as his father Amadeus the RED (*see* COLOURFUL
CHARACTERS), the younger Amadeus retired in 1434 to a monastery in La Ripaille. Here his religious austerity impressed his
subjects so much that they dubbed him 'the Hermit of La Ripaille'
and Rome so much that they elected him pope. After ten years,
however, the quiet ways of Pope Felix V proved unpopular with
the kings of France, England and Sicily, and Amadeus was pres-
sured to resign. Peacefully he accepted the demotion to the lesser
role of cardinal, and died two years later in Geneva.

¶ *Henry the* Parricide

Henry V, king of Germany, 1086–1125

The nickname 'the Parricide' does Henry an injustice since he
did not kill his father. Instead, with the help of ecclesiastical and
lay magnates, he merely imprisoned him and extorted from him
the renunciation of his rights as ruler. The disgraced Henry IV
was then allowed to escape to Liège, where he died. Lower

Rhineland peasant farmers, not caring a jot about the intrigue behind his death, trooped past his displayed corpse in order to touch it with their seed corn in the hope of a good harvest.

¶ *Charles the* Parson's Emperor
Charles IV, king of Germany and Bohemia and Holy Roman Emperor, 1316–78

In his autobiography, *Mirror of Princes*, Charles relates how one day he met his old tutor Peter Roger, who had overseen his religious education while he was growing up in the court of Charles the FAIR (*see* GALLIC PRACTICE). The teacher, now a cardinal, told his former pupil that 'one day you will be king of the Romans', to which Charles replied, 'but before that you will be pope'. Both predictions came true.

With a motto of 'Piously to see what is right', Charles kept on good terms with popes throughout his life, a religious bond for which anti-papal elements of his court mocked him as 'the Parson's Emperor' or 'the Pope's Errand-Boy'. However, Charles had the last laugh, his coronation as emperor of the Holy Roman Empire taking place on Easter Day 1355. Peter Roger – Pope Clement VI – had died three years earlier, but was undoubtedly there in spirit.

¶ *Edgar the* Peaceable
Edgar, king of the English, *c.*943–75

England during the reign of Edgar was eerily quiet. The blood-thirsty 'Erik Bloodaxe' was dead, and the Vikings were licking their wounds back in Scandinavia. On the domestic front Edgar's wives, including Athelfleda the WHITE DUCK, were producing healthy sons such as Edward the MARTYR and Ethelred the UNREADY, and the only notable violence, such as the destruction of Thanet in 969, was on the orders of the king himself. Free from the pressures of military conflict, therefore, Edgar had time for grand displays of his power. The *Anglo-Saxon Chronicle* waxes lyrical about his sumptuous coronation ceremony at Bath in 973, and elsewhere we learn of a second carefully arranged show

Edgar the Peaceable

of royal authority that same year, when eight Celtic kings acknowledged Edgar's overlordship by seating him at the helm of a boat and rowing him along the River Dee. Further order and stability were brought about through reforms of the monastic and monetary systems, and it is therefore of little surprise to read chronicler John of Worcester's description of Edgar as '*pacificus*'.

Some commentators, however, argue that *pacificus* should be rendered 'the Peacemaker' rather than 'the Peaceable' since the source of such national calm was not a serene monarch but the threat of military action should anyone step out of line. As the aggression against Thanet demonstrated, Edgar was always ready to remind people, brutally if necessary, who was in control.

¶ *Edgar the* Peacemaker *see* Edgar the PEACEABLE

¶ *Edward the* Peacemaker *see* Edward the CARESSER

¶ *Casimir the* Peasants' King *see* Casimir the GREAT

¶ *Frederick the* Penniless
Frederick IV, duke of Austria, 1384–1439

The Holy Roman Emperor Sigismund the LIGHT OF THE WORLD threw Frederick in jail for supporting the antipope John XXIII. From behind bars, Frederick must have viewed his future with distinct unease. He had few supporters, fewer possessions and no money whatsoever.

'The Penniless' was an obvious nickname, and one that he desperately tried to shake off when he was freed and had regained power. Despite amassing an impressive treasury (much of the revenue coming from Austria's new silver mines) and owning a considerable amount of land, the name frustratingly stuck until his dying day. The story that he built the magnificent 'Goldenes Dachl', or 'Golden Roof', in Innsbruck purely to demonstrate his new, healthier financial situation is appealing but sadly has no basis in fact.

¶ *Diana the* People's Princess
Diana, princess of Wales, 1961–97

In its coverage of the outpouring of grief that followed Diana's death in 1997 the media frequently used two immediately recognizable nicknames to represent the princess's character and popularity.

During a television interview Diana had once remarked that although she would never be the queen of England, she hoped she could become the queen of people's hearts, and soon the nickname of 'the Queen of Hearts' became common parlance. A frequent memento at the hundreds of makeshift memorials erected on the news of her death in France was the queen of hearts playing card. Myriad photographs, meanwhile, of Princess Diana among crowds, on her knees in front of children or sitting at the end of hospital beds revealed a princess who had the common touch, for which the media termed her 'the People's Princess' – a phrase used by Prime Minister Tony Blair in an informal interview on the morning after her death and embraced by a nation in mourning.

¶ *John the* Perfect
John II, king of Portugal, 1455–95

In 1481 John considered the gifts of land and cash that his father, 'Alfonso the African', had made to certain nobles to be over-generous. So, in a deliberate policy to limit the nobles' control, he abolished several of the privileges that they had previously enjoyed. The third duke of Braganza objected vociferously to these restrictions. He was immediately arrested and, after a summary trial, beheaded, and overnight the considerable estates of Braganza became crown property. John then foiled another 'conspiracy' by stabbing to death his brother-in-law, Diego, the duke of Viseu, with his own hands. Perfect? Hardly.

His nickname of 'the Perfect' has its origins in an early sixteenth-century political treatise by Niccolò Machiavelli. In *Il Principe*, Machiavelli describes the qualities of a perfect prince, and some of his readers considered John to fit the model to a tee. But this was some twenty years after John had died. Many of his contemporaries, who knew him better, dubbed him 'the Tyrant'.

¶ *Le* Petit Albert *see* Albert the GREAT

¶ *Alfonso the* Philosopher *see* Alfonso the
ASTRONOMER

¶ *Louis the* Pious

Louis I, king of France and Holy Roman Emperor,
778–840

Piety was not top of the agenda for the teenage Louis, who by
the age of sixteen had become the father of two children by two
mistresses. But when his father Charles the GREAT died in 814,
Louis, who had been crowned the year before without the benefit
of clergy, saw one of his main tasks as the continued Christianiz-
ation of the empire. Much of his early legislation therefore con-
centrated on the monastic and ecclesiastical reform of a vast
territory that he considered a gift from God, and for which he
was chiefly responsible.

Piety later played second fiddle to political necessity. When
King Bernard of Italy challenged his authority, for instance, Louis
had him blinded. Moreover, in order to prevent any dynastic
challenges, he had his half-brothers tonsured and secured in
monasteries. Such unchristian behaviour finally caught up with
him when, in 833, a coalition of his sons, the pope and several
leading clergy drove him to a monastery and only freed him
after he acknowledged his sins and agreed to do penance for all
eternity.

Piety also sometimes slipped into superstition. Bewildered
and terrified by the sight of Halley's Comet in 837, Louis asked his
astronomer what the phenomenon meant. The courtier, who was
a good Christian, answered that stars in the sky should not be
trusted since 'God was the final arbiter of the fates of both the stars
and the Franks.' Nevertheless, Louis stayed up all night and, when
dawn finally arrived, commanded that alms should be distributed
to the poor in celebration that the gods had been kind.

Louis's nickname derives from his famed generosity. One of
his biographers, Thegan, wrote that he gave away houses to
faithful subjects, restored property that his father had confiscated
from Frisians and Saxons and renounced all claims on Church
lands. As a result of such piety, tension and instability in Frankish
Gaul increased dramatically.

❡ *Robert the* Pious

Robert II, king of France, *c.*970–1031

Many of our perceptions of Robert emanate from his biography, written by his chaplain, Helgaud, monk of Fleury. Naive and semi-hagiographical it may be, but other contemporary chronicles support Helgaud's depiction of Robert as a devout, virtuous and generous king who actively supported the Church and granted privileges to monasteries. Helgaud said that Robert could have been mistaken for a monk, while a fellow chronicler tells of how Robert threw his cloak over two lovers embracing each other a little too enthusiastically for his liking.

Not everything he did delighted the Church, however. Take, for instance, the time he burned down the monastery of Saint-Germain in Auxerre simply because it stood in the way of his soldiers. And then there were his marriages. After repudiating Rozala of Flanders (but keeping much of her land, much to the chagrin of her son 'Baldwin Handsome-Beard'), he lived openly with one Bertha of Blois before marrying her in 997. A few years later he dumped Bertha – possibly through uncharacteristic religious scruples, probably because she had produced no children – and married Constance, daughter of the count of Arles. His new bride, however, turned out to be an unscrupulous battleaxe of a woman, and Robert, hoist by his own petard, had his Christian qualities of patience and endurance sorely tested for the rest of his days.

❡ *Geoffrey* Plantagenet

Geoffrey V, count of Anjou, 1113–51

Of all the world's flora, Geoffrey liked to wear a sprig of broom, or *planta genista*, in his cap. His son, who became Henry CURT-MANTLE of England, inherited the soubriquet, which became the name of the royal dynasty.

¶ *Lady Wu the* Poisoner

Wu Hou, empress of China, 625–705

The winsome Wu arrived in court in 638 and joined the corps of junior concubines. Driven by insatiable imperial ambition, however, she soon rose out of servile anonymity and into the history books as one of the most powerful – and most barbarous – figures of the Tang dynasty.

Her first step to achieve her dynastic ambition was to strangle her own baby and pin the murder on a rival. She then gradually won the affections of the new emperor, Kao Tsung, and eventually became his favourite concubine. But being someone's plaything was not for Wu, and she contrived to achieve the top position in the land, whatever the cost. On her way to power, she is said to have:

- poisoned a sister, a niece and a son
- forced another son to hang himself
- had four grandchildren whipped to death
- ordered the execution of two stepsons, and sixteen of their male heirs
- killed four daughters-in-law, one by starvation
- executed thirty-six government officials and generals and
- overseen the slaughter of 3,000 families.

Once enthroned in 660, the new empress lost little time in exacting revenge on those who had opposed her elevation. The former empress Wang and the senior concubine were singled out for special treatment, being mercilessly flogged, dismembered and then tossed into a vat full of wine to die.

With the emperor frequently ill, and politically inferior, Wu enjoyed absolute control, styling herself among other things as 'Holy Mother' and 'Divine Sovereign'. And she ran China with consummate ability, encouraging agricultural advancement, independent thinking and commercial efficiency. China had not been so prosperous – or so peaceful – for generations.

The Popish and Protestant Dukes

James II, king of England and Ireland, and VII, king of Scotland, 1633–1701
James Scott, first duke of Monmouth, 1649–85

During the Civil War, James, the duke of York, holed up in France, and he only returned to England when the Commonwealth under NOSE ALMIGHTY had foundered and James's brother, Charles the MERRY MONARCH, had been restored to power. Assessing his qualities in comparison with those of his older brother, the English found James to be distinctly second best. Whereas Charles was jolly and genial, James was grindingly dull.

But it was his lack of religious tolerance rather than his lack of personality that infuriated a nation and eventually brought about his downfall. James converted to Catholicism in 1670, a fact made public knowledge three years later, when he resigned as Lord High Admiral in opposition to the Test Act, a bill that prevented Catholics from holding positions of authority. From this moment on, the heir apparent was known scathingly by many of his future subjects as 'the Popish Duke'. Things got worse for James in 1678 when an anti-Catholic protester called Titus Oates stated under oath that he had uncovered a massive plot

¶ Poor Fred
Frederick Louis, prince of Wales, 1707–51

When they came to England in 1714, the future king George the GREAT PATRON OF MANKIND and Princess Caroline of Ansbach left their seven-year-old son in Germany and did not see him again until he arrived in England in 1728 as a grown man. By then they had had more children, and they rejected Frederick to murder Charles and to replace him with James and his Catholic supporters. While most of Oates's charges were utter fabrication, they nevertheless fuelled anti-papal sentiment, and in 1685, when Charles died and James ascended the throne, opinions on having a Catholic English monarch polarized a nation.

On the one hand there were the king and his followers. On the other were Protestants who claimed that Charles's illegitimate son James, the first duke of Monmouth, was the rightful heir. Monmouth – dubbed 'the Protestant Duke' to balance the king's epithet – led a military campaign to seize power. The rebellion was quickly snuffed out, however, as was Monmouth, who was captured and beheaded.

King James forged ahead with his mission to make England Catholic. With what some consider recklessness, he promoted his religious friends to positions of importance and had the 'Bloody Assizes' punish any Protestants who dared to rebel. When in 1688 James's wife, Mary of Modena, gave birth to a boy and thus put paid to any hopes that the crown would pass to the Protestant children of James's first marriage, Parliament invited the Protestant William of Orange and his wife, Mary, to save England from a Catholic future. James and his family fled to France where they nurtured their son James the WARMING-PAN BABY to become a pretender to the English throne.

both as a son and as a person, referring to him as a 'foundling' and nicknaming him 'Griff' because he had the appearance of the ugly mythical beast the griffin. Poor Fred.

Frederick incurred the wrath of his father over his womanizing and wastrel ways. He also incurred the wrath of his mother to the point that she is reported to have said about him, 'That wretch! That villain! I wish the ground would open at this moment and sink the monster to the lowest hole in hell!' Poor Fred.

Living in virtual exile with his wife, Augusta of Saxe-Gotha, with whom he had eight children, including FARMER GEORGE, Frederick, unlike his father, made an attempt to assimilate himself into English life. He studied the rules of cricket and, although not a proficient player himself, became a committed patron of the game. It is alleged that during a match a ball struck him on the head and killed him. Poor Fred.

He is buried at Westminster Abbey. Not found on his tomb is the popular anonymous epigram that was written shortly after his death:

> Here lies poor Fred
> Who was alive, and is dead
> Had it been his father
> I had much rather.

❡ *Charles the* Pope's Errand-Boy
see Charles the PARSON'S EMPEROR

❡ *James the* Popish Duke *see the* POPISH
AND PROTESTANT DUKES

❡ *John the* Posthumous
John I, king of France, 1316

Official histories record that John was the posthumous son of Louis the QUARRELLER and lived only five days before being succeeded by his uncle, 'Philip the Tall'. Unofficial and more colourful histories state that barons loyal to the king, fearing Philip would murder him, substituted a dead child in his cot and whisked him off to Siena. There, Giannino Baglioni, as he was known, became a merchant banker, but was killed soon after he was informed of his true identity.

§ *Ptolemy the* Pot-Bellied *see* PTOLEMAIC
KINGS

§ Pretty Witty Nell *see* Eleanor the WITTY

§ *Rudolph the* Prince of Alchemy
Rudolph II, Holy Roman Emperor, 1552–1612

Rudolph was prone to severe bouts of depression, and his tactic
for dealing with the demands of the external world was to shut
himself away in his castle in Prague and literally put his fingers
in his ears. This was not the kind of behaviour that his subjects
wanted to see in their emperor.

In between his attacks Rudolph was clear-headed, but as the
sixteenth century came to a close his periods of lucidity
decreased. Eventually he was forced to bow to the inevitable and,
entrusting the government of his empire to his ministers, retired
to his fortress. Without the worries of office, he was then able to
devote himself to the study of alchemy and the search for the
Philosopher's Stone. At his court astrologers, soothsayers, necro-
mancers and mathematicians all attempted to transmute base
metals into gold, but to no avail.

In his final years 'the Prince of Alchemy' became ever more
eccentric, attending Mass in a secret chapel wearing chains, walking about with the fingers of a dead man in his pocket, and
collecting dwarves. In the end he went completely mad.

§ *George the* Prince of Whales *see* George
the BEAU OF PRINCES

Ptolemaic Kings

Beginning with the accession of Ptolemy the Saviour in 323 BC and ending with the death of Cleopatra in 30 BC, the Ptolemaic dynasty is a deeply convoluted and somewhat neglected 300-year stretch of Egyptian history. Nicknames of a few of the earlier Ptolemaic kings reflect the intimate relationships among the Egyptian royal family. Those of the later rulers (whose precise dates and even numerals are keenly disputed) suggest an increasingly feeble monarchy. The first dozen kings are listed below.

Ptolemy I the Saviour
*c.*367–*c.*283 BC

The inhabitants of Rhodes supposedly awarded Ptolemy the divine title of 'Soter' after his forces saved their island in 304 BC by lifting a year-long siege led by Antigonus the ONE-EYED.

Ptolemy II the Brother-Loving
308–246 BC

As well as caring deeply for his brothers, Ptolemy also loved his sister, Arsinoe II. He loved her so much, in fact, that he married her.

Ptolemy III the Benefactor
282–211 BC

Dubbed 'Euergetes' because, as well as extending the kingdom almost as far as Babylon, he sponsored learning and the arts and was famed for initiating the construction of a great temple at Edfu.

Ptolemy IV the Lover of His Father
*c.*238–205 BC

Ptolemy 'Philopater' may have loved his dead father, but he had little time for any of his other relatives, not least his mother, whom he as-sassinated at the inauguration of his reign, and his sister, whom he married and then murdered.

Ptolemy V the Illustrious
*c.*210–180 BC

Hardly illustrious, Ptolemy 'Epiphanes' was controlled by inept guardians when he was a boy-king and incompetent advisers when an adult. As a result, Egypt lost nearly all its foreign possessions during his sorry reign.

Ptolemy the Lover of his Father

Ptolemy VI the Lover of His Mother
*c.*180–145 BC

Ptolemy VI's nickname of 'Philometor' refers to his role as joint head of state with his mother, Cleopatra I, until her death in 176 BC.

Ptolemy VII the New Lover of His Father
d. 144 BC

Sources are muddled as to the place of this king in the Ptolemaic royal sequence. It seems that he ruled sometime in 145 BC after the death of his father, whom he apparently loved, and later was executed when his widowed mother married his uncle, whom he possibly did not love so much.

Ptolemy VIII the Pot-Bellied
d. 116 BC

This Ptolemy wanted to be known as 'the Benefactor', but it was not to be. Alexandrians dubbed their brutal king 'the Malefactor', especially after his expulsion of all Greek intellectuals from the city, while his more common nickname was 'Physkon', meaning 'the Pot-Bellied' or 'Fatso'.

Ptolemy IX the Chickpea
d. 81 BC

Although also known as 'Fatso', Ptolemy IX was more famously known by the mysterious and intriguing appellation 'Chickpea'. The Greek essayist and biographer Plutarch states that it was given irreverently. Perhaps, as with the Roman orator Cicero, he was so named because he had a chickpea-shaped wart at the end of his nose.

¶ **Prinny** *see* George the BEAU OF PRINCES

¶ *James the* Protestant Duke *see* the POPISH AND PROTESTANT DUKES

¶ *Eleanor the* Protestant Whore *see* Eleanor the WITTY

Ptolemy X the Son of a Bitch
d. 88 BC

Ptolemy X was dubbed 'Kokke', an epithet that in polite circles might be translated as 'Son of a Bitch'. The bitch in question was the obstreperous Cleopatra III, with whom he briefly ruled before having her assassinated.

Ptolemy XI Alexander II
d. 80 BC

This Ptolemy, also known as Alexander II, ruled Egypt for only a few days and thus did not have time to acquire a nickname, pejorative or otherwise.

Ptolemy XII the Flute Player
*c.*112–51 BC

Unimpressed by his desire to be recognized as a god, the Egyptians dubbed their king 'Auletes' in reference to his delight in accompanying choruses on the flute, the favourite instrument of the goddess Isis.

¶ *Charles the* Proud Duke
Charles Seymour, sixth duke of Somerset, 1662–1748

A favourite of BRANDY NAN, Charles was an outlandishly vain despot. His inordinate fondness for court ceremony and supremely arrogant understanding of people's 'places' in society earned him both his soubriquet and his famous characterization by essayist Thomas Macaulay as 'a man in whom the pride of birth and rank amounted almost to a disease'. Apparently the duke of Somerset never allowed his children to sit in his presence, and only conversed with his servants through signs.

¶ *Philip the* Prudent
Philip II, king of Spain, 1527–98

Philip's contemporaries used such terms as 'melancholy' and 'phlegmatic' to describe this king, who seldom revealed his emotions. Certainly, he never acted in haste – indeed he was notoriously tardy in making decisions. According to his court secretary Cabrera de Córdoba, he would infuriate his ministers with his catchphrase of 'I and time shall arrange matters as we can', and by holding on to important papers 'until they wilted'.

Scholars disagree as to his political prudence. Some consider his quiet reserve to be nothing more than timidity and lack of resolve. Others see it as good common sense. Certainly his prudence appears to have failed him when he sent his armada against GOOD QUEEN BESS in 1588: it was soundly defeated and then shattered to smithereens by storms.

¶ Puddle-Nell *see* Eleanor the WITTY

[Q]

¶ *Louis the* Quarreller
Louis X, king of France, 1289–1316

Louis quarrelled a lot, especially with his advisers. Once he lashed out at some of them when they suggested that he should not indulge in cold wine immediately after an overheated ball game – a practice, perhaps, that may have led to his death from pleurisy while still in his twenties. Louis was also known as 'le Hutin', sometimes translated as 'the Stubborn'. The *hutinet* was a small mallet used by coopers that made a magnificent bonging noise but did not give very forcible blows. Some have suggested that this second epithet therefore refers not to any character trait but rather to a brief reign that was busy yet lacked any significant impact.

¶ Queen Dick
Richard Cromwell, English statesman, 1626–1712

Oliver 'NOSE ALMIGHTY' Cromwell was particularly concerned with the welfare of his son Richard, known as Dick, whom he suspected of being something of a weak vessel. To this end he undertook some matchmaking and negotiated a union between Dick and one Dorothy Mayor (whom Cromwell senior called 'Doll').

Queen Dick

Dick was a sweet and oversensitive young man, and the contemporary verdict on him was that he was an amiable, if spineless, individual. In middle age Dick was still the same genial but incompetent country gentleman. His brother-in-law, Viscount Fauconberg, used a genteel, biblical turn of phrase when he wrote of Dick's fine qualities 'even if his sheaf be not as Joseph's, to which all the rest bow'. Others were less polite, going so far as to question whether Oliver, the great military leader, could really be the father of such a loveable nincompoop. His nickname 'Queen Dick' and the contemporary phrase 'as queer as Dick's hatband' allude to a widespread suspicion that Richard Cromwell was homosexual.

¶ Queen Goosefoot *see* Bertha BIGFOOT

¶ *Diana the* Queen of Hearts *see* Diana the PEOPLE'S PRINCESS

¶ *Elizabeth the* Queen of Hearts *see* the WINTER MONARCHS

¶ *Mary the* Queen of Tears
Mary, second wife of King James II of England, 1658–1718

Mary of Modena had cause to weep. Between 1675 and 1682 she gave birth to five children, all of whom quickly died, with the blame popularly being conferred upon her husband, 'James the Popish Duke' (*see* the POPISH AND PROTESTANT DUKES), who had regularly suffered from venereal disease. In 1688 she finally gave birth to her sixth child, a healthy boy. Any royal aspirations she may have held for him, however, were soon dashed as a cynical nation, calculating that he had been born a month prematurely, presumed that he was not hers at all but had been substituted for yet another stillborn child in order to preserve the

Catholic succession. This rampant suspicion led to the invasion of William III, 'the Gallic Bully'. Mary, with James the WARMING-PAN BABY in her arms, tearfully escaped to a life of exile in France.

¶ *Zenobia the* Queen of the East
Zenobia, queen of Palmyra, *fl*. third century

When King Odenathus died in 269, the Romans thought that Palmyra in Syria would continue as a vassal state under Aurelian the RESTORER OF THE WORLD. They were mistaken. Queen Zenobia, now the sole ruler, immediately declared independence from Rome and began a military campaign that eventually saw her troops conquer Egypt and much of Asia Minor.

Zenobia, who styled herself 'the Queen of the East', was a true warrior queen, often at the vanguard of her troops as they went into battle. In 274, however, her military ambitions were thwarted. Imperial forces pushed her army all the way back to Palmyra itself and captured her as she tried to flee from her palace on a dromedary. After a brief spell of captivity in Rome, Zenobia married a senator and lived out her days as a socialite on an estate near modern-day Tivoli.

¶ *Elizabeth the* Queen of the Sea
see GOOD QUEEN BESS

¶ *Queen* Sarah
Sarah Jennings, first duchess of Marlborough, 1660–1744

Princess Anne, later BRANDY NAN, and Sarah, the first duchess of Marlborough, were devoted to each other. Sharing a common dislike of William III, 'the Gallic Bully', they privately wrote to each other as Mrs Morley and Mrs Freeman respectively, and dreamed of the day when Anne would be queen and Sarah the most powerful woman in English politics since GOOD QUEEN BESS.

On Anne's accession a gossiping public were quick to recognize that the power of the throne lay not with their queen but with Sarah, and so honoured the duchess with a royal nickname. Political differences, however, conspired to force the two 'queens' inexorably apart: Anne favoured the Tories, whom she saw as the only party serious about the Church, while Sarah was an ardent Whig. In 1710 Anne dismissed her aide, and a relationship of extraordinary sympathy ended in mutual contempt.

¶ *Queen* Venus
Margaret of Valois, queen of France, 1553–1615

Margaret's nickname refers to her string of romantic liaisons, many of which were conducted during her marriage to Henry the GREAT. After a brief affair with the extremist Catholic duke of Guise, the daughter of Henry the WARLIKE (*see* GALLIC PRACTICE) reluctantly married the Protestant Henry in 1572, with the king all but physically forcing her to make the responses at their wedding. Her next serious lover was Joseph, Viscount de la Môle, an unsavoury character renowned for his sexual prowess. Popular rumour has it that when he was beheaded for treason, Margaret buried his remains secretly at night. As he had been quartered as well as beheaded it must have been a messy business. Others allege that Margaret embalmed de la Môle's head, had it set with jewels and placed it in a lead casket which she then interred with her own hands.

Happily divorced and living on a guaranteed income, by middle age Margaret had grown monstrously fat, and in her vast skirts would routinely block doorways. Her old-fashioned clothes, over-rouged cheeks and flabby jowls made her an object of derision. Her massive blonde wig, for which blond footmen were hired and shaved whenever she needed a new coiffure, was the talk of the town. And yet her lovers, whom she is rumoured to have regularly beaten, were prolific. Oddly enough, she got on well with Henry's second wife, Marie de Medici, who allowed her children to call this very strange woman 'Aunt'.

[R]

¶ *William the* Rake of Piccadilly
William Douglas, fourth duke of Queensbury, 1724–1810

As a young man, William pursued his passion for wine, women and the races with such reckless abandon that he made eighteenth-century London society gasp. When William continued pursuing the same passions with unrelenting ardour even into his eighties, early nineteenth-century London reeled at his behaviour: he was the consummate dirty old man.

His love of a bet was legendary. He once won a wager that he could make a letter travel fifty miles in an hour, by stuffing the letter into a cricket ball and having twenty men throw it back and forth as fast as they could. And while his colours were a mainstay at horse-racing meets for many decades, it was his myriad and shameless dalliances with women, regardless of their position or marital status, that earned him his notoriety and nickname.

From the balcony of his house at 138 Piccadilly, William would leer at and ogle the passing women and have his groom take notes to those who caught his eye. To the dismay of genteel England, many young women would accept his invitation to be entertained at his expense. Towards the end of his extremely long life, which he ascribed in part to his habit of bathing in milk, 'Old Q' would still drive out in his signature dark green clothes and make passes at women. When the poet Leigh Hunt saw him in the early 1800s, he 'wondered at the longevity of his dissipation and the prosperity of his worthlessness'.

❡ *Louis a* Reborn Alexander *see* Louis the
LION

❡ *Amadeus the* Red *see* COLOURFUL
CHARACTERS

❡ *Erik the* Red
Erik, Viking explorer, 935–1001

Redheaded Erik often saw red. Such was his temper that he was convicted of manslaughter both in his native land of Norway and later in Iceland, and was banished from both for three years respectively. Erik decided to spend his exile exploring a new land that had been sighted some fifty years earlier by a Norwegian sailor called Gunnbjorn, and so in 980 he set sail for terra incognita.

He found a territory uninhabited by man but flush with bears, foxes and caribou, and as soon as his period of exile was over he returned to Breidafjord in Iceland waxing lyrical about this new country, which was prime for colonization. The place had to be named, of course, and, though some may mock given its vast expanse of ice, Erik called the country 'Greenland' after the deep-green fjords and lakes and verdant slopes of the south-west.

❡ *Otto the* Red *see* Otto the BLOODY

❡ *Thorstein the* Red *see* COLOURFUL
CHARACTERS

❡ *Sigismund the* Red Demon *see* Sigismund
the LIGHT OF THE WORLD

Red and Black Douglases

The Douglas clan, one of the mightiest of all Scottish families, has produced several noblemen whose deeds and consequent nicknames can be found throughout this book. But how the name 'Douglas' came into being is worthy of note itself.

There are two main schools of thought. According to that proposed by the eighteenth-century antiquary George Chalmers, a nobleman called 'Theobald the Fleming' journeyed in 1147 from Flanders to Scotland, where the abbot of Kelso granted him some land to live on. The abbot also gave him the rights to a river known as 'the dark stream', or '*dhu-glas*', from which the clan name 'Douglas' is supposedly derived. A second theory holds that during a battle between the forces of King Solvathius and Donald the WHITE (*see* COLOURFUL CHARACTERS) Solvathius noticed a knight of surpassing bravery. When the king asked the identity of the man, somebody replied, '*Sholto du glasse*', a phrase which has been variously translated as 'Behold yonder grey-haired black man' or 'Behold the black, grey man', and the words *du glasse* were quickly fused into 'Douglas'.

Both these views are based more on conjecture than fact. Of considerably greater certainty is that in the late fourteenth century the Douglas family split into two factions. On one side were the descendants of Archibald the GRIM, known as the 'Black Douglases', possibly because of Archibald's 'terrible dark countenance in warfare', inherited from his semi-legendary forebear. On the other side were the 'Red Douglases' of Angus, named possibly because of the colour of their hair, which ran through the clan. Of the two households, the Black Douglases initially enjoyed greater influence and were the unrivalled power in the south of Scotland at the turn of the fourteenth and fifteenth centuries. After the death of William, the eighth earl of Douglas, in 1452, Black Douglas power waned and the leadership of the Douglases shifted to the 'Reds' of Angus, including such luminaries as BELL THE CAT and his grandson Archibald GREYSTEEL.

¶ *Elizabeth the* Red-Nosed Princess
see COLOURFUL CHARACTERS

¶ *Aurelian the* Restorer of the World
Aurelian, Roman emperor, 214–75

In 270 Aurelian, otherwise known as Lucius Domitius Aurelianus, inherited an empire in a shambles. In the space of fifteen years mismanagement, rebellion and barbarian invasion had reduced imperial territories by two-thirds, and his task of reinstating the empire to its former glory was nothing short of Herculean.

He started immediately, expelling the Vandals from Roman land and forcing the last remaining Goths back over the Danube River, for which he received the title 'Gothicus Maximus', or 'the Greatest Goth'. In 272 he addressed the lost eastern provinces of the empire, now ruled by Zenobia the QUEEN OF THE EAST, where he was delighted to find resistance to be minimal. The so-called Palmyrene cities fell like ninepins before his troops, and Zenobia was ferried to Rome and displayed in golden chains before hundreds of thousands of cheering citizens. For this achievement Aurelian was given the title 'Restitutor Orientis', or 'the Restorer of the Orient'.

Finally the victorious Aurelian turned his attention to the west and, thanks in part to the treachery of Tetricus, the commander of the Gallic Empire, he speedily recovered Gaul and Britain. He returned to Rome in triumph and won his last honorific from the Senate – that of 'Restitutor Orbis' or 'the Restorer of the World'. In just four years he had done what some had deemed impossible, giving new life and hope to an empire that was on its knees. Certainly Aurelian was impressed with his own achievements, describing himself on his coins as 'Deus et Dominus', 'God and Lord'.

¶ *Edward the* Robber
Edward IV, king of England, 1442–83

Edward was publicly dubbed 'the Robber' after his slaughter of the forces of Henry the MARTYR at Towton, where he confiscated much of the land belonging to Lancastrian sympathizers. Privately, others saw him as a robber of something far more precious than land and claimed that he was ruled not by his brain but by another organ of his body. Edward was a handsome monarch. He had a winning smile and a mane of golden brown hair, and stood just over six feet three inches with his boots off . . . and he got his boots off a lot.

There is ample evidence that he was a debauched womanizer of the worst kind. According to his contemporary Dominic Mancini, Edward 'was licentious in the extreme . . . [and] pursued with no discrimination the married and the unmarried, the noble and lowly'. Sir Thomas More adds that 'he was of youth greatly given to fleshly wantonness', while the French critic Philip de Commynes suggests that his death, of an unknown illness at age forty, was due to his excessive 'devotion to pleasure'.

Until the twentieth century the general consensus among historians was that Edward had no merits at all. For some, his 'robbing' of the life of his brother George, first duke of Clarence, who was allegedly drowned in a vat of malmsey wine, epitomized a degenerate, cruel life. A few modern historians, however, have portrayed him in a more flattering light, as an astute leader who brought a measure of political stability into a divided realm, his talents in the bedroom matched by his skill at domestic government.

❡ *Erik the* Romantic
Erik XIV, king of Sweden, 1533–77

Erik asked both GOOD QUEEN BESS and Mary the MERMAID to marry him. They both turned him down. He then

Erik the Romantic

popped the question to a number of German princesses. They, too, declined. His many proposals earned him nothing more than a nickname. Erik did eventually tie the knot, with Karin ('Kitty') Mansdatter, his mistress, but his reign was noted more for his insanity than his romance, with Erik stabbing courtiers for no reason, claiming to be his brother John, the duke of Finland, and sentencing two guards to death for 'annoying the King'. An indignant John deposed Erik and threw him in prison where, tradition has it, someone poisoned his pea soup.

❡ Ruby Nose *see* NOSE ALMIGHTY

❡ *Otto* Rufus *see* Otto the BLOODY

❡ *William* Rufus
William II, king of England, c.1056–1100

In the summer of 1100 a charcoal burner was travelling through the New Forest when he happened across the still-warm body of his king. Reverently he lugged it on to his cart and hauled it to Winchester, where it was buried with due, but not elaborate, ceremony. The nation hardly shed a tear for their mean, selfish and now-dead king.

In life William had been a cruel and coarse dandy of a man who had little taste for anything beyond hunting and military exercise, and who alarmed many of his subjects with his crass ostentation. Once, for example, when one of his chamberlains produced a new pair of shoes for him, William asked what they had cost. 'Three shillings!' he exclaimed. 'You son of a whore! Since when has a king worn shoes as cheap as those! Go and buy me some for a mark of silver!' The chamberlain duly left court, but went and bought a second, equally priced, pair of shoes and lied that they had indeed cost a mark.

William may well have thought that he cut a dash, what with his shoes, fashionable clothing and long hair with its centre parting, but all his subjects saw was a short, stocky, pot-bellied tyrant, a vain, blasphemous cynic whose only notable features were his red hair (for which he received the moniker 'Rufus') and his ruddy complexion, which became particularly inflamed when he was excited.

With tolerable certainty we can accept that a nobleman called Walter Tirel fired the arrow that killed William. Whether it was deliberate or an accident, with the arrow first glancing off a hart and then ricocheting off a tree before ending up in the king, is a matter for debate.

[**S**]

❡ *William the* Sailor King
William IV, king of England, 1765–1837

In 1779, at the age of fourteen, William went to sea. Starting as a humble able seaman, he rose through the ranks, seeing action off Cape St Vincent, participating in the relief of Gibraltar and serving under Nelson in the West Indies. In 1788 he took command of his own frigate.

Like many a sailor, William had a girl in every port. His 'best girl' was actress Dorothea Jordan, with whom he lived for twenty years, but he left her when she took to the bottle. At the age of sixty-five he finally added the title of 'King' to that of 'Lord High Admiral'. By now the former sailor appeared, at least from a distance, like a respectable old admiral. When one came nearer, however, it was obvious that this garrulous, undignified grouch with a curiously pear-shaped head had neither the bearing nor manners of a grand old man of the sea. William drank and gambled to excess, spat in public and was considered to be extremely dim.

In polite circles William may have been called 'the Sailor King', but popularly he was known as 'Silly Billy'. Once, it is alleged, he was visiting Bedlam asylum for the insane when a patient pointed at him and yelled out, 'Silly Billy! Silly Billy!' The name stuck.

❡ *George the* Sailor Prince
George V, king of England, 1865–1936

The fifteen years that Prince George spent as a naval officer on HMS *Britannia* and HMS *Bacchante* were the making of him as king. Fifteen years of discipline, doing what he was told and saluting others instead of being saluted himself moulded him into a young man with a categorical sense of duty.

George had no desire to be king, but on the death of his elder brother Albert (known as 'Eddy' to the family) he was prepared to live the life that a nation expected of him. Although a private man, preferring stamp collecting to public display, he visited the Grand Fleet no fewer than five times during the First World War, and made even more visits to his army.

'The Sailor Prince' will always be associated with the seaside resort of Bognor Regis in West Sussex. In 1928 George spent some weeks in Bognor recuperating after a severe bout of septicaemia. Eight years later as he lay dying, his wife, Queen Mary, suggested he might visit the town again. George's reply was 'Bugger Bognor!' – allegedly his last words.

¶ *Erik the* Saint
Erik IX, king of Sweden, d. 1160

Under the guidance of an Englishman called Henry who became the first bishop of Uppsala, Erik strove to promote his Christian faith among the Swedes. He erected churches, appointed preachers and, notably, promoted marriage as an institution in which wives as well as husbands had a right to family property. Using evangelical methods similar to those of 'Vladimir the Great' (*see* GREAT ... BUT NOT THAT GREAT), he led an expedition to Finland where he forced the inhabitants, at the point of a sword, to be baptized.

Back home in Uppsala, Erik was on his way home after hearing Mass when a Danish prince hacked him to death, and it is widely held that a spring immediately appeared on the very spot where he was murdered. Almost overnight his bones became an object of veneration, and 'St Erik' became the patron saint of Sweden. A statue of the holy king – a young knight carrying the sword and banner of the realm – became an obligatory accessory in all churches, a memorial to a pious monarch and a symbol of dawning nationalism.

¶ *Louis the* Saint

Louis IX, king of France, 1214–70

In his *Life of Saint Louis*, John, lord of Joinville, writes of the king's considerable wisdom, a trait for which many dubbed him 'the Solomon of France'. The tall, good-humoured Louis would often hold court in the wood at Vincennes, where, leaning against an oak tree, he would listen to people's complaints and administer justice, a practice that won him considerable public acclaim. But it is for his piety and religious devotion that he is most remembered.

In moral uprightness Louis led by example. He heard Mass daily, and the sermons that he loved to hear inspired him to go on crusades, during which his sufferings merely increased his faith. Back in France he upbraided John of Joinville for saying that he would rather commit thirty mortal sins than become a leper, and indeed Louis shocked his subjects by publicly kissing lepers' hands. In 1254 he passed laws making blasphemy, gambling and prostitution criminal offences.

Some thought such piety unbecoming in a king. His simple attire of woollen tunic and sleeveless jacket was deemed too modest for a monarch, while his lavish generosity to the Church and the poor was considered unattractive self-aggrandizement. Soft-spoken Louis, canonized less than thirty years after his death, took such complaints in his stride. 'I would rather have such excessive sums as I spend,' he countered, 'devoted to almsgiving for the love of God than used in empty ostentation and the vanities of this world.'

¶ *Frederick the* Sand Dealer *see* Frederick the GREAT

¶ *Ptolemy the* Saviour *see* PTOLEMAIC KINGS

¶ *Arthur the* Saviour of the Nations
see Arthur the IRON DUKE

¶ *Francis the* Scarred
Francis, second duke of Guise, 1519–63

Adored by his troops and feared by his enemies, Francis fought in the army of Francis the FATHER OF LETTERS and received the scar that won him his nickname at the siege of Boulogne in 1545. Later, in 1552, he distinguished himself at the defence of Metz against the emperor Charles the HARLEQUIN, but in 1563 was mortally wounded by a Huguenot assassin as he prepared to besiege Orléans.

¶ *Henry the* Scarred
Henry I, third duke of Guise, 1550–88

In a remarkable, indeed unique, father-and-son nickname double, Henry, son of Francis the SCARRED, also received a massive scar in battle and won the nickname 'le Balafré' for his injuries. His scar was from a frightful gash to his face that he received at the battle of Dormans in 1577. Henry was assassinated by the bodyguard of Henry the MAN-MILLINER, who stabbed him to death, burned his body and flung his ashes into the Loire. Like his father, then, Henry lived by the sword, was nicknamed by the sword and died by the sword.

¶ *John the* Scot
John, Irish nobleman, *fl.* ninth century

John's full name of 'John Scotus Eriugena' helps to explain this anomaly of nomenclature, since the latter two words go some way to identify the Irishman's place of origin. In the ninth century the Latin word *Scotus* rather unhelpfully meant both 'Irish' and 'Scottish' depending on the circumstances. *Eriugena*, however, was far more specific. It is a word that appears to have been concocted by John himself, meaning 'born in Ireland, or Erin'.

John, who was well known for his humorous banter, was a companion, chamberlain and adviser on theological matters to Charles the BALD. Once, writes the chronicler William of Malmesbury, Charles and John were sitting at a table, both having eaten and drunk to excess. Seeing John do something that mildly offended French taste, Charles rebuked him, saying, 'What separates a drunkard from a Scot?' to which the wag John replied, 'Just a table.'

Eventually John tired of the French court and came to the court of Alfred the GREAT in England, where he became a tutor, his students including the young prince himself. His teaching clearly did not go down as well as his jokes, since a few years later some of his pupils stabbed him to death with their pens.

¶ *Attila the* Scourge of God

Attila, king of the Huns, 406–53

To the Romans and Greeks, the Huns were an ugly bunch. The fifth-century Roman Ammianus Marcellinus compared them with the 'stumps, rough hewn . . . that are used in putting sides into bridges'. Attila, their short and swarthy king, with his beady eyes, big head and flat nose, was no exception.

To historians of the time, Attila was more than just physically unattractive. According to many religious sources, he was 'Flagellum Dei', or 'the Scourge of God', while pagan chronicles dubbed him 'the Terror of the World'. These grim epithets stemmed from the apparent barbarism of the Scythian hordes as they overwhelmed much of Europe. Attila and his men ravaged vast areas between the Rhine and the Caspian Sea, exacted draconian tributes from the emperor 'Theodosius the Calligrapher', and even invaded Italy, sacking modern-day Padua, Verona and Milan.

A Greek writer called Priscus visited the court of Attila and sat and ate at a banquet with him in 448. His description of the event suggests that by then the Scourge of God was not the fearsome monster portrayed by earlier chroniclers. 'In every-thing,' Priscus recalls, 'Attila showed himself temperate – his cup was of wood, while to the guests were given goblets of gold and silver. His dress, too, was quite simple, affecting only to be clean.'

¶ *Charles the* Scourge of God *see* Charles the AFFABLE

¶ *Charles* A Second Charlemagne
see Charles the HARLEQUIN

¶ *Sancho the* Settler *see* NOBLE PROFESSIONS

¶ *Wilfrid the* Shaggy
Wilfrid, founding father of Catalan political independence, d. 897

En route to the Carolingian court, Wilfrid's father, also called Wilfrid, was killed during a brawl with some Frankish soldiers. In outrage, Wilfrid junior, described in the twelfth-century *Gesta Comitum Barcinonensium* as 'the Shaggy' or 'the Hairy' owing to the unusually luxuriant growth of hair on his body, made for Charles's court to demand revenge. And so it was that Wilfrid the Shaggy came face to face with Charles the BALD. Little is known of the conversation except that Charles apologized profusely.

According to the *Gesta*, Wilfrid was the proud founder of Catalonia and, like many of his regional contemporaries, de-fended his territories against Muslim aggression and strove to repopulate deserted territory. Wilfrid continued to show family loyalty when he founded and endowed two monasteries and named his own children as abbot and abbess.

¶ *Isabella the* She-Wolf of France
Isabella, wife of King Edward II of England, 1292–1358

One of the vilest women of her age, Isabella did not merely

Isabella the **She-Wolf of France**

dislike her husband Edward CARNARVON, she detested the very ground on which he walked. And so, together with her lover Roger of Mortimer, she invaded England in 1327 and arranged for Edward's murder at Berkeley Castle. The manner of his death, the thrusting of a hot iron into his bowels, still makes the squeamish wince nearly 700 years later. Back then, it won for her the awesome title 'the She-Wolf of France', an epithet employed by the eighteenth-century poet Thomas Gray, when he wrote of her as a:

> She-wolf of France, with unrelenting fangs
> That tear'st the bowels of thy mangled mate.

Isabella's son Edward the BANKRUPT replaced Carnarvon on the English throne.

¶ Shockhead *see* Harold FAIRHAIR

¶ *Pepin the* Short
Pepin III, king of the Franks, *c.*714–68

Pepin may have been short – by most accounts about four and a half feet tall – but his influence was extensive. Once he had exchanged his mayoral hat at the palace of the last Merovingian king, Childeric the STUPID, for the Frankish crown, he vigorously protected his vast lands from all would-be trespassers and even helped the papal forces to defend Rome against the Lombards.

Pepin, the son of Charles the HAMMER, may have been short, but with his wife Bertha BIGFOOT was the proud parent of Charles the GREAT, one of the tallest kings history has ever recorded.

¶ *Paul the* Silent *see* Harald and the HAIR SHIRT

¶ *William the* Silent
William I, prince of Orange, 1533–84

William the Silent – 'Willem de Zwijger' or 'Guillaume le Taciturne' if you prefer – was far from taciturn, let alone silent. In fact, he was a most affable, cheerful and delightful fellow and spoke Latin, French, German, Flemish and Spanish regularly and fluently. His soubriquet stems from the discretion he demonstrated in some of his dealings with Henry the WARLIKE (*see* GALLIC PRACTICE) and Philip the PRUDENT, most notably when he kept his own counsel on the news that the two kings were planning to send thousands of Spanish troops to rid the Netherlands of 'heretics' (i.e. Protestants). Churlish critics interpret William's silence as sulking because he had not been asked to join their plot, but others counter that this would be wholly out of character for such an adroit politician and the courageous leader of the revolt against Spanish domination.

Many Dutch today regard William as their national hero. Even though he mainly spoke French, he is hailed as 'the Father of the Fatherland' for his role in steering Holland to independence from Spanish control. The Dutch national anthem was written in recognition of his achievements and, despite having a flag of red, white and blue, Holland has orange as its national colour, reflecting William's lineage.

¶ *Charles the* Silly
Charles VI, king of France, 1368–1422

In his early twenties Charles was tall and strong, with fair hair falling in thick curls to his shoulders. He was a lover of the outdoor life but was also a patron of the arts and, together with his wife Isabella the GREAT SOW, hosted luxurious gatherings at court despite the Hundred Years War that raged around them. For his gallantry and generosity some dubbed him 'the Well-Beloved'. But then, on 5 August 1392, he went berserk.

Fuelled by alcohol or suffering from sunstroke, he lost his head in the forest of Le Mans and killed four men before his sword broke and he could be tied up. From then on, his attacks came with monotonous regularity and, as his mental health deteriorated, he was renamed 'the Silly' and eventually 'the Mad'. Aware in lucid moments of his condition, Charles officially handed over authority of the running of the country to his porcine wife.

¶ Silly Billy *see* William the SAILOR KING

¶ *John the* Silly Duke
John Churchill, first duke of Marlborough, 1650–1722

Marlborough was an outstanding soldier, a brilliant diplomat and the long-suffering husband of the imperious QUEEN SARAH. The French considered him to be rather dashing and called him 'the Handsome Englishman'. General Turenne, his commander in the 1670s, declared that he 'was no less distinguished for the singular graces of his person than for his brilliant courage and consummate ability both as a soldier and a statesman'. Voltaire praised him for 'that serenity of soul in danger, which the English call a cool head'. By contrast, the English called him 'the Silly Duke', because he would habitually cry 'Oh, silly! Silly!' whenever he heard some bad news.

❡ *Lulach the* Simpleton *see* Lulach the FOOL

❡ *Basil the* Slayer of the Bulgars
Basil II, Byzantine emperor, *c.*957–1025

Basil was short and blue-eyed and had a habit of twirling his bushy whiskers around his fingers when angry. He was a formidable opponent, and Samuel, the Bulgarian tsar, was unsurprisingly very concerned when in 1014 he learned that Byzantine forces were once more advancing towards his capital city, Ochrida. Spies told him that Basil was twirling his whiskers furiously and was in no mood for a peace offering.

Nothing, however, could have prepared Samuel for the spectacle that he confronted when his men returned from battle in the Belasica Mountains. Basil, it transpired, had not only defeated Samuel's army but also blinded the 14,000 prisoners, leaving one eye to each hundredth man in order that they could lead their comrades back home. On staring at 27,860 bloody eye sockets, Samuel died of shock.

❡ *Harald the* Smooth Talker *see* Harald and the HAIR SHIRT

❡ *Frederick the* Snow King *see* the WINTER MONARCHS

❡ *Elizabeth the* Snow Queen *see* the WINTER MONARCHS

❡ Softsword *see* John LACKLAND

❡ *Louis the* Solomon of France *see* Louis the SAINT

The Sons of Tancred

Tancred de Hauteville was a Norman nobleman of little note. Several of his twelve sons, however, achieved considerable notoriety through their exploits in southern Italy. Three of the children who found fame and fortune in the Mediterranean acquired nicknames that reveal their different paths to success.

William the Iron Arm
Count of Apulia, d. 1046

In about 1035 William and his brothers Drogo and Humphrey left France to join the mercenary Norman army in southern Italy where William soon became count of Apulia. He earned his nickname of 'il Bracchio di Ferro' during the siege of the Muslim-occupied city of Syracuse. According to one biographer, the count was not only a 'lamb in society and an angel in council' but also a 'lion in war', and with his 'iron arm' is said to have 'unhorsed and transpierced' the city's hapless emir.

Robert the Cunning
Duke of Apulia, c.1015–85

That same year Robert 'Guiscard' – sometimes translated as 'the Weasel' but more commonly as 'the Cunning' – headed south from France with four horsemen and a couple of dozen followers on foot. Once in the Mediterranean he initially led the life of a robber baron and supported himself by cattle rustling. By 1053, however, he had amassed a considerable army and defeated the forces of Pope Leo IX at the battle of Cività. The pope himself was taken prisoner, but, in a cunning plan, Robert and his men knelt and asked for his blessing, knowing that an alliance with the papacy could be an advantage in the future. Indeed it was. Six years later Pope Nicholas II formally invested Robert with all the lands he had conquered.

Robert was not satisfied with being just the duke of Apulia, Calabria and (by his own decree) Sicily. Various military exploits followed, including an invasion of Rome and an expedition through Greece to fight the Byzantine emperor Alexius I. It was on this final campaign that he made a deep impression upon Anna, the emperor's daughter. In *The Alexiad* Anna describes Robert as 'In temper tyrannical, in mind most cunning . . . and subordinate to nobody in the world.' Anna was also impressed with Robert's physique. In breathless tones she tells us that 'his stature was so lofty that he surpassed even the tallest, his complexion was ruddy, his hair flaxen . . . [and] his eyes all but emitted sparks of fire.'

Roger the Great Count
Count of Sicily, 1031–1101

Roger, Tancred's youngest, decided that he would like to rule the island of Sicily rather than a region on the Italian mainland, and in 1061, after a spell as a bandit and a horse thief, his campaign to conquer the entire island began in earnest.

It was no easy task. Starting with a mere hundred knights and facing fierce Muslim resistance, he made painstakingly slow progress. For thirty long years he laboriously laid siege to each and every town until finally, in 1091, the island was his and he was on a par with most of the monarchs in Europe. Extremely proud of his achievements Roger deemed the title of 'count' that came with the crown of Sicily to be demeaning, and so instead he gave himself the title 'the Great Count'.

Some contemporary historians write how Roger demonstrated general tolerance to Sicily's vanquished Muslim population by allowing them to maintain their magistrates and mosques. The count's other epithet, 'the Terror of the Faithless', suggests that he made it unequivocally clear that Sicily was a Christian realm.

¶ *Ptolemy the* Son of a Bitch
see PTOLEMAIC KINGS

¶ *Charles the* Son of the Last Man
see Charles the MERRY MONARCH

¶ *Louis the* Springer
Louis, margrave of Thuringia, 1042–1128

Convicted of murder, Louis was imprisoned deep in the impregnable Giebichenstein Castle near Halle – the Colditz or Alcatraz of its day. After two years of incarceration he managed to escape by climbing to the top of the battlements and 'springing' into the River Saale below. For his courage, the emperor pardoned him and gave him his nickname as well as his liberty.

¶ *Sitric the* Squint-Eyed
Sitric, king of Dublin and York, d. 927

When Sitric 'Cáech' signed a treaty with the powerful Athelstan the GLORIOUS in order to prevent any hostilities, part of the agreement was that Sitric had to accept Christianity and marry Althelstan's sister Edith. The glorious Athelstan should have noticed the deception behind those squinty eyes. Within months of the nuptials Sitric renounced the faith and sent Edith packing to a convent.

¶ *Robert the* Steward *see* NOBLE
PROFESSIONS

¶ *Sigurd the* Stout
Sigurd II, earl of Orkney, d. 1014

In 1013 Sigurd, the mighty earl of Orkney, was asked by 'Sitric Silkenbeard', the Norse king of Dublin, for help in his battle against the Irish high king Brian Bóru. Sitric promised that if they were victorious, Sigurd would become the high king. With such a prize Sigurd could not refuse, and the battle took place on 23 April 1014. Brian Bóru was killed, but Sigurd, possibly not helped by his plump physique, also lost his life.

¶ *Augustus the* Strong
Augustus II, king of Poland, 1670–1733

As duke of several territories, including Saxony and Meissen, Augustus possessed the means to rule without having to ask for financial support. As an elector of the Holy Roman Empire, he wielded considerable influence. Moreover, as commander of the imperial armies in a number of campaigns, he had a distinguished military reputation. All in all, he looked a fitting successor to the great John the WIZARD, but it is for his love life rather than for his leadership that Augustus is best remembered.

His romances formed one of the wonders of the age, attesting no less to his catholic and cosmopolitan taste than to his phenomenal stamina. After a series of youthful adventures abroad, where he had variously disguised himself as a matador and a monk, he returned to Dresden in 1693 to the charms of his bride, Eberdine, to the labours of electoral office, and to the cultivation of a covey of concubines whom his courtiers classified for public consumption as 'official', 'confidential' or 'top secret'.

Augustus was the father of some 300 children. Gossip-mongers have it that the abandoned mistress of the British ambassador to Saxony, who turned to him for comfort, was the only woman he was unable to seduce in fifty years of amorous endeavour. His nickname, it is held, was awarded after he slept with his own mother at the royal hunting-lodge at Mauritzburg.

The political ventures of 'Augustus the Strong' were less successful than his sexual forays. By the end of his reign Poland had declined from a thrusting major European power to a flaccid protectorate of Russia.

¶ Strongbow
Richard, son of Gilbert de Clare, second earl of Pembroke, d. 1176

Richard's strength and skill at archery knew no equal. It is said that his arms were so long that, when standing fully upright, he could touch his knees with the palms of his hands.

¶ *Louis the* Stubborn *see* Louis THE

QUARRELLER

¶ *Childeric the* Stupid
Childeric III, Merovingian king, d. 755

In the second quarter of the eighth century the mayors of the Merovingian palace, Pepin the SHORT and his brother Carloman, grew aware that their growing power was making the other Frankish leaders increasingly agitated, so Pepin and his brother looked around for a puppet figure who would nominally be king but allow them to continue in absolute command. Childeric was their man. Playing no part in public business whatsoever, he simply did as he was told.

The royal annals do not dwell on whether he was intellectually challenged. They are content merely to record that in 747, when Carloman died and Pepin decided to crown himself king, Childeric was 'retired' to a monastery.

¶ *Ferdinand the* Summoned
Ferdinand IV, king of Castile and León, 1285–1312

Apart from his troops' capture of Gibraltar from the Moors in 1309, Ferdinand's reign is of little note. His place in Spanish history is enshrined, however, due to the legend behind his sudden death. In 1312 Ferdinand condemned to death two brothers, John and Peter Carvajal, for a minor offence. As they faced their executioners, the prisoners vociferously proclaimed their innocence and summoned Ferdinand to appear before God within thirty days. Preparing for a raid on Granada, the king was very much alive and well thirty days later. The following morning, however, 'el Emplazado' – 'the Summoned' – was found dead in his bed.

¶ *Louis the* Sun King
Louis XIV, king of France, 1638–1715

When Louis ascended the throne at the age of five, a party of grumbling nobles orchestrated violent unrest – known as 'le Fronde' – against his quasi-regent Cardinal Mazarin. In celebration of the defeat of these upstart aristocrats, Mazarin commissioned a ballet entitled *Le Ballet de la Nuit*, in which Louis danced the central role of the Rising Sun, while the princes of the Fronde were portrayed as rebellious divinities making obeisance to their prancing monarch. In so doing, Louis employed dance as a weapon of state and also won his nickname of 'le Roi Soleil'.

Later, Louis delighted in appearing at various balls in his opulent courts as Apollo, the god of the sun, and incorporated the sun as part of his heraldic device, thus conveying to one and all his personal brilliance and that of the Bourbon dynasty. By the end of his reign, however, political clouds were forming over a nation whose place in the sun was increasingly unsure.

¶ *Fulk the* Surly
Fulk IV, count of Anjou, 1043–1109

Disgruntled at inheriting little more than the Chateau of Vihiers from his uncle Geoffrey Martel while his elder brother 'Geoffrey the Bearded' received the province of Anjou, Fulk 'le Réchin' swiftly imprisoned Geoffrey and claimed the region as his own.

Still dissatisfied with his lot, he then spent much of his life in battle against local barons and the forces of the duke of Normandy. Life hit rock bottom for the surly count, however, when the enormously fat Philip the AMOROUS 'ran' off with his wife.

¶ **Sweet Nell** *see* Eleanor the WITTY

[T]

¶ *Ivan the* Terrible
Ivan IV, tsar of Russia, 1530–84

When Ivan was only three his father died, leaving control of Russia in the hands of the senior members of the aristocracy known as boyars. For ten years these boyars utterly neglected their prince, to the extent that he became a beggar in his own palace. He was washed, dressed in fine clothes and put on display only when it was necessary to show a visiting dignitary that Russia was stable. The only person to whom little Ivan could turn was his nurse, Agrafena, and when she was forcibly removed to a convent he was utterly lost and alone – more 'Ivan the Traumatized' than 'Ivan the Terrible'. Such an upbringing may go some way to explain his dark deeds of later life.

His terrible rule began on 29 December 1543 when he summoned the boyars together, berated them for their inhumanity and had their leader thrown into an enclosure with a pack of starving hounds. The dogs immediately set upon the screaming man and ate him. The large crowd of Muscovites who witnessed the event were deeply impressed, and the cowering boyars acknowledged that Ivan had complete power.

It is said that Ivan's troops bestowed upon him the term of 'Grozny', meaning 'the Terrible' or more accurately 'the Awesome', after their victory over the Tatar stronghold of Kazan in 1562. Be that as it may, Ivan is popularly known as 'the Terrible' for his barbarism. Below are just some of the acts for which he is held responsible.

• He hurled dogs and cats from the Kremlin walls just to watch them suffer.

- He roamed the streets knocking down old people at will.
- He raped women, and disposed of his victims by having them hanged, thrown to bears or buried alive.
- He imprisoned his uncle in a dungeon and left him to starve.
- He had a peasant woman strip naked and then used her as target practice.
- He drowned a host of beggars en masse in a lake.
- He forced a boyar to sit on a barrel of gunpowder and then blew him to bits.
- He happened across his pregnant daughter-in-law in her underwear and beat her with his staff because he considered her attire indecent.
- He boiled his treasurer alive in a cauldron.
- He killed his own son in a fit of temper.

His most heinous crime of all was ordering the massacre of the 60,000 citizens of Novgorod. After the archbishop was sewn up in a bearskin and hunted to death by a pack of dogs, the 'Oprichniki', Ivan's black-uniformed secret police, embarked on their wholesale slaughter. Observers reported that so many bodies clogged the Volkhov River that it overflowed its banks.

As well as a callous heart, Ivan also had a calloused forehead, a condition caused by his throwing himself before icons and banging his head on the floor in acts of extreme devotion. He deeply loved his wife, Anastasia, calling her his 'little heifer', and when she died after a lingering disease, he underwent an emotional collapse and repeatedly hit his head on the floor in full view of the court. In 1584, after a forty-year reign of terror, Ivan was settling down to play a game of chess when he suddenly collapsed and died.

❡ *Attila the* Terror of the World *see* Attila the SCOURGE OF GOD

¶ *James the* Thistle

James IV, king of Scotland, 1473–1513

Although James was rather easily duped into signing away valuable crown lands (most notably to the Campbell and Gordon clans), he was a truly popular king, and it was his very shortcomings as a ruler – his fun-loving spirit and generosity – that won the hearts of his people.

James the Thistle

James ascended the throne when he was only fifteen, and dancing, hunting and hawking were the preferred pastimes in the court of the young monarch. Carefree with his money and extravagant with his wine bill, he was also a great religious enthusiast. He ate no meat on Wednesdays and Fridays, refused to mount a horse on Sundays and would not allow anything to interfere with his annual pilgrimage to the remote shrines of St Ninian and St Duthac. All this deeply impressed the courtier-poet William Dunbar, who, in his work *The Thrissil and the Rose*, dubbed his king 'Thrissil', or 'Thistle', after the national flower, and the young queen Margaret, daughter of Henry the ENGLISH SOLOMON (*see* ENGLISH EPITHETS), 'that sweit meik Rois'.

Whatever James did, he did with energy. Internationally he improved his nation's position within European politics, while domestically he improved the education system and licensed Scotland's first printers. Passionately interested, meanwhile, in dentistry and surgery, he once paid a man fourteen shillings to be allowed to extract one of the man's teeth, and another nearly two pounds to be allowed to let his blood.

More moonstruck than military, James died at the battle of Flodden Field when he accompanied his spearmen in a reckless downhill charge, his costly heroism helping to make him one of Scotland's most popular monarchs of all time. Perhaps more pathetic than James's sorry death, however, was that of his son, Alexander, the archbishop of St Andrews, a man so short-sighted that in order to read he had to hold a book at the end of his nose. Out of love and loyalty to his earthly father, he joined him on the battlefield. One hopes and expects that his demise was swift.

¶ *Anne of a* Thousand Days *see* Anne the GREAT WHORE

¶ *Bejazet the* Thunderbolt
Bejazet I, sultan of the Turks, 1347–1403

For the speed with which he transported his army from one continent to another, Bejazet was nicknamed 'Yildirim', meaning 'Lightning' or 'the Thunderbolt' – an epithet doubly suitable, as Edward Gibbon states, owing to the 'fiery energy of his soul' as well as the 'rapidity of his destructive march'.

Bejazet was certainly never one to let grass grow under his feet. On the battlefield of Kosovo, where his father Murad was killed, his first act as the new sultan was to order the death of his own younger brother Yakub, whom he deemed too popular with the troops. The hapless Yakub was found and immediately strangled with a bowstring. Having quickly avenged his father's death by a wholesale massacre of Serbian nobility, Bejazet turned his attentions to Asia Minor – a hasty act that was to prove his undoing. At the battle at Ankara he finally met his match in 'Timur the Tatar', who, legend has it, kept Bejazet in chains at night, used him literally as a footstool and had the sultan's wife strip and serve him naked at his table. Bejazet's spirit was crushed by such humiliations, and eight months after being captured he was dead from an apoplectic seizure.

❡ **Tiddy-Doll** *see* Napoleon the LITTLE
CORPORAL

❡ **Toom Tabard**
John Balliol, king of Scotland, 1249–1315

To win the Scottish throne from a number of contenders, John had to pledge allegiance to Edward the HAMMER OF THE SCOTS. Once in power, however, he found Edward's demands too stringent and refused to continue to pay him homage, forging instead the 'Auld Alliance' with France. Edward reacted swiftly, launching an attack against Scotland and decisively winning the only battle of the campaign, at Dunbar in April 1296. In early July the chastened John formally surrendered.

John's nickname of 'Toom Tabard', meaning 'Empty Surcoat' or 'Empty Jacket', stems from the humiliation that he then suffered. It is alleged that John was publicly cashiered – discharged from service with ignominy – by having the royal blazon from his coat ripped off before a jeering public.

❡ *Albert with the* Tress *see* Albert THE
ASTROLOGER

❡ *Theobald the* Troubadour *see* NOBLE
PROFESSIONS

❡ *Abu Bakr the* Truthful *see* Abu Bakr the
UPRIGHT

❡ **Tum Tum** *see* Edward the CARESSER

¶ *George the* Turnip-Hoer
George I, king of England, 1660–1727

Apart from a penchant for truffles George had no interest at all in the finer things of life. Averse to pomp and ceremony, the dour and matter-of-fact monarch preferred instead to concentrate on affairs of state and the prudent development of a well-ordered economy. Common sense was the royal watchword, indicated perhaps by his enquiry as to the cost of transforming the beautiful and ornate St James's Park into a turnip field.

¶ *Alexander the* Two-Horned *see* Alexander the GREAT

¶ *Christian the* Tyrant
Christian II, king of Denmark, Norway and Sweden, 1481–1559

In 1517, when already king of Denmark and Norway, Christian decided to conquer Sweden and become its king. After a couple of military setbacks he won a decisive battle at Bogesund in January 1520 at which Sten Sture, the Swedish regent, was mortally wounded. Christian's coronation took place in November the same year. Six days of feasting later, the intemperate king then orchestrated an atrocity which will for ever sully his fame.

Despite a solemn and sweeping declaration of amnesty for all who had opposed him, Christian, with the decidedly unchristian archbishop Gustav Trolle at his side, accused Sture's followers of heresy. Without trial, they were all found guilty; two bishops were dragged to the market-place and beheaded and nearly a hundred nobles and prominent burghers were killed in what became known as 'the Stockholm Massacre'. The body of Sten Sture was disinterred and, together with those of the recently murdered, thrown on to a pyre and burned. For this outrage

Christian acquired the unwelcome but deserved epithets 'the Cruel', 'the Nero of the North' and 'the Tyrant'.

¶ *John the* Tyrant *see* John the PERFECT

[**U**]

§ *Edward the* Uncle of Europe *see* Edward
the CARESSER

§ *Arnulf the* Unfortunate
Arnulf III, count of Flanders, 1055–71

Arnulf was unfortunate to grow up in a time when it was the
norm for sixteen-year-old boys to fight in battle. Arnulf died,
aged sixteen, at the battle of Kassel while fighting against his
uncle, 'Robert the Frisian'.

§ *Louis the* Universal Spider
Louis XI, king of France, 1423–83

With the aid of his assistant 'Tristan the Gossip', Louis was a
consummate king of spin, creating an elaborate web of international relations and intrigue that trapped unwary politicians
and uncertain monarchs into making concessions or agreeing to
his harsh demands. The wily John II of Aragon, known for his
own political parleying, warned that Louis was 'the inevitable
conqueror in all negotiations', while the Milanese ambassadors
to the French court, men who prided themselves on their diplomatic sophistication, found Louis to be the 'subtlest man alive'.

Yet, less than a generation after his death, he was remembered
not so much for his political mastery as for his cruelty and
repression. Legend has it that he delighted in drinking infants'
blood and listening to the screams of people being tortured.
More believable were stories of his harsh treatment of his servants
who had their ears sliced off for simple acts of dishonesty, and

his ill-treatment of some pigs which he had incorporated into a kind of porcine piano. Pigs of various sizes were attached to a keyboard and when the keys were pressed, spikes would jab the pigs, making them squeal in pain and almost in tune.

Ugly, indiscreet and manipulative, Louis claimed to be a devout Christian and wore a leaden statuette of the Virgin Mary in his hat.

¶ *Ethelred the* Unready
Ethelred II, king of England, 968–1016

Ethelred was something of a reluctant monarch, and, according to historian Henry of Huntingdon, his reign was destined to be disastrous from the moment he urinated in the font at his baptism.

As every schoolchild knows, he is remembered as 'the Unready'. Fewer are perhaps aware that the nickname does not refer to any lack of preparation on his part but is instead an ironic play on his name, with *athel* meaning 'noble' and *raed* meaning 'counsel'. 'Unready' here means 'poorly advised', and by his own admission Ethelred did indeed receive poor guidance. His unsuccessful attempts to defend the country through diplomacy rather than force, his unproductive political marriage to Emma the GEM OF NOR-

Ethelred the Unready

MANDY and his unpopular levy of a tax called 'the Danegeld' to buy off Viking raids, he agreed were all products of woeful counsel.

The worst advice Ethelred probably took was to endorse what became known as the St Brice's Day Massacre on 13 November 1002, when he ordered the killing of every Dane living in England.

Whether this decree was fulfilled to the letter is unclear. What *is* clear is that the event prompted Sven FORKBEARD to invade England. By 1013 Sven had been accepted as king and Ethelred had fled to Normandy. Ethelred returned to rule after Sven's death in 1014, but died himself in 1016, leaving the country to his son Edmund IRONSIDE.

¶ *Elizabeth an* Untamed Heifer *see* GOOD QUEEN BESS

¶ *Abu Bakr the* Upright
Abu Bakr, Muslim caliph, *c.*573–634

Abu Bakr – the name itself means 'the Father of the Maiden' in reference to his daughter Aisha, whom Muhammad married at an age 'when she was still playing with dolls' – was the prophet's closest friend. Abu Bakr succeeded Muhammad as the first caliph in 632 and began compiling the Qur'an. Such was his earnest holiness during his two-year reign that he earned the title 'as-Siddiq', meaning 'the Truthful' or 'the Upright'.

[V]

¶ *Osman the* Victorious
Osman I, founder of the Ottoman Empire, 1259–1326

On his deathbed Osman encouraged his son Orhan to 'Rejoice my soul with a series of victories.' Given his father's extraordinary success in expanding the Ottoman dynasty, primarily at Byzantine expense, it was going to be hard for Orhan to emulate even half of his father's achievements.

Osman was a simple soul who lived largely in the saddle and commanded a number of Turkish nomadic tribes that captured 'infidel' territories in order to increase the land under Islamic control. His first major victory, however, was not military but marital. He told his future father-in-law that he had experienced a dream in which he had seen the city of Constantinople as a jewelled ring on his (Osman's) finger. The father-in-law was impressed and handed over his daughter, confident that Osman's vision of personal power could mean nothing but good for him and his family. Successfully married, Osman could now turn his attention to military conquest.

Villages, then cities and then entire regions slowly but surely fell under his sway, until his greatest victory in 1326 when, after a ten-year siege, the great Byzantine city of Bursa capitulated. The Ottomans now had a real capital from which to pursue their imperial designs.

The news of the fall of Bursa reached Osman as he lay dying. To his son he left a vast area of the globe ripe for Ottoman expansion, and also his few personal but much cherished possessions, including his turban, a few pieces of red muslin and a salt cellar.

¶ *Waldemar the* Victorious
Waldemar II, king of Denmark, 1170–1241

With BARBAROSSA reluctantly acknowledging Danish independence from Germany, and with a guarantee of no further military trouble from Norway, Waldemar felt comfortable enough to lead his forces personally in a crusade against Estonia, where success upon success made him master of much of the Baltic states. His greatest achievement was the final subjugation of the Estonians at the battle of Reval (modern-day Tallinn) in 1219, at which the Danish gained not only a famous victory but also their national symbol. According to legend, a red cloth with a white cross just happened to fall from the sky during the engagement, and from that day on the 'Dannebrog' has been Denmark's national flag.

¶ *Napoleon the* Violet Corporal
see Napoleon the LITTLE CORPORAL

¶ *Elizabeth the* Virgin Queen *see* GOOD
QUEEN BESS

❧ *Hereward the* Wake

Hereward, Saxon thane, *fl.* eleventh century

In the third quarter of the eleventh century pockets of resistance to William the CONQUEROR's new Norman regime remained throughout the north and west of England, and especially in the fenland of East Anglia, where the Saxon thane Hereward stoutly defended the city of Ely. Stories of Hereward's heroics abound. Some chronicles state, for example, that in 1068 Hereward returned to his family estate only to find the house occupied by a Norman and his brother's decapitated head impaled above the doorway. That night, armed with what he could carry, he allegedly ambushed and killed fifteen Norman soldiers and substituted their heads for his brother's.

In 1071 William mustered his crack troops against Hereward's rebels and launched an offensive upon Ely. The island garrison eventually surrendered, but Hereward managed to escape into the fen country to become a semi-legendary resistance fighter on a par with Robin Hood.

The name 'the Wake' was not attached to Hereward until the fourteenth century, when he appears in the *Chronicle of Abbot John* as 'le Wake'. The nickname does not mean 'the Vigilant' as some profess, but actually refers to the Wake family who, at the time of Abbot John's work, claimed to have inherited their lands from Hereward following a series of marriages involving his alleged descendants. The Wake family's claim has not been substantiated.

❧ *Henry the* Warlike *see* GALLIC PRACTICE

¶ *James the* Warming-Pan Baby

James Stuart, pretender to the English throne, 1688–1766

A disaffected Protestant England dismissed all Jacobite claims that James Stuart was the rightful heir to the throne. Instead it counterclaimed that this so-called 'son' of James II (*see* the POP-ISH AND PROTESTANT DUKES) and Mary the QUEEN OF TEARS was in actuality a substitute for Mary's stillborn child, smuggled into the royal bedchamber in a warming pan. Catholic France was much more amenable to the claims of 'James III', and Louis the SUN KING lent his support to 'the Old Pretender' as James made a number of half-hearted attempts to gain his crown. After a distinguished career with the French army in the War of the Spanish Succession for which he earned the soubriquet 'le Chevalier de St George', James retired to Italy. There his wife Mary gave birth to the 'Young Pretender', BONNIE PRINCE CHARLIE.

¶ *Robert the* Weasel *see* the SONS OF

TANCRED

¶ *Charles the* Well-Beloved *see* Charles the

SILLY

¶ *Louis the* Well-beloved

Louis XV, king of France, 1710–74

In 1744 Louis set out to join his forces in the second campaign of the War of the Austrian Succession. At the city of Metz he fell violently ill, and for several days lay on what many feared was his deathbed. On the news of his recovery the delighted French people acclaimed their king as 'Louis le Bien-Aimé'. It is a curiously unsuitable nickname for a monarch who received an extremely bad press from his contemporaries, not least because of his scandalous private life.

In 1725 Louis married Marie Leszczynska, a Polish princess,

and together they had ten children. But monogamy was not for Louis, and in 1732 the first in a string of mistresses appeared. His affairs with all three of the Nesle sisters and the former high-class prostitute Jeanne Bécu generated howls of outrage from the press of the day. But it was his liaison with Jeanne Poisson, better known as Madame Pompadour, that caused the greatest offence. It was alleged that when she could no longer satisfy the king herself, she furnished him with a succession of young women (and some very young girls) whom she kept in a house known as the 'Deer Park'.

There were some things that Louis could do as well as anybody. He was noted, for instance, for his skill in cutting off the top of a boiled egg with one blow of his fork, and he made a point of being served boiled eggs whenever he dined in public. In almost everything else, however, he failed to impress. France was insulted by his sexual antics and dismayed at his abysmal foreign policy that saw the country abandon all its territories in the New World. Well-beloved, in sum, he was not.

¶ *Donald the* White *see* COLOURFUL CHARACTERS

¶ *Athelfleda the* White Duck

Athelfleda, queen of England, d. *c.*964

Athelfleda married her childhood sweetheart Edgar the PEACE-ABLE and together they had a son, Edward the MARTYR. Histories diverge as to whether she died in childbirth or separated from Edgar after finding out about his affair with a woman called Wulfryth, whom he later banished to a nunnery. No one is exactly sure about the reason for her nickname either, although some propose that 'the White Duck' or 'the Little White Duck' was simply Edgar's pet name for his first love.

❡ **White Hands** *see* COLOURFUL
CHARACTERS

❡ *Mary the* **White Queen** *see* Mary the
MERMAID

❡ *Victoria the* **Widow of Windsor**
Victoria, queen of the United Kingdom, 1819–1901

Rudyard Kipling, author of *The Jungle Book* and other classics,
is somewhat responsible for this nickname. He wrote a poem in
1890 that contained the lines:

> 'Ave you 'eard o' the Widow of Windsor
> With a hairy gold crown on 'er 'ead?

After her husband Albert the GOOD died of typhoid Victoria
spent the rest of her life, much of it at Windsor Castle, wearing
the black of mourning. There were some good times in her forty
years of widowhood, however, notably her deep affection for her
'gillie', or attendant, John Brown, who became her personal aide.
Rumours spread that the two had secretly married, and some
gave the queen of Great Britain and Ireland and empress of India
the additional title 'Mrs Brown'. Certainly their relationship was
close. In her personal diary of 1884 she wrote, 'I like his strength,
his weight, this feeling of security. He calls me Woman; I call
him Man . . . He treats me roughly, he scolds me, he gives me
orders and I am happy that he does so.'

Victoria also earned the soubriquet of 'the Grandmother of
Europe' since on her death her descendants occupied most of
the thrones of that continent.

The Winter Monarchs

Frederick V, elector Palatine and king of Bohemia, 1596–1632
Elizabeth, queen of Bohemia, 1596–1662

In 1619 the Protestant estates of Bohemia rebelled against the Catholic authorities and offered the crown of Bohemia to Frederick and his wife, Elizabeth. Some of their followers considered this a foolish idea, and suggested that they should heed Catholic taunts that they would be 'the Snow King' and 'the Snow Queen' – only on the throne while snow was on the ground. Others, citing promised support from the Protestant Union and Frederick's father-in-law James the WISEST FOOL IN CHRISTENDOM, encouraged the couple to accept. Frederick and Elizabeth chose the latter course.

The expected aid, however, never materialized, and just two months after their coronation their troops lost a crushing defeat at the battle of White Mountain. Jesuit prophecies that the couple would melt away from Bohemia as snow vanished with the first rays of spring sunshine proved accurate. Mocked as 'the Winter King' and 'the Winter Queen' – monarchs that reigned for just one season – they fled to exile in Holland.

Frederick was distraught. Elizabeth, however, refused to be downhearted, and her constant good-natured disposition while in the Low Countries garnered her a second epithet, 'the Queen of Hearts'.

¶ *Frederick the* Winter King *see* the
WINTER MONARCHS

¶ *Elizabeth the* Winter Queen *see* the
WINTER MONARCHS

¶ *Albert the* Wise *see* Albert the LAME

¶ *Alfonso the* Wise *see* Alfonso the
ASTRONOMER

¶ *Frederick the* Wise
Frederick III, elector of Saxony, 1463–1525

Frederick was a pious man and owned a collection of holy relics
supposedly including scraps from Jesus's swaddling clothes, a hair
of his beard and remains of some of the innocents slaughtered by
King Herod. As well as a keen collector, Frederick was also a
fierce promoter of scholarship and, despite his own Catholicism,
supported and protected the reformer Martin Luther against
Catholic charges of heresy. His reputation for deliberation and
even-handedness won him the titles 'the Wise' and 'the Learned',
although his cautious nature earned him the soubriquet 'the
Hesitater' from (a rather ungrateful) Luther.

¶ *James the* Wisest Fool in Christendom
James I, king of England, and VI, king of Scotland, 1566–
1625

James had a tongue too big for his mouth, legs too weak for his
body, and lifeless, buglike eyes that rolled around inside his head.
He pranced about in padded green clothing, with a hunting horn
rather than a sword dangling at his side. He rode abominably,

swore horribly and wrote some of the dullest treatises of all time. Many people, among them the author Charles Dickens, would have us believe that the only son of Mary the MERMAID was a complete and utter buffoon and an impossible pedant. This is an unnecessarily harsh portrait. That said, his character did contain shocking defects:

- He was outstandingly vain, and adored having courtiers grovel before him.
- He was vindictive: he hunted in a repulsive way, slaughtering his prey with a scary, furious glee.
- He was unhygienic: he never washed and as a result itched insufferably. Always sweating, sneezing or blowing his nose, he avoided water like the plague.
- He was cruel to animals: when Philip of Spain gave him five camels and an elephant, he put the camels on display in St James's Park but hid the elephant away, feeding it with a gallon of wine each day until it refused to drink water.
- He was coarse: when some of his subjects once came to pay their respects and see him face to face, he responded, 'God's wounds! I will pull down my breeches and they shall also see my arse.'

And yet James was no fool. As a young man he studied Greek, French and Latin, and he regularly consulted his library of classical and religious writings. Narrow-minded he may have been, yet he was still able to quote Aristotle freely, expound at great length on his favourite topic, witchcraft, and write poetry, political treatises and translations of some thirty psalms. Aware of his learned background, the duke of Sully, French envoy to the English court, dubbed him 'the Wisest Fool in Europe', but when the King James Version of the Bible appeared, a translation commissioned at James's behest, the epithet was broadened to 'the Wisest Fool in Christendom'.

¶ *James the* Wisest Fool in Europe
see James the WISEST FOOL IN CHRISTENDOM

¶ *Eleanor the* Witty
Eleanor 'Nell' Gwyn, mistress of King Charles II of England, 1650–87

Of all the mistresses of Charles the MERRY MONARCH – and there were many – the public took only one to their hearts, namely the petite, brown-eyed and high-spirited Nell Gwyn.

After a childhood serving brandy in a brothel and selling oranges at the Drury Lane Theatre in London, Nell worked as a comedienne until she left the stage for Charles in 1669. Her infectious wit and gleeful lewdness won her a host of nicknames and the acclaim of a public otherwise cool to the monarch's paramours. Many knew her as 'Sweet Nell', others as 'Pretty Witty Nell', while the scholar Robert Whitcomb described her as having the beauty of Venus, spirit of Hercules, wisdom of Apollo and wit of Mercury. Such extravagant praise must have softened the pain of her less flattering epithets, 'Puddle-Nell' and 'the Protestant Whore'.

Nell had an extravagant lifestyle – she bought her house on fashionable Pall Mall in cash – and by the time of Charles's death she was universally in debt. Aware of this, the king, on his deathbed, begged his brother to 'not let poor Nelly starve', and so she was given a modest annual income until her own death from a stroke when in her late thirties.

¶ *John the* Wizard
John III, king of Poland, 1629–96

John III, or John Sobieski, is a Polish hero most famous for his rescue of Vienna from a Turkish invading force in the late summer of 1683. With the Turks heading his way, the pusillani mous emperor 'Leopold the Great' (*see* GREAT . . . BUT

NOT THAT GREAT) skulked off to his Bavarian fortress, leaving the Viennese to their fate. But up stepped John, with his large moustache, diamond-encrusted fur cap and, as always, a scimitar strapped to his side. On 12 September, with his force of some 70,000 men, John routed the 'infidel' and wrote a message to the pope: '*Veni, Vidi, Deus Vicit*' – 'I came, I saw, God conquered.' The Turks simply could not understand how they had lost,

John the Wizard

and named John 'the Wizard' in the belief that he possessed supernatural powers.

Sobieski may have relieved Vienna, but he proved unable to extract any tangible benefits for Poland from the victory. Possessing little of the ambition of Louis the SUN KING or the conquering spirit of Peter the GREAT, the wizard simply lacked the magic needed to prevent his homeland from tumbling into vassalage after his death.

¶ *Alexander the* Wolf of Badenoch
Alexander Stewart, lord of Badenoch, 1343–*c*.1405

When the bishop of Moray censured the lord of Badenoch for adultery, he cannot possibly have expected Alexander's reaction. With a posse of Gaelic thugs Alexander ransacked the town of Forres before moving on to Elgin and burning the cathedral to the ground. As a result, the lupine lord, elsewhere known as 'Big Alexander', was excommunicated. A fictional account of the unsavoury exploits and amorous adventures of Alexander the Wolf of Badenoch can be found in a novel of the same name by the Victorian author Thomas Lauder. Readers may also wish to peruse some of Lauder's other works, including 'Account of a

Toad Found in the Trunk of a Beech' and 'An Account of the Worm with which the Stickleback is Infested'.

¶ *Frederick the* Wonder of the World
Frederick II, king of Germany and Holy Roman Emperor, 1194–1250

'Covered with red hair . . . bald and short-sighted. Had he been a slave, he would not have fetched 200 dirhams at market.' This first-hand description of Frederick by the Syrian historian Ibn al-Jawz suggests that the emperor, given his appearance, was of little value. But looks can deceive. Frederick was in fact one of the most remarkable of all medieval rulers.

Even his birth and upbringing were remarkable. In order to stop any dispute as to his legitimacy, Constance of Sicily gave birth to him publicly in a market-place. Both Constance and Frederick's father, Henry the CRUEL, died before Frederick was four years old, and he came under the guardianship of Pope Innocent III. The pontiff, however, neglected him and Frederick spent much of his childhood roaming the streets of Rome like an urchin. At the age of fourteen he was cleaned up and married to the daughter of the king of Aragon.

After his coronation two years later Frederick stayed in Sicily when he wasn't on crusade. It is here, in his island kingdom, that his reputation as the 'Stupor Mundi' – 'the Wonder', or more accurately 'the Astonishment of the World' – was cultivated. Among his many achievements, Frederick:

- could speak nine languages and was literate in seven;
- wrote poetry of considerable merit;
- compiled a manual on the art of falconry and wrote the first modern book on ornithology;
- introduced the concept of zero to European arithmetic;
- founded the University of Naples;
- issued regulations on the practice of pharmacy throughout Europe; and

- published a collection of laws for his realm. With minor modifications this work, known as the *Liber Augustalis*, remained the basis of Sicilian law well into the nineteenth century.

But Frederick did have his critics. An Italian contemporary called Salimbene wrote that, while he admired the emperor immensely, there were certain aspects of his character that he found distasteful. Cruelty was one of them. Once, for example, he cut off the thumb of a notary who had spelt his name 'Fredericus' instead of 'Fridericus'. The king was also prone to engage in macabre experiments in which humans were the guinea pigs. Here are just three of these investigations:

- He gave two men supper and then sent one to bed and the other out to hunt. After a few hours he brought them back to his court and had them disembowelled in his presence to see which one had digested the food more rapidly (apparently it was the former).
- He locked convicted criminals in an airtight room until they suffocated, and then, as he opened the door, looked for evidence of their souls escaping.
- In his search to see if humans are born with a 'natural' language, he abandoned several babies in the wild to grow up without human contact. The children all died.

It was the Church, however, who condemned the emperor with greatest fury. Although a Christian, Frederick denounced Jesus as a fraud, mocked many fundamental doctrines and maintained a harem. Many of his fellow believers denounced him as 'the Hammer of Christianity'. Pope Gregory IX went further, excommunicating him twice and calling him 'the Antichrist'.

❡ *Elizabeth the* World's Wonder *see* GOOD QUEEN BESS

¶ *Wenceslas the* Worthless

Wenceslas, king of Germany and Bohemia, 1361–1419

This Wenceslas was in power some 400 years after the 'Good King Wenceslas' of carol fame, who was duke of Bohemia in the tenth century. As periods in European history go, the end of the fourteenth century was downright awful. In Germany the worthless Wenceslas held sway, Charles the SILLY ruled France, Richard the COXCOMB flapped about in England and two popes, one in Rome and the other in Avignon, were discrediting each other. Of all those in supreme authority at the time, however, Wenceslas deserves special mention as the most contemptible. Here, in no particular order, are ten reasons why he deserved his nickname.

- He extracted revenue through arbitrary fines.
- He was constantly enmeshed in bitter family rivalries.
- He angered Church leaders in Bohemia, not least when he orchestrated the drowning of the vicar general of Prague in the River Moldau.
- He promoted totally inexperienced friends to senior governmental positions, thereby infuriating the Bohemian nobility.
- He failed conspicuously to keep the peace in either Germany or Bohemia.
- He failed to heal the Great Schism within the papacy, and even failed to remain constant to one side.
- He failed to achieve imperial coronation.
- He routinely drank to excess, earning himself the additional nickname 'the Drunkard'.
- He murdered his wife by setting a dog on her.
- He allegedly roasted his cook alive for serving up a ragout that Wenceslas deemed second-rate.

Europe became a slightly brighter place when, eventually deposed by his half-brother Sigismund the LIGHT OF THE WORLD, Wenceslas died, mercifully without any heirs.

[Y]

¶ *Charles the* Young Pretender *see* BONNIE PRINCE CHARLIE

[Z]

¶ Zeus-Ammon *see* Alexander the GREAT

List of Entries by First Name

[**A**]

Abdul Hamid II, sultan of the Ottoman Empire, 1842–1918
The DAMNED
Bloody Abdul

Abu Bakr, Muslim caliph, c.573–634
The UPRIGHT
The Father of the Maiden
The Truthful

Agnes, countess of Dunbar and March, c.1312–69
BLACK AGNES

Akbar, emperor of India, 1542–1605
The GREAT
The Guardian of Mankind

Albert, prince consort of Queen Victoria of the United Kingdom, 1819–61
The GOOD

Albert II, duke of Austria, 1289–1358
The LAME
The Wise

Albert III, duke of Austria, 1349–95
The ASTROLOGER
Albert with the Tress
The Braided

Albertus Magnus, German nobleman, c.1200–1280
The GREAT
Le Petit Albert

Alexander II, emperor of Russia, 1818–81
The EMANCIPATOR
Little Father

Alexander III, king of Macedonia, 356–323 BC
The GREAT
Macedonia's Madman
The Two-Horned
Zeus-Ammon

Alexander III, king of Scotland, 1241–86
The GLORIOUS

Alexander Stewart, lord of Badenoch, 1343–c.1405
The WOLF OF BADENOCH
Big Alexander

Alfonso I, king of Portugal, *c.*1109–85
The CONQUEROR

Alfonso II, king of Asturias, 759–842
The CHASTE

Alfonso IV, king of Asturias and León, d. 933
The MONK

Alfonso IV, king of Portugal, 1291–1357
The FIERCE

Alfonso X, king of Castile and León, 1221–84
The ASTRONOMER
The Learned
The Philosopher
The Wise

Alfred, king of Wessex, 849–99
The GREAT

Alfred d'Orsay, French nobleman, 1801–52
The LAST OF THE DANDIES

Amadeus VI, count of Savoy, 1334–83
The GREEN

Amadeus VII, count of Savoy, 1360–91
The RED

Amadeus VIII, duke of Savoy, 1383–1451

The PACIFIC
The Hermit of La Ripaille

Anne, duke of Joyeuse, 1561–87
The KING'S KING

Anne Boleyn, queen of England, *c.*1507–36
The GREAT WHORE
Anne of a Thousand Days

Anne, queen of England, 1515–57
The MARE OF FLANDERS

Anne, queen of England, 1665–1714
BRANDY NAN
Mrs Morley

Anthony, Burgundian nobleman, 1421–1504
The GREAT BASTARD
The Great

Antigonus I, king of Macedonia, 382–301 BC
The ONE-EYED

Archibald Douglas, third earl of Douglas, *c.*1328–1400
The GRIM

Archibald Douglas, fourth earl of Douglas, *c.*1369–1424
The LOSER

Archibald Douglas, fifth earl of Angus, *c.*1449–*c.*1513
BELL THE CAT

Archibald Douglas, sixth earl of Angus, *c.*1489–1557
Archibald GREYSTEEL

Aristides, Athenian statesman, *c.*530–468 BC
The JUST

Arnulf III, count of Flanders, 1055–71
The UNFORTUNATE

Arthgal, first earl of Warwick, *fl.* fifth century
The BEAR

Arthur Wellesley, duke of Wellington, 1769–1852
The IRON DUKE
Beaky
Conky
The Great Duke
Old Nosey
The Saviour of the Nations

Athelfleda, queen of England, d. *c.*964
The WHITE DUCK
The Little White Duck

Athelstan, king of the English, 895–939
The GLORIOUS

Attila, king of the Huns, 406–53
The SCOURGE OF GOD
The Terror of the World

Aud, Norse queen, *fl.* 850s
The DEEP-MINDED

Augustus II, king of Poland, 1670–1733
The STRONG

Aurelian, Roman emperor, 214–75
The RESTORER OF THE WORLD
The Greatest Goth
The Restorer of the Orient

[**B**]

Baldwin IV, king of Jerusalem, 1161–85
The LEPER

Basil II, Byzantine emperor, *c.*957–1025
The SLAYER OF THE BULGARS

Bejazet I, sultan of the Turks, 1347–1403
The THUNDERBOLT
Lightning

Bertrada, queen of the Franks, *c.*720–83
Bertha BIGFOOT
Queen Goosefoot

Boleslav III, prince of Poland, 1085–1138
The CROOKED-MOUTHED

Boleslav IV, prince of Poland, *c.*1120–73
The CURLY

Boleslav V, prince of Poland, 1226–79
The BASHFUL
The Chaste

[C]

Casimir III, king of Poland, 1310–70
The GREAT
The Peasants' King

Catherine II, empress of Russia, 1729–96
The GREAT
The Little Mother of All the Russians
The Modern Messalina

Charles I, duke of Burgundy, 1433–77
The BOLD
The Audacious

Charles, mayor of the palace of Austrasia, c.688–741
The HAMMER

Charles I, king of England, 1600–1649
The LAST MAN
The Man of Blood
The Martyr

Charles I (Charlemagne), king of the Franks and Lombards and Holy Roman Emperor, c.742–814
The GREAT

Charles II, king of England, 1630–85
The MERRY MONARCH
The Black Boy
The Blackbird
Old Rowley
The Son of the Last Man

Charles II, king of France, 823–77
The BALD
The Most Christian King

Charles II, king of Spain, 1661–1700
The BEWITCHED

Charles III, Frankish king and Holy Roman Emperor, 839–88
The FAT
Little Charles

Charles IV, king of France, 1294–1328
The FAIR

Charles IV, king of Germany and Bohemia and Holy Roman Emperor, 1316–78
The PARSON'S EMPEROR
The Pope's Errand-Boy

Charles V, Holy Roman Emperor, 1500–1558
The HARLEQUIN
A Discrowned Glutton
A Second Charlemagne

Charles VI, king of France, 1368–1422

The SILLY
The Mad
The Well-Beloved

Charles VIII, king of France,
1470–98
The AFFABLE
The Scourge of God

Charles XII, king of Sweden,
1682–1718
The MADMAN OF THE NORTH
The Alexander of the North

Charles Seymour, sixth duke
of Somerset, 1662–1748
The PROUD DUKE

Charles Edward Stuart,
pretender to the English
throne, 1720–88
BONNIE PRINCE CHARLIE
The Highland Laddie
The Young Pretender

Childeric III, Merovingian
king, d. 755
The STUPID

Christian II, king of
Denmark, Norway and
Sweden, 1481–1559
The TYRANT
The Cruel
The Nero of the North

Christian III, king of
Denmark, 1503–59
The FATHER OF HIS PEOPLE

Christina, queen of Sweden,
1626–89
The MIRACLE OF NATURE

Christopher III, king of
Denmark, Norway and
Sweden, 1418–48
The KING OF BARK

Claude, queen consort of
Francis I of France, 1499–1524
The HANDSOME QUEEN

Clovis I, Merovingian king,
c.466–511
The GREAT

Clovis II, Merovingian king,
c.634–57
The DO-NOTHING KING

Constantine I, emperor of
Rome, c.280–337
The GREAT

Constantine III, king of
Scotland, d. 997
The BALD

Cyrus II, Persian ruler,
c.585–c.529 BC
The GREAT

[**D**]

David, king of Georgia,
1073–1125
The BUILDER

David Kalakaua, king of
Hawaii, 1836–91
The MERRY MONARCH
The Last King of Paradise

Demetrius II, king of Georgia,
1269–89
The DEVOTED
The Man Who Sacrificed His
    Head

Denis, king of Portugal,
1261–1325
The FARMER

Diana, princess of Wales,
1961–97
The PEOPLE'S PRINCESS
The Queen of Hearts

Donald III, king of Scotland,
c.1033–99
The WHITE

Duncan I, king of Scotland,
c.1001–40
The GRACIOUS

[**E**]

Edgar, king of England,
c.1052–c.1125
The OUTLAW
The Atheling

Edgar, king of the English,
c.943–75
The PEACEABLE
The Peacemaker

Edmund I, king of the
English, 921–46
The MAGNIFICENT
The Deed-Doer

Edmund II, king of England,
c.993–1016
Edmund IRONSIDE

Edward, king of England,
c.962–78
The MARTYR

Edward, king of England,
c.1003–66
The CONFESSOR

Edward, king of Wessex,
d. 924
The ELDER

Edward, prince of Wales,
1330–76
The BLACK PRINCE

Edward I, king of England,
1239–1307
The HAMMER OF THE SCOTS
Edward Longshanks
The English Justinian
The Father of the Mother of
    Parliaments
The Lawgiver

Edward II, king of England,
1284–1327
Edward CARNARVON

Edward III, king of England,
1312–77
The BANKRUPT

Erik IX, king of Sweden,
d. 1160
The SAINT

Erik XIV, king of Sweden,
1533–77
The ROMANTIC

Ernest, duke of Austria,
1383–1424
The IRON-HANDED

Ethelred II, king of England,
968–1016
The UNREADY

[**F**]

Ferdinand I, king of Portugal,
1345–83
The INCONSTANT
The Handsome

Ferdinand II, king of Aragon,
1452–1516
The CATHOLIC

Ferdinand II, king of the Two
Sicilies, 1810–59
BOMBA

Ferdinand IV, king of Castile
and León, 1285–1312
The SUMMONED

Francis, second duke of Guise,
1519–63
The SCARRED

Francis I, king of France,
1494–1547
The FATHER OF LETTERS
The Maecenas of France

Frederick I, king of Germany
and Holy Roman Emperor,
c.1123–90
BARBAROSSA
The Father of His Country

Frederick II, king of Germany
and Holy Roman Emperor,
1194–1250
The WONDER OF THE WORLD
The Antichrist
The Hammer of Christianity

Frederick II, king of Prussia,
1712–86
The GREAT
Alaric-Cotin
Old Fritz
The Sand Dealer

Frederick II, margrave of
Brandenburg, 1413–71
Frederick IRONTOOTH

Frederick III, elector of
Saxony, 1463–1525
The WISE
The Hesitater
The Learned

Frederick IV, duke of Austria,
1384–1439
The PENNILESS

Frederick V, elector Palatine
and king of Bohemia,
1596–1632
The WINTER KING
The Snow King

Frederick Louis, prince of
Wales, 1707–51
POOR FRED
Griff

Frederick William IV, king of
Prussia, 1795–1861
CLICQUOT

Fulk III, count of Anjou,
c.970–1040
The BLACK

Fulk IV, count of Anjou,
1043–1109
The SURLY

Fyodor I, tsar of Russia,
1557–98
The BELLRINGER

[**G**]

Geoffrey V, count of Anjou,
1113–51
Geoffrey PLANTAGENET

George, prince of Denmark,
1653–1703
EST-IL-POSSIBLE?

George I, king of England,
1660–1727
The TURNIP-HOER

George II, king of England,
1683–1760
The GREAT PATRON OF
MANKIND

George III, king of England,
1738–1820
FARMER GEORGE
The Button-Maker

George IV, king of England,
1762–1830
The BEAU OF PRINCES
The Fat Adonis at Fifty
The Fat Adonis at Forty
The Prince of Whales
Prinny

George V, king of England,
1865–1936
The SAILOR PRINCE

Godred, king of Man and
Dublin, c.1040–95
WHITE HANDS

Gorm, king of Denmark,
d. c.958
The OLD

Götz von Berlichingen,
German knight, 1480–1562
IRON-HAND

[**H**]

Haakon I, king of Norway,
c.920–c.961
The GOOD

Haakon II, king of Norway,
*c.*1147–62
The BROAD-SHOULDERED

Haile Sellassie I, emperor of
Ethiopia, 1892–1975
The LION OF JUDAH

Halfdan III, king of Norway,
d. *c.*860
The BLACK

Harald, king of the Danes,
*c.*910–*c.*985
Harald BLUETOOTH

Harald I, earl of Orkney,
d. 1131
The SMOOTH TALKER

Harold, king of Norway,
*c.*860–*c.*940
Harold FAIRHAIR
Shockhead

Harold I, king of England,
d. 1040
Harold HAREFOOT

Harold II, king of England,
*c.*1020–66
The LAST OF THE SAXONS

Haroun al-Rashid, caliph
of the Abbasid dynasty,
*c.*766–809
The JUST

Heneage Finch, first earl of
Nottingham, 1621–82
The DISMAL

Henry, prince of Portugal,
1394–1460
The NAVIGATOR

Henry, prince of Wales,
1594–1612
OUR ENGLISH MARCELLUS

Henry I, count of
Champagne, 1152–81
The LIBERAL

Henry I, duke of Guise,
1550–88
The SCARRED

Henry I, king of England,
1069–1135
Henry BEAUCLERC

Henry I, king of Germany,
*c.*876–936
The FOWLER

Henry I, king of Navarre,
*c.*1210–74
The FAT

Henry II, king of England,
1133–89
Henry CURTMANTLE

Henry II, king of France,
1519–59
The WARLIKE

Henry III, king of France,
1551–89
The MAN-MILLINER

Henry IV, king of England,
1366–1413
Henry BOLINGBROKE

Henry IV, king of France,
1553–1610
The GREAT
The King of Brave Men

Henry V, king of England,
1387–1422
The ENGLISH ALEXANDER

Henry V, king of Germany,
1086–1125
The PARRICIDE

Henry VI, king of England,
1421–71
The MARTYR
Ill-Fated Henry

Henry VI, king of Germany,
1165–97
The CRUEL

Henry VII, king of England,
1457–1509
The ENGLISH SOLOMON

Henry VIII, king of England,
1491–1547
BLUFF KING HAL
The Defender of the Faith
Old Copper Nose

Henry Percy, English
nobleman, 1364–1403
Harry HOTSPUR

Hereward, Saxon thane,
fl. eleventh century
The WAKE

Hugh, Lord of Douglas,
1294–1342
The DULL

Humphrey, duke of
Gloucester, 1391–1447
GOOD DUKE HUMPHREY

Hywel ap Gruffyth, Sir, Welsh
nobleman, b. *c.*1284
Hywel of the HORSESHOES

Hywel, king of Wales,
*c.*882–950
The GOOD

[**I**]

Isabella, queen of Castile and
Aragon, 1451–1504
The CATHOLIC

Isabella, queen consort of
Charles VI of France,
1371–1435
The GREAT SOW

Isabella, wife of King
Edward II of England,
1292–1358
The SHE-WOLF OF FRANCE

Ivan IV, tsar of Russia,
1530–84
The TERRIBLE
The Awesome

Ivar, king of Dublin and York, c.794–872
The BONELESS

Iyasu I, emperor of Ethiopia, d. 1706
The GREAT

[**J**]

James I, king of England, and VI, king of Scotland, 1566–1625
The WISEST FOOL IN CHRISTENDOM
The Wisest Fool in Europe

James II, king of England and Ireland, and VII, king of Scotland, 1633–1701
The POPISH DUKE

James II, king of Scotland, 1430–60
The FIERY FACE

James IV, king of Scotland, 1473–1513
The THISTLE

James V, king of Scotland, 1512–42
The ILL-BELOVED
The King of the Commons

James Douglas, Scottish nobleman, 1286–1330
The BLACK DOUGLAS
The Good Sir James

James Douglas, second earl of Douglas, c.1358–88
The DEAD MAN WHO WON A FIGHT

James Douglas, seventh earl of Douglas, c.1371–1443
The GROSS

James Scott, first duke of Monmouth, 1649–85
The PROTESTANT DUKE

James Stewart, first earl of Moray, c.1531–70
The GOOD REGENT

James Stewart, second earl of Moray, d. 1592
The BONNY EARL

James Stuart, pretender to the English throne, 1688–1766
The WARMING-PAN BABY
Le Chevalier de St George
The Old Pretender

Jamshid, king of Persia, fl. eighth century BC
The ILLUSTRIOUS

Jane Grey, queen of England, 1537–54
The NINE DAYS' QUEEN

Joan, countess of Kent, 1328–85
The FAIR MAID OF KENT

Joan, queen of Castile and Aragon, 1479–1555
The MAD

Joan, queen of Scotland, 1321–62
Joan MAKEPEACE

John, duke of Bedford, 1389–1435
John with the LEADEN SWORD

John, duke of Burgundy, 1371–1419
The FEARLESS

John, duke of Lancaster, 1340–99
John of GAUNT

John, Irish nobleman, *fl.* ninth century
The SCOT

John, king of England, 1167–1216
John LACKLAND
Dollheart
Softsword

John I, king of France, 1316
The POSTHUMOUS

John II, king of France, 1319–64
The GOOD

John II, king of Portugal, 1455–95
The PERFECT
The Tyrant

John III, king of Poland, 1629–96
The WIZARD

John Balliol, king of Scotland, 1249–1315
TOOM TABARD

John Churchill, first duke of Marlborough, 1650–1722
The SILLY DUKE
The Handsome Englishman

John Zisca, Bohemian reformer, 1360–1424
The ONE-EYED

[**K**]

Kamehameha I, king of Hawaii, 1758–1819
The GREAT
The Napoleon of the Pacific

[**L**]

Ladislaus I, king of Poland, *c.*1260–1333
The ELBOW-HIGH

Leo II, Roman emperor of the East, *c.*401–74
The BUTCHER

Llewellyn, king of Gwynedd, *c.*1173–1240
The GREAT

Louis, margrave of Thuringia, 1042–1128
The SPRINGER

Louis I, king of France and
Holy Roman Emperor,
778–840
The PIOUS

Louis IV, king of the east
Franks, 893–911
The CHILD

Louis IV, king of France,
921–54
The FOREIGNER

Louis V, king of France,
967–87
The INDOLENT
The Sluggard

Louis VI, king of France,
1081–1137
The FAT

Louis VIII, king of France,
1187–1226
The LION
A Reborn Alexander

Louis IX, king of France,
1214–70
The SAINT
The Solomon of France

Louis X, king of France,
1289–1316
The QUARRELLER
The Stubborn

Louis XI, king of France,
1423–83
The UNIVERSAL SPIDER

Louis XII, king of France,
1462–1515
The FATHER OF THE PEOPLE

Louis XIII, king of France,
1601–43
The JUST

Louis XIV, king of France,
1638–1715
The SUN KING

Louis XV, king of France,
1710–74
The WELL-BELOVED

Louis XVI, king of France,
1754–93
The BAKER
The Locksmith King
Monsieur Veto

Louis XVIII, king of France,
1755–1824
The KING OF SLOPS
The Bread-Soup King
Bungy Louis
The Desired

Louis Philip I, king of France,
1773–1850
The CITIZEN KING
The King of the Barricades

Lulach, king of Scotland,
c.1031–58
The FOOL
The Simpleton

[M]

Magnus I, king of Norway
and Denmark, 1024–47
The GOOD

Magnus III, king of Norway,
c.1073–1103
Magnus BARELEGS

Magnus VI, king of Norway,
1238–80
The LAW-MENDER

Malcolm III, king of Scotland,
c.1031–93
Malcolm BIGHEAD

Malcolm IV, king of Scotland,
1141–65
The MAIDEN

Manuel I, king of Portugal,
1469–1521
The FORTUNATE
The Grocer King

Margaret of Valois, queen of
France, 1553–1615
QUEEN VENUS

Margaret, queen-elect of
Scotland, 1283–90
The MAID OF NORWAY

Maria Louisa, queen of Spain,
1751–1819
DONA JUANA

Maria Theresa, archduchess of
Austria and queen of Hungary
and Bohemia, 1717–80
The MOTHER OF HER
COUNTRY

Marie Antoinette, queen
consort of France, 1755–93
The BAKER'S WIFE
The Austrian Wench
Madame Deficit
Madame Veto

Mary, queen of Scotland,
1542–87
The MERMAID
The White Queen

Mary, second wife of King
James II of England, 1658–1718
The QUEEN OF TEARS

Mary I, queen of England,
1516–58
BLOODY MARY

Mehmed II, sultan of the
Ottoman Empire, 1432–81
The CONQUEROR

Merfyn, king of Gwynedd,
c.780–844
The FRECKLED

Michael III, Byzantine
emperor, 838–67
The DRUNKARD

Michael V, Byzantine
emperor, d. c.1042
The CAULKER

[N]

Napoleon Bonaparte, emperor of the French, 1769–1821
The LITTLE CORPORAL
Boney
The Corsican General
The Eagle
The Nightmare of Europe
Tiddy-Doll
The Violet Corporal

Napoleon François Bonaparte, titular king of Rome, 1811–32
The EAGLET

Nicholas I, tsar of Russia, 1796–1855
The IRON TSAR
The Gendarme of Europe

[O]

Oliver Cromwell, Lord Protector of the Commonwealth, 1599–1658
NOSE ALMIGHTY
Copper Nose
Crum-Hell
King Oliver
Nosey
Old Ironsides
Old Noll
Ruby Nose

Omar I, second caliph, c.581–644
The COMMANDER OF THE FAITHFUL

Osman I, founder of the Ottoman Empire, 1259–1326
The VICTORIOUS

Otto, duke of Austria, d. 1339
The JOLLY

Otto, king of Bavaria, 1848–1916
The MAD

Otto II, king of Germany and Holy Roman Emperor, 955–83
The BLOODY
The Red
Rufus

[P]

Paul II, earl of Orkney, d. c.1138
The SILENT

Pepin, Frankish prince, d. 811
The HUNCHBACK

Pepin III, king of the Franks, c.714–68
The SHORT

Peter I, king of Portugal, 1320–67
The CRUEL
The Just

Peter I, tsar of Russia, 1672–1725
The GREAT

Peter IV, king of Aragon,
1319–87
The CEREMONIOUS
Peter of the Dagger

Philaretos, Byzantine
nobleman, 702–92
The MERCIFUL

Philip I, duke of Orléans,
1747–93
CITIZEN EQUITY

Philip I, king of Castile,
1478–1506
The HANDSOME

Philip I, king of France,
1052–1108
The AMOROUS

Philip II, duke of Burgundy,
1342–1404
The BOLD

Philip II, duke of Orléans,
1674–1723
The GODLESS REGENT

Philip II, king of France,
1165–1223
The MAGNANIMOUS
Philip Augustus

Philip II, king of Spain,
1527–98
The PRUDENT

Philip III, duke of Burgundy,
1396–1467
The GOOD

Philip III, king of France,
1245–85
The BOLD
The Daring

Philip IV, king of France,
1268–1314
The FAIR

Philip VI, king of France,
1293–1350
The LUCKY

Ptolemy I, king of Egypt,
c.367–c.283 BC
The SAVIOUR

Ptolemy II, king of Egypt,
308–246 BC
The BROTHER-LOVING

Ptolemy III, king of Egypt,
282–211 BC
The BENEFACTOR

Ptolemy IV, king of Egypt,
c.238–205 BC
The LOVER OF HIS FATHER

Ptolemy V, king of Egypt,
c.210–180 BC
The ILLUSTRIOUS

Ptolemy VI, king of Egypt,
c.180–145 BC
The LOVER OF HIS MOTHER

Ptolemy VII, king of Egypt,
d. 144 BC
The NEW LOVER OF HIS
FATHER

Ptolemy VIII, king of Egypt, d. 116 BC
The POT-BELLIED
The Benefactor
Fatso
The Malefactor

Ptolemy IX, king of Egypt, d. 81 BC
The CHICKPEA
Fatso

Ptolemy X, king of Egypt, d. 88 BC
The SON OF A BITCH

Ptolemy XI, king of Egypt, d. 80 BC
ALEXANDER II

Ptolemy XII, king of Egypt, c.112–51 BC
The FLUTE PLAYER

[R]

Ramiro II, king of Aragon, d. 1154
The MONK

René I, duke of Anjou and king of Sicily, 1409–80
GOOD KING RENÉ

Richard, son of Gilbert de Clare, second earl of Pembroke, d. 1176
STRONGBOW

Richard I, king of England, 1157–99
The LIONHEART

Richard II, king of England, 1367–1400
The COXCOMB

Richard III, king of England, 1452–85
Richard CROOKBACK

Richard Cromwell, English statesman, 1626–1712
QUEEN DICK

Richard Neville, sixteenth earl of Warwick, 1428–71
The KINGMAKER

Robert, duke of Apulia, c.1015–85
The CUNNING
The Weasel

Robert I, king of Scotland, 1274–1329
The BRUCE

Robert II, duke of Normandy, c.1054–1134
Robert CURTHOSE
Gambaron

Robert II, king of France, c.970–1031
The PIOUS

Robert II, king of Scotland,
1316–90
The STEWARD
Auld Blearie

Robert III, king of Scotland,
c.1337–1406
JOHN OF YESTERYEAR

Robert Devereux, second earl
of Essex, 1567–1601
The ENGLISH ACHILLES

Roger I, count of Sicily,
1031–1101
The GREAT COUNT
The Terror of the Faithless

Rosamund Clifford, mistress
of King Henry II of England,
c.1140–c.1176
FAIR ROSAMUND

Rudolph II, Holy Roman
Emperor, 1552–1612
The PRINCE OF ALCHEMY

Rupert, prince of the
Palatinate, 1619–82
The MAD CAVALIER

[S]

Saladin, Saracen leader,
c.1138–93
The CHIVALROUS SARACEN

Sancho I, king of Castile and
Léon, d. 967
The FAT

Sancho I, king of Portugal,
1154–1211
The SETTLER

Sarah Jennings, first duchess
of Marlborough, 1660–1744
QUEEN SARAH
Mrs Freeman

Sigismund, Holy Roman
Emperor, 1368–1437
The LIGHT OF THE WORLD
The Red Demon

Sigurd I, earl of Orkney,
d. 892
The MIGHTY

Sigurd I, king of Norway,
c.1089–1130
The CRUSADER

Sigurd II, earl of Orkney,
d. 1014
The STOUT

Sitric, king of Dublin and
York, d. 927
The SQUINT-EYED

Sophia Charlotte, mistress of
King George I of England,
1675–1725
The ELEPHANT

Suleiman I, sultan of the
Ottoman Empire, 1495–1566
The MAGNIFICENT
The Lawgiver

Sven I, king of Denmark and England, *c.*960–1014
Sven FORKBEARD

[**T**]

Theobald, king of Navarre, 1201–53
The TROUBADOUR

Theodosius I, Roman emperor of the East and West, 347–95
The GREAT

Thomas Cromwell, first earl of Essex, *c.*1485–1540
The HAMMER OF THE MONKS

Thorstein, Norse king of Scotland, d. 900
The RED

[**V**]

Victor Emmanuel II, king of Italy, 1820–78
The GALLANT KING
Guaff

Victoria, queen of the United Kingdom, 1819–1901
The WIDOW OF WINDSOR
The Grandmother of Europe
Mrs Brown

Vlad Tepes, prince of Wallachia, *c.*1431–76
The IMPALER
Dracula

[**W**]

Waldemar II, king of Denmark, 1170–1241
The VICTORIOUS

Wenceslas, king of Germany and Bohemia, 1361–1419
The WORTHLESS
The Drunkard

Wilfrid, founding father of Catalan political independence, d. 897
The SHAGGY
The Hairy

William, count of Apulia, d. 1046
The IRON ARM

William I, king of England, *c.*1028–87
The CONQUEROR
The Bastard

William I, king of Scotland, 1143–1214
The LION

William I, king of Sicily, 1120–66
The BAD

William I, prince of Orange, 1533–84
The SILENT
The Father of the Fatherland

William II, king of England,
*c.*1056–1100
William RUFUS

William IV, king of England,
1765–1837
The SAILOR KING
Silly Billy

William Douglas, fourth duke
of Queensbury, 1724–1810
The RAKE OF PICCADILLY
Old Q

Wu Hou, empress of China,
625–705
Lady Wu the POISONER
Divine Sovereign
Holy Mother

[**Y**]

Yung-cheng, emperor of
China, 1678–1735
The IMMORTAL

[**Z**]

Zenobia, queen of Palmyra, *fl.*
third century
The QUEEN OF THE EAST

Bibliography

R. Absalom, *Italy since 1800: A Nation in the Balance?* (London: Longman, 1995).

R. Andrews, *The Columbia Dictionary of Quotations* (New York: Columbia University Press, 1993).

M. Ashley, *The Life and Times of William I* (London: Weidenfeld & Nicolson, 1973).

—, *The Mammoth Book of British Kings and Queens* (London: Constable & Robinson, 1998).

R. Barber, *Edward, Prince of Wales and Aquitaine: A Biography of the Black Prince* (Woodbridge: The Boydell Press, 2003).

F. Barlow, *William Rufus* (London: Methuen, 1983).

C. Barnett, *Bonaparte* (Ware, Hertfordshire: Wordsworth, 1997).

C. L. Barnhart (ed.), *The New Century Cyclopedia of Names* (New York: Appleton-Century-Crofts, 1954).

R. Bartlett, *The Making of Europe: Conquest, Colonization and Cultural Change 950–1350* (London: Penguin, 1994).

—, *England Under the Norman and Angevin Kings, 1075–1225* (Oxford: Oxford University Press, 2000).

H. Belloc, *Characters of the Reformation: Historical Portraits of 23 Men and Women and Their Place in the Great Religious Revolution of the 16th Century* (Rockford, IL: TAN Books and Publishers, 1992).

G. Benecke, *Maximilian I (1459–1519): An Analytical Biography* (London: Routledge & Kegan Paul, 1982).

V. L. Benes and N. G. J. Pounds, *Poland* (London: Ernest Benn, 1970).

L. E. Berry and R. O. Crumney (eds.), *Rude & Barbarous Kingdom: Russia in the Accounts of Sixteenth-Century English Voyagers* (Madison: University of Wisconsin Press, 1968).

M. R. Best and F. H. Brightman (eds.), *The Book of Secrets of Albertus Magnus* (Oxford: Oxford University Press, 1973).

B. Bevan, *Henry IV* (London: The Rubicon Press, 1994).

—, *King William III: Prince of Orange, the First European* (London: The Rubicon Press, 1997).

C. Bingham, *James V: King of Scots, 1512–1542* (London: Collins, 1971).

—, *The Stewart Kingdom of Scotland 1371–1603* (London: Weidenfeld & Nicolson, 1974).

—, *James VI of Scotland* (London: Weidenfeld & Nicolson, 1979).

T. N. Bisson, *The Medieval Crown of Aragon: A Short History* (Oxford: Oxford University Press, 1986).

H. Bolitho, *Albert: Prince Consort* (London: David Bruce & Watson, 1970).

S. Bradford, *King George VI* (London: Weidenfeld & Nicolson, 1989).

E. C. Brewer, *Historic Note-Book with an Appendix of Battles* (London: Smith, Elder, 1891).

R. Briggs, *Early Modern France: 1560–1715*, 2nd edn (Oxford: Oxford University Press, 1998).

P. H. Brown, *A Short History of Scotland*, new edn ed. H. W. Meikle (Edinburgh: Oliver & Boyd, 1951).

D. Buisseret, *Henry IV* (London: Allen & Unwin, 1984).

R. Burek (ed.), *Poland: An Encyclopedic Guide* (Warsaw: Polish Scientific Publishers, 2000).

A. Burn, *Persia and the Greeks: The Defence of the West, c. 546–478 BC*, 2nd edn (London: Duckworth, 1970).

A. Cameron and P. Garnsey (eds.), *The Cambridge Ancient History: Volume XIII, The Late Empire, A.D. 337–425* (Cambridge: Cambridge University Press, 1998).

T. Carlyle, *Early Kings in Norway* (New York: Merrill & Baker, n.d.).

R. Chamberlin, *Charlemagne: Emperor of the Western World* (London: Grafton, 1986).

P. Champion, *Louis XI*, trans. W. S. Whale (London: Cassell, 1929).

D. G. Chandler, *Napoleon* (Barnsley: Leo Cooper, 2001).

C. E. Chapman, *A History of Spain: Founded on the Historia de España y de la Civilización Española of Rafael Altamira* (New York: The Free Press, 1965).

R. D. Charques, *A Short History of Russia* (London: Phoenix, 1956).

Ching Ping and D. Bloodworth, *The Chinese Machiavelli: 3000 Years of Chinese Statecraft* (London: Secker & Warburg, 1976).

T. Claydon, *William III* (Harlow: Pearson Education, 2002).

I. Cloulas, *Charles VII et le mirage italien* (Paris: Albin Michael, 1986).

R. Collins, *The Arab Conquest of Spain, 710–797* (Oxford: Blackwell, 1989).

—, *Early Medieval Spain: Unity in Diversity, 400–1000*, 2nd edn (Basingstoke: Macmillan, 1995).

A. Comnena, *The Alexiad: Being the History of the Reign of Her Father, Alexius I, Emperor of the Romans, 1081–1118 A.D.*, trans. E. A. S. Dawes (London: Kegan Paul, Trench, Turner, 1928).

C. Cook, *Macmillan Dictionary of Historical Terms*, 2nd edn (London and Basingstoke: Macmillan, 1989).

M. A. Cook, *A History of the Ottoman Empire to 1730* (Cambridge: Cambridge University Press, 1976).

C. Cope, *Phoenix Frustrated: The Lost Kingdom of Burgundy* (London: Constable, 1986).

F. J. Coppa (ed.), *Dictionary of Modern Italian History* (Westport, CT: Greenwood Press, 1985).

H. B. Cotterill, *Medieval Italy during a Thousand Years (305–1313)* (London: George G. Harrap, 1915).

E. L. Cox, *The Green Count of Savoy: Amadeus VI and Transalpine Savoy in the Fourteenth Century* (Princeton: Princeton University Press, 1967).

D. Crystal (ed.), *The Cambridge Biographical Encyclopaedia*, 2nd edn (Cambridge: Cambridge University Press, 2000).

—, *The Penguin Concise Encyclopedia* (London: Penguin, 2003).

J. Danstrup, *A History of Denmark*, 2nd edn (Copenhagen: Wivels Forlag, 1947).

H. E. Davidson and P. Fisher, *Saxo Grammaticus: History of the Danes, Books I–IX* (Woodbridge: D. S. Brewer, 1980).

N. Davies, *God's Playground: A History of Poland* (New York: Columbia University Press, 1982).

A. Delahunty, *Oxford Dictionary of Nicknames* (Oxford: Oxford University Press, 2003).

A. G. Dickens, *The Courts of Europe: Politics, Patronage and Royalty – 1400–1800* (New York: McGraw Hill, 1977).

C. Dickens, *A Child's History of England* (London: J. M. Dent, 1908).

W. C. Dickinson, *Scotland: From the Earliest Times to 1603* (London: Thomas Nelson & Sons, 1961).

G. Donaldson, *Scottish Kings*, 2nd rev. edn (London: B. T. Batsford, 1977).

G. Donaldson and R. S. Morpeth, *A Dictionary of Scottish History* (Edinburgh: John Donald, 1977).

W. Doyle (ed.), *Old Regime France: 1648–1788* (Oxford: Oxford University Press, 2001).

F. R. H. du Boulay, *Germany in the Later Middle Ages* (London: The Athlone Press, 1983).

P. Dukes, *A History of Russia: Medieval, Modern, Contemporary c. 882–1996*, 3rd edn (Basingstoke: Macmillan, 1998).

A. H. Dunbar, *Scottish Kings: A Revised Chronology of Scottish History, 1005–1625* (Edinburgh: David Douglas, 1899).

P. E. Dutton, *The Politics of Dreaming in the Carolingian Empire* (Lincoln: University of Nebraska Press, 1994).

P. Earle, *The Life and Times of Henry V* (London: Weidenfeld & Nicolson, 1972).

P. B. Ebrey, *The Cambridge Illustrated History of China* (Cambridge: Cambridge University Press, 1996).

E. W. Egan, C. B. Hintz and L. F. Wise (comps. and eds.), *Kings, Rulers and Statesmen*, rev. edn (New York: Sterling, 1976).

J. H. Elliott, *Imperial Spain 1469–1716* (London: Penguin, 1990).

O. Elton (trans.), *The First Nine Books of the Danish History of Saxo Grammaticus* (London: David Nutt, 1894).

The Encyclopedia Americana, International Edition (New York: Americana Corporation, 1977).

C. Erickson, *Bloody Mary: The Life of Mary Tudor* (London: Robson, 2001).

I. H. Evans, *Brewer's Dictionary of Phrase and Fable*, new rev. edn (London: Cassell, 1981).

H. Fichtenau, *The Carolingian Empire*, trans. P. Muntz (Toronto: University of Toronto Press, 1978).

M. I. Finley, D. M. Smith and C. Duggan, *A History of Sicily* (London: Chatto & Windus, 1986).

D. J. V. Fisher, *The Anglo-Saxon Age c. 400–1042* (London: Longman, 1973).

C. P. Fitzgerald, *The Empress Wu* (London: The Cresset Press, 1968).

M. Foot, *The Pen and the Sword* (London: MacGibbon & Kee, 1957).

P. Foote and D. M. Wilson, *The Viking Achievement: The Society and Culture of Early Medieval Scandinavia* (London: Sidgwick & Jackson, 1980).

J. Foxe, *Acts and Monuments of the Church Containing the History and Sufferings of the Martyrs, Part One* (Whitefish, MT: Kessinger, 2004).

A. Fraser, *King Charles II* (London: Weidenfeld & Nicolson, 1979).

—, *Cromwell: Our Chief of Men* (London: Methuen, 1985).

C. Freeman, *Egypt, Greece and Rome: Civilizations of the Ancient Mediterranean* (Oxford: Oxford University Press, 1996).

B. Freestone, *Harrap's Book of Nicknames and Their Origins: A Comprehensive Guide to Personal Nicknames in the English-speaking World* (London: Harrap, 1990).

A. R. Frey, *Sobriquets and Nicknames* (Boston: Ticknor, 1888).

E. M. Gerli (ed.), *Medieval Iberia: An Encyclopedia* (New York: Routledge, 2003).

M. T. Gibson and J. L. Nelson (eds.), *Charles the Bald, Court and Kingdom*, 2nd rev. edn (Aldershot: Variorum, 1990).

D. E. Gould, *Historical Dictionary of Stockholm* (Lanham, MD, and London: The Scarecrow Press, 1997).

A. J. Grant, *The French Monarchy (1483–1789)* (Cambridge: Cambridge University Press, 1931).

M. Grant, *The Twelve Caesars* (London: Weidenfeld & Nicolson, 1975).

R. Gray (ed.), *The Cambridge History of Africa* (Cambridge: Cambridge University Press, 1975).

D. Green, *Queen Anne* (London: Collins, 1970).

M. Greengrass, *France in the Age of Henri IV: The Struggle for Stability* (London: Longman, 1984).

E. Gregg, *Queen Anne* (New Haven and London: Yale University Press, 2001).

A. Guérard, *The Life and Death of an Ideal: France in the Classical Age* (New York: George Braziller, 1956).

J. R. Hale, *Florence and the Medici* (London: Phoenix Press, 2001).

O. Halecki, *A History of Poland*, rev. edn (London: Routledge & Kegan Paul, 1978).

E. M. Hallam and J. Everard, *Capetian France, 987–1328*, 2nd edn (Harlow: Pearson Education, 2001).

C. Hallendorff and A. Schück, *History of Sweden*, trans. L. Yapp (London: Cassell, 1929).

B. Hamilton, *The Leper King and His Heirs: Baldwin IV and the Crusader Kingdom of Jerusalem* (Cambridge: Cambridge University Press, 2000).

J. R. Hamilton, *Alexander the Great* (London: Hutchinson, 1973).

J. S. Hamilton and P. J. Bradley (eds.), *Documenting the Past: Essays in Medieval History Presented to George Peddy Cuttino* (Woodbridge: The Boydell Press, 1989).

P. Hanks, F. Hodges, A. D. Mills and A. Room, *The Oxford Names Companion* (Oxford: Oxford University Press, 2002).

R. Hatton, *George I: Elector and King* (London: Thames & Hudson, 1978).

S. C. Hawkes (ed.), *Weapons and Warfare in Anglo-Saxon England* (Oxford: Oxford University Committee for Archaeology, 1989).

D. Hay, *Europe in the Fourteenth and Fifteenth Centuries* (London: Longman, 1966).

J. Haywood, *Encyclopaedia of the Viking Age* (London: Thames & Hudson, 2000).

H. Hearder and D. P. Waley (eds.), *A Short History of Italy: From Classical Times to the Present Day* (Cambridge: Cambridge University Press, 1963).

F. Heer, *The Holy Roman Empire*, trans. J. Sondheimer (London: Phoenix Press, 2002).

C. Hibbert, *Charles I* (London: Weidenfeld & Nicolson, 1968).

—, *The Rise and Fall of the House of Medici* (London: Penguin, 1979).

—, *Queen Victoria: A Personal History* (London: HarperCollins, 2000).

J. N. Hillgarth, *The Spanish Kingdoms 1250–1516* (Oxford: Clarendon Press, 1976).

R. H. Hodgkin, *A History of the Anglo-Saxons* (Oxford: Oxford University Press, 1935).

The Holy Bible, New Revised Standard Version, anglicized edn (Oxford: Oxford University Press, 1989).

M. Hoskin (ed.), *The Cambridge Illustrated History of Astronomy* (Cambridge: Cambridge University Press, 1997).

W. Hubatsch, *Frederick the Great of Prussia: Absolutism and Administration* (London: Thames & Hudson, 1975).

M. E. Hudson and M. Clark, *Crown of a Thousand Years: A Millennium of British History Presented as a Pageant of Kings and Queens* (Sherborne, Dorset: Alphabooks, 1978).

H. Inalcik, *The Ottoman Empire: The Classical Age 1300–1600* (London: Weidenfeld & Nicolson, 1973).

J. Israel, *The Dutch Republic: Its Rise, Greatness, and Fall, 1477–1806* (Oxford: Oxford University Press, 1995).

E. W. Ives, *Anne Boleyn* (Oxford: Blackwell, 1986).

G. M. Jackson, *Women Rulers throughout the Ages: An Illustrated Guide* (Oxford: ABC-CLIO, 1999).

J. M. Jeep (ed.), *Medieval Germany: An Encyclopedia* (New York: Garland, 2001).

E. Jenkins, *Elizabeth the Great* (London: Victor Gollancz, 1958).

J. Jesch, *Women in the Viking Age* (Woodbridge: The Boydell Press, 1991).

A. H. M. Jones and E. Monroe, *A History of Ethiopia* (London: Oxford University Press, 1955).

B. Jones and M. V. Dixon (eds.), *The Macmillan Dictionary of Biography* (London: Macmillan, 1985).

G. Jones, *Eirik the Red and Other Icelandic Sagas* (London: Oxford University Press, 1961).

—, *A History of the Vikings*, rev. edn (Oxford: Oxford University Press, 1964).

W. G. Jones, *Denmark* (London: Ernest Benn, 1970).

G. P. Judd IV, *Hawaii: An Informal History* (New York: Collier, 1961).

A. P. Kazhdan (ed.), *The Oxford Dictionary of Byzantium* (Oxford: Oxford University Press, 1991).

J. Keay and J. Keay (eds.), *Collins Encyclopaedia of Scotland* (London: HarperCollins, 1994).

P. M. Kendall, *Louis XI* (London: Allen & Unwin, 1971).

J. P. Kenyon, *The Stuarts* (Glasgow: Collins, 1970).

J. B. Kinross, *The Ottoman Centuries: The Rise and Fall of the Turkish Empire* (London: Jonathan Cape, 1977).

B. Klimaszewski, *An Outline of Polish Culture* (Warsaw: Interpress, 1984).

R. S. Kuykendall, *A History of Hawaii* (New York: Macmillan, 1926).

Y. Labonde-Mailfert, *Charles VIII et son milieu (1470–1498): La jeunesse au pouvoir* (Paris: Librairie C. Klincksieck, 1975).

—, *Charles VIII: Le vouloir et la destinée* (Paris: Fayard, 1986).

P. Lagassé (ed.), *The Columbia Encyclopedia*, sixth edn (New York: Columbia University Press, 2000).

K. Larsen, *A History of Norway* (Princeton: Princeton University Press, 1948).

E. Latham, *A Dictionary of Names, Nicknames and Surnames of Persons, Places and Things* (London: Routledge, 1904).

K. S. Latourette, *The Chinese: Their History and Culture*, rev. edn (New York: Macmillan, 1964).

M. R. Lee Jr, *Government by Pen: Scotland under James VI and I* (Urbana: University of Illinois Press, 1980).

E. Le Roy Ladurie, *The Royal French State: 1400–1610*, trans. J. Vale (Oxford: Blackwell, 1994).

P. S. Lewis, *Later Medieval France: The Polity* (London: Macmillan, 1968).

R. Lindsay, *House of Lorraine* (London: Mills & Boon, 1959).

P. Linehan, *History and the Historians of Medieval Spain* (Oxford: Oxford University Press, 1993).

H. V. Livermore, *A New History of Portugal*, 2nd edn (Cambridge: Cambridge University Press, 1976).

J. E. Lloyd, *A History of Wales: From the Earliest Times to the Edwardian Conquest* (London: Longman, 1911).

H. W. Lockot, *The Mission: The Life, Reign and Character of Haile Sellassie I*, (London: Hurst, 1989).

E. Longford (ed.), *The Oxford Book of Royal Anecdotes* (Oxford: Oxford University Press, 1989).

H. Luke, *The Making of Modern Turkey: From Byzantium to Angora* (London: Macmillan, 1936).

M. Lynch, *Scotland: A New History* (London: Century, 1991).

— (ed.), *The Oxford Companion to Scottish History* (Oxford: Oxford University Press, 2001).

A. Mackay, *Spain in the Middle Ages: From Frontier to Empire, 1000–1500* (London: Macmillan, 1977).

R. L. Mackie, *King James IV of Scotland: A Brief Survey of His Life and Times* Edinburgh: (Oliver & Boyd, 1958).

F. Maclean, *A Concise History of Scotland* (London: Thames & Hudson, 1970).

J. O. Maenchen-Helfen, *The World of the Huns: Studies in Their History and Culture* (Berkeley: University of California Press, 1973).

B. Martin, *William the Silent: A Biography for Boys and Girls* (London: Independent Press, 1952).

H. Maxwell, *A History of the Houses of Douglas* (London: Freemantle, 1902).

J. McCarthy, *The Ottoman Turks: An Introductory History to 1923* (Harlow: Addison Wesley Longman, 1997).

U. McGovern (ed.), *Chambers Biographical Dictionary*, 7th edn (Edinburgh: Chambers Harrap, 2002).

R. McKitterick, *The Frankish Kingdoms under the Carolingians, 751–987* (London: Longman, 1983).

— (ed.), *The New Cambridge Medieval History: Volume II, c. 700–c. 900* (Cambridge: Cambridge University Press, 1995).

S. McMahon (ed.), *The Poolbeg Book of Children's Verse* (Swords, County Dublin: The Poolbeg Press, 1987).

R. T. McNally and R. Florescu, *In Search of Dracula: The Enthralling History of Dracula and Vampires* (London: Robson, 1995).

C. Mercer, *Alexander the Great* (London: Cassell, 1962)

R. B. Merriman, *Suleiman the Magnificent, 1520–1566* (New York: Cooper Square, 1966).

R. Mitchison, *A History of Scotland*, 3rd edn (London: Routledge, 1999).

W. R. Morfill, *Poland* (London: T. Fisher Unwin, 1893).

J. Morgan, C. O'Neill and R. Harré, *Nicknames: Their Origins and Social Consequences* (London: Routledge & Kegan Paul, 1979).

O. M. Morgan, *A History of Wales* (Liverpool: Edward Howard, 1911).

J. Morwood (ed.), *The Pocket Oxford Latin Dictionary* (Oxford: Oxford University Press, 1994).

J. L. Motley, *William the Silent* (London: Blackie, 1911).

W. A. Neilson (ed.), *Webster's Biographical Dictionary* (Springfield, MA: G. & C. Merriam, 1974).

J. L. Nelson, *Charles the Bald* (London: Longman, 1992).

— (ed.), *Rulers and Ruling Families in Early Medieval Europe: Alfred, Charles the Bald and Others* (Aldershot: Aldgate, 1999).

D. Nicholas, *Medieval Flanders* (London: Longman, 1992).

R. Nicholson, *Scotland: The Later Middle Ages* (Edinburgh: Oliver & Boyd, 1974).

H. Nicolson, *King George the Fifth: His Life and Reign* (New York: Doubleday, 1953).

S. Oakley, *The Story of Sweden* (London: Faber & Faber, 1966).

—, *The Story of Denmark* (London: Faber & Faber, 1972).

J. F. O'Callaghan, *A History of Medieval Spain* (Ithaca: Cornell University Press, 1975).

Z. Oldenbourg, *The Crusades*, trans. A. Carter (London: Weidenfeld & Nicolson, 1998).

R. Oliver and M. Crowder (eds.), *The Cambridge Encyclopaedia of Africa* (Cambridge: Cambridge University Press, 1981).

S. Pankhurst, *Ethiopia: A Cultural History* (Woodford Green, Essex: Lalibela House, 1955).

J. Paterson, *James the Fifth or the 'Gudeman of Ballangeich': His Poetry and Adventures* (Edinburgh: William P. Nimmo, 1861).

H. Paul, *Queen Anne* (London: Hodder & Stoughton, 1912).

A. Pavlov and M. Perrie, *Ivan the Terrible* (Harlow: Pearson Education, 2003).

S. G. Payne, *A History of Spain and Portugal* (Madison: University of Wisconsin Press, 1973).

J. Peddie, *Alfred: Warrior King* (Stroud, Gloucestershire: Sutton, 1999).

Pere III of Catalonia [Pedro IV of Aragon], *Chronicle*, trans. M. Hillgarth, ed. J. N. Hillgarth (Toronto: Pontifical Institute of Mediaeval Studies, 1980).

P. Pierson, *The History of Spain* (Westport, CT: Greenwood Press, 1999).

A. Plowden, *Lady Jane Grey: Nine Days Queen* (Stroud, Gloucestershire: Sutton, 2003).

G. Plumptre, *Edward VII* (London: Pavilion, 1995).

A. L. Poole, *From Domesday Book to Magna Carta, 1087–1216*, 2nd edn (Oxford: Oxford University Press, 1955).

R. G. Popperwell, *Norway* (London: Ernest Benn, 1972).

C. Prouty and E. Rosenfeld, *Historical Dictionary of Ethiopia and Eritrea*, 2nd edn (Metuchen, NJ, and London: The Scarecrow Press, 1994).

S. Ratcliffe (ed.), *People on People: The Oxford Dictionary of Biographical Quotations* (Oxford: Oxford University Press, 2001).

B. F. Reilly, *The Kingdom of León-Castile under Alfonso VI, 1065–1109* (Princeton: Princeton University Press, 1988).

L. Reiners, *Frederick the Great: An Informal Biography*, trans. L. P. R. Wilson (London: Oswald Wolff, 1960).

T. Reuter, *Germany in the Early Middle Ages c. 800–1056* (London: Longman, 1991).

— (ed.), *The New Cambridge Medieval History, Volume III, c. 900–c. 1024* (Cambridge: Cambridge University Press, 1999).

P. Rex, *Hereward: The Last Englishman* (Stroud, Gloucestershire: Tempus, 2005).

D. T. Rice, *The Byzantines* (London: Thames & Hudson, 1962).

T. T. Rice, *Elizabeth: Empress of Russia* (London: Weidenfeld & Nicolson, 1970).

P. Riché, *The Carolingians: A Family Who Forged Europe*, trans. M. I. Allen (Philadelphia: University of Pennsylvania Press, 1993).

A. J. Roderick (ed.), *Wales through the Ages, Volume I, From the Earliest Times to 1485* (Llandybie, Carmarthenshire: C. Davies, 1959).

W. J. Rose, *Poland: Old and New* (London: G. Bell & Sons, 1948).

R. Rosen, *Georgia: A Sovereign Country of the Caucasus* (Kowloon: Odyssey Publications, 1991).

C. Ross, *Edward IV* (London: Methuen, 1983).

P. Russell, *Prince Henry 'the Navigator': A Life* (New Haven: Yale University Press, 2000).

P. E. Russell, *Spain: A Companion to Spanish Studies* (London and New York: Methuen, 1973).

—, *Portugal, Spain and the African Atlantic, 1343–1490: Chivalry and Crusade from John of Gaunt to Henry the Navigator* (Aldershot: Variorum, 1995).

B. Saklatvala, *The Origins of the English People* (New York: Taplinger, 1970).

J. H. M. Salmon, *Society in Crisis: France in the Sixteenth Century* (London: Methuen, 1975).

G. Sanford and A. Gozdecka-Sanford, *Historical Dictionary of Poland* (Metuchen, NJ,: The Scarecrow Press, 1994).

J. H. Saraiva, *Portugal: A Companion History*, trans. U. Fonss, ed. I. Robertson and L. C. Taylor (Manchester: Carcanet, 1997).

J. J. Scarisbrick, *Henry VIII*, new edn (New Haven: Yale University Press, 1997).

S. Schama, *Citizens: A Chronicle of the French Revolution* (New York: Alfred A. Knopf, 1989).

F. Schevill, *The Great Elector* (Hamden, CT: Archon, 1965).

H. Sellassie, *My Life and Ethiopia's Progress, 1892–1937*, trans. and ann. E. Ullendorff (Oxford: Oxford University Press, 1977).

L. E. Seltzer et al., *The Columbia Lippincott Gazetteer of the World* (New York: Columbia University Press, 1952).

D. Seward, *The First Bourbon: Henry IV of France and Navarre* (London: Constable, 1971).

—, *Prince of the Renaissance: The Life of François I* (London: Sphere, 1974).

S. P. Shannon, *Kings' Names: An Encyclopaedia of Rulers' Nicknames* (Grantham: Barny, 2001).

H. S. Sharp, *Handbook of Pseudonyms and Personal Nicknames* (Metuchen, NJ, and London: The Scarecrow Press, 1973).

S. Shaw, *History of the Ottoman Empire and*

Modern Turkey (Cambridge: Cambridge University Press, 1976).

D. Sinor, *History of Hungary* (London: Allen & Unwin, 1959).

D. M. Smith, *Cavour and Garibaldi 1860: A Study in Political Conflict* (Cambridge: Cambridge University Press, 1954).

—, *A History of Sicily 800–1715* (London: Chatto & Windus, 1968).

—, *Italy: A Modern History*, new rev. edn (Ann Arbor: University of Michigan Press, 1969).

—, *Victor Emanuel, Cavour, and the Risorgimento* (Oxford: Oxford University Press, 1971).

—, *Italy and Its Monarchs* (New Haven: Yale University Press, 1989).

J. P. Spielman, *Leopold I of Austria* (London: Thames & Hudson, 1977).

J. Spurr, *England in the 1670s* (Oxford: Blackwell, 2000).

J. C. Squire, *William the Silent* (London: Methuen, 1912).

D. C. Stedman, *The Black Douglases* (London: Thomas Nelson & Sons, 1913).

A. Steel, *Richard II* (Cambridge: Cambridge University Press, 1962).

A. A. Stomberg, *A History of Sweden* (London: Allen & Unwin, 1932).

L. Strachey, *Queen Victoria* (London: Penguin, 1971).

D. Sturdy, *Alfred the Great* (London: Constable, 1995).

Suger, *The Deeds of Louis the Fat*, trans. R. Cusimano and J. Moorhead (Washington: The Catholic University of America Press, 1992).

J. Sumption, *The Albigensian Crusade* (London: Faber & Faber, 1978).

P. Sykes, *A History of Persia*, 3rd edn (London: Routledge & Kegan Paul, 1969).

R. Tabrah, *Hawaii: A Bicentennial History* (New York: W. W. Norton, 1980).

J. R. Tanner, C. W. Previté-Orton and Z. N. Brooke (eds.), *The Cambridge Medieval History* (Cambridge: Cambridge University Press, 1929).

J. M. Thompson, *Lectures on Foreign History 1494–1789*, rev. edn (Oxford: Blackwell, 1956).

S. M. Toyne, *The Scandinavians in History* (London: Edward Arnold, 1948).

G. Treasure (ed.), *Who's Who in British History: Beginnings to 1901* (London: Fitzroy Dearborn, 1998).

K. W. Treptow and M. Popa, *Historical Dictionary of Romania*, European Historical Dictionaries No. 15 (Lanham, MD, and London: The Scarecrow Press, 1996).

J. P. Trevelyan, *A Short History of the Italian People: From the Barbarian Invasions to the Present Day* (London: Allen & Unwin, 1956).

M. J. Trow, *Vlad the Impaler: In Search of the Real Dracula* (Stroud, Gloucestershire: Sutton, 2003).

D. Twitchett and J. K. Fairbank (eds.), *The Cambridge History of China* (Cambridge: Cambridge University Press, 1979).

J. Van der Kiste, *William and Mary* (Stroud, Gloucestershire: Sutton, 2003).

S. B. Várdy, *Historical Dictionary of Hungary*, European Historical Dictionaries No. 18 (Lanham, MD, and London: The Scarecrow Press, 1997).

A. Vauchez (in association with B. Dobson and M. Lapidge), *Encyclopedia of the Middle Ages* (Cambridge: James Clarke, 2000).

R. Vaughan, *Philip the Good: The Apogee of Burgundy* (London: Longman, 1970).

—, *John the Fearless: The Growth of Burgundian Power* (Woodbridge: The Boydell Press, 2002).

I. W. Walker, *Harold: The Last Anglo-Saxon King* (Stroud, Gloucestershire: Sutton, 1997).

T. Walter (ed.), *The Mourning for Diana* (Oxford: Berg, 1999).

W. L. Warren, *Henry II* (London: Eyre Methuen, 1973).

D. R. Watson, *The Life and Times of Charles I* (London: Weidenfeld & Nicolson, 1972).

G. Way and R. Squire, *Scottish Clan and Family Encyclopedia* (Glasgow: HarperCollins, 1994).

H. Webster, *A History of the Ancient World: From Earliest Times to the Fall of Rome* (London: George G. Harrap, 1915).

C. V. Wedgwood, *William the Silent* (London: Jonathan Cape, 1967).

M. Weiner, *The French Exiles: 1789–1815* (London: John Murray, 1960).

A. Weir, *Henry VIII: King and Court* (London: Jonathan Cape, 2001).

A. Wheatcroft, *The Ottomans* (London: Penguin, 1993).

D. L. Wheeler, *Historical Dictionary of Portugal*, European Historical Dictionaries No. 1 (Metuchen, NJ, and London: The Scarecrow Press, 1993).

C. Wilkinson, *Prince Rupert the Cavalier* (London: George G. Harrap, 1934).

William of Malmesbury, *The Deeds of the Bishops of England*, trans. D. Preest (Woodbridge: The Boydell Press, 2002).

S. W. Williams, *The Middle Kingdom: A Survey of the Geography, Government, Literature, Social Life, Arts, and History of the Chinese Empire and Its Inhabitants* (New York: Scribners, 1898).

D. H. Willson, *King James VI and I* (London: Jonathan Cape, 1956).

M. Wood, *In Search of the Dark Ages* (London: BBC Worldwide, 2001).

C. Woodham-Smith, *Queen Victoria: Her Life and Times* (London: Hamish Hamilton, 1972).

J. W. Zophy (ed.), *The Holy Roman Empire: A Dictionary Handbook* (Westport, CT, and London: Greenwood Press, 1980).

E. J. Zürcher, *Turkey: A Modern History* (London: I. B. Tauris, 1993).

Index